Authentic Legends

More than one hundred million people are estimated to be involved in the cult of the orishas. This religion originated in Cuba, where the religious practices of Yoruba slaves mixed with the Catholic beliefs of their new masters to become what is now known as Santería—also called the worship of saints.

This African-Cuban syncretic mixture resulted in a rich body of lore about the Santería deities, known as orishas. The lively tales in this book comprise many of the colorful legends of the orishas and their interrelationships. Each orisha is identified with a natural force—seas, rivers, winds, fire, thunder and lightning, volcanoes—and each represents a concept such as justice, fate, war, passion, love, wisdom, or peace.

The orishas also represent the best and the worst traits of humankind, and one of their functions is to teach us lessons about living and remind us of our duties in this world. Their adventures illustrate an important message: if we find harmony in nature and in each other, life can be a wonderful journey.

Worship of the orishas is still very much alive today, not only in Nigeria but in Cuba, Brazil, and the United States. González-Wippler wrote these English versions of the patakis from the Spanish with a skill that clarifies these tales' archetypal significance while retaining all of their glorious life and vibrancy.

About the Author

Migene González-Wippler was born in Puerto Rico and has degrees in psychology and anthropology from the University of Puerto Rico and from Columbia University. She has worked as a science editor for the Interscience Division of John Wiley, the American Institute of Physics and the American Museum of Natural History, and as an English editor for the United Nations in Vienna, where she lived for many years. She is a cultural anthropologist and lectures frequently at colleges in New York. She is the noted author of many books on religion and mysticism, including the widely acclaimed *Santería: African Magic in Latin America*, *A Kabbalah for the Modern World*, *The Complete Book of Spells, Ceremonies & Magic*, *The Complete Book of Amulets & Talismans*, and *Dreams and What They Mean to You*.

To Write to the Author

If you wish to contact the author or would like more information about this book, please write to the author in care of Llewellyn Worldwide, and we will forward your request. Both the author and publisher appreciate hearing from you and learning of your enjoyment of this book and how it has helped you. Llewellyn Worldwide cannot guarantee that every letter written to the author can be answered, but all will be forwarded. Please write to:

Migene González-Wippler
c/o Llewellyn Worldwide
P.O. Box 64383-328, St. Paul, MN 55164-0383, U.S.A.

Please enclose a self-addressed, stamped envelope for reply, or $1.00 to cover costs.
If outside the U.S.A., enclose international postal reply coupon.

Free Catalog from Llewellyn

For more than ninety years Llewellyn has brought its readers knowledge in the fields of metaphysics and human potential. Learn about the newest books in spiritual guidance, natural healing, astrology, occult philosophy, and more. Enjoy book reviews, new age articles, a calendar of events, plus current advertised products and services. To get your free copy of *Llewellyn's New Worlds of Mind and Spirit*, send your name and address to:

Llewellyn's New Worlds of Mind and Spirit
P.O. Box 64383-328, St. Paul, MN 55164-0383, U.S.A.

WORLD RELIGION & MAGIC SERIES

LEGENDS OF SANTERÍA

A New, Expanded, and Revised Publication
of *Tales of the Orishas*

Migene González-Wippler

1994
Llewellyn Publications
St. Paul, Minnesota 55164-0383

FIRST EDITION
First Printing, 1994

Illustrations by Joseph Francis Wippler
Cover design by Alexandra Lumen
Book design and layout by Trish Finley

Library of Congress Cataloging-in-Publication Data
González-Wippler, Migene.
    Legends of Santería / Migene González-Wippler.
        p.   cm. — (Llewellyn's world religion & magic series)
    "A new, expanded, and revised publication of Tales of the Orishas."
    Includes bibliographical references.
    ISBN 1-56718-328-X
    1. Santería. 2. Orixás. 3. Yoruba (African people)—Folklore.
I. González-Wippler, Migene. Tales of the orishas. II. Title.
III. Series.
BL2532.S3G65   1994
299'.67—dc20   94-9352
                                                                      CIP

Llewellyn Publications
A Division of Llewellyn Worldwide, Ltd.
P.O. Box 64383, St. Paul, MN 55164-0383

Llewellyn's World Religion & Magic Series

At the core of every religion, at the foundation of every culture, there is MAGIC.

Magic sees the world as alive, as the home which humanity shares with beings and powers both visible and invisible with whom and which we can interface to either our advantage or disadvantage—depending upon our awareness and intention.

Religious worship and communion is one kind of magic, and just as there are many religions in the world, so are there many magical systems.

Religion and magic are ways of seeing and relating to the creative powers, the living energies, the all-pervading spirit, the underlying intelligence that is the universe within which we and all else exist.

Neither religion nor magic conflicts with science. All share the same goals and the same limitations: always seeking truth, and forever haunted by human limitations in perceiving that truth. Magic is "technology" based upon experience and extrasensory insight, providing its practitioners with methods of greater influence and control over the world of the invisible before it impinges on the world of the visible.

The study of world magic not only enhances your understanding of the world in which you live, and hence your ability to live better, but brings you in touch with the inner essence of your long evolutionary heritage and most particularly—as in the case of the magical system identified most closely with your genetic inheritance—with the archetypal images and forces most alive in your whole consciousness.

Other Books by Migene González-Wippler

The Santería Experience
The Complete Book of Amulets & Talismans
The Complete Book of Spells, Ceremonies & Magic
Dreams and What They Mean to You
A Kabbalah for the Modern World
Rituals and Spells of Santería
Santería: African Magic in Latin America
Santería: The Religion
The Seashells
Powers of the Orishas
Peregrinaje (in Spanish)

This book is dedicated to
Fernando Ybaé

Acknowledgements

I wish to express my appreciation to all the santeros and santeras who have shared with me their great knowledge of the legends or patakis of Santería.

I especially want to thank in memoriam, Eduardo Pastoriza (Changó Lari), who was one of the best-known priests of Changó in the United States, for many of the Changó legends; Pancho Mora (Ifá Moro), a babalawo and high priest of Orunla, who is said to have brought Santería to the United States; and Fernando Sierra (Oyeye-I), a priest of Obatalá for twenty-five years, who was the greatest source of Santería lore I have ever known, and the principal racounteur behind the legends. To all of them, in the throne of Olofi, *maferefun* and *aché*.

I also wish to express my deep gratitude to the Oba Oriaté Willie García, a high priest of Obatalá for twenty-four years, who is one of the best-known santeros in the New York metropolitan area and the principal storyteller behind the patakis in Part II.

Pataki: one of the many legends of Santería, relating the origins of the orishas, their interrelationships, and the roles they are believed to play in the creation of the world and the destiny of humanity.

Changó. We greet you: "Good morning."
The bushrat awakens.
The elder of Koso awakens on the ground.
Changó, when I awakened this morning,
I saluted the king of Oluleje.
When I awakened,
I knelt down to greet Awo,
Who was made a king in the land of Likii;
I greeted *shere*;
I greeted the mouth of *aja*;
I greeted Moro,
King of the *ehuru* birds.
Whoever deceives me, deceives Changó,
The son of Yemayá;
Changó, who throws away the tray of a trader;
Changó, who chases away the king
And householder alike.
Changó is my lord,
Who blesses the wise and maddens the fool.

(Owoade P.C.)

Contents

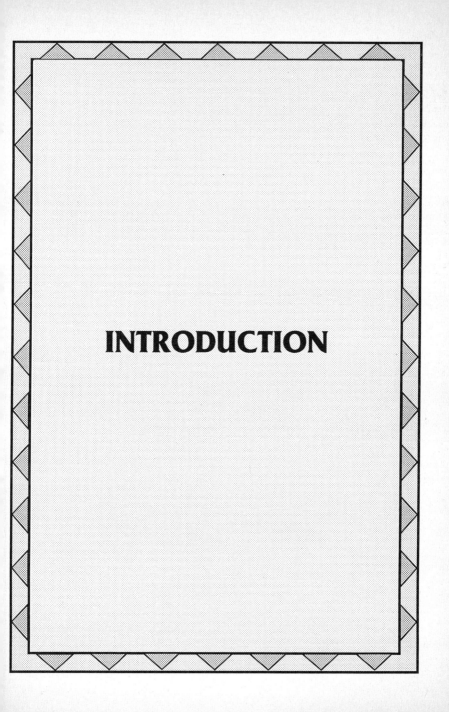

INTRODUCTION

The origins of the orishas and the various legends that explain those origins are the subject of a great deal of animated controversy among the santeros. The legends or patakis that relate the adventures of the deities and their interrelationships are not as much in question as how the deities themselves came into being and why they are the way they are.

When this book was first published, the patakis that I chose to include in the book told one version of the creation of the orishas and how they relate to each other and to humanity. But in Santería there are many contradicting stories about the origins of the orishas, and for that reason I decided to add a new section to this second edition of the work, relating a second version of the creation of the world and stories of the most popular Santería deities.

The new section presents the creation of the world and of the orishas through several patakis that are in direct opposition to some of those presented in the first part of the book. It is difficult to ascertain which versions reflect the beliefs of the vast majority of the followers of Santería. Their opinions seem to be mixed. These additional legends are presented because they are important to the understanding of the religion and its philosophy, which is largely based on the personalities of the orishas and their interrelationships.

Among the many basic differences in the two versions of the legends is the concept of Obatalá as the first created being. In Part I, Oloddumare creates Obatalá first and gives him a wife called Oddudúa. In Part II, Oddudúa is created first and is male instead of female. Obatalá does not come into being until much later in this second version.

The concept of Olosi, which is not presented in Part I, permeates the beliefs of Santería, and yet, this shadowy and malicious creature—such a clear syncretism of the Christian devil—is hardly ever mentioned by the santeros. His presence is acknowledged and his destructive actions are recognized, but his name is never uttered and there are no active ebbós or spells to guard against his nefarious influence. This is because Eleggua is in charge of keeping Olosi at bay, and the santeros rely on the power of Eleggua to neutralize Olosi's presence. This legend is also presented in Part II.

The birth of the other orishas and the fulfillment of Oloddumare's plan, culminating in the creation of humanity, are explained in an entirely new form in the second part. The origin of these patakis, like those of the first part, can be traced to the oddus of the seashells and to Yoruba mythology, but there are also elements in the patakis that can be traced to Cuban myths and the Christian influence, which is such an important part of Santería.

The Yorubas

The Yoruba people of southwestern Nigeria and the neighboring republics of Benin (Dahomey) and Togos number more than ten million. They are subdivided into more than twenty groups, each of which was traditionally an autonomous kingdom. In spite of the many differences between the various subgroups, enough cultural links remain to indicate that they all belong to the same ethnic group. This is particularly true of their language which according to scholars has been spoken by the Yorubas for several thousand years.

The antiquity of the Yorubas is based not only on linguistic evidence, but also on archeological studies that seem to indicate that the tribes migrated from the East, perhaps from the Upper Nile, in the beginning of the Christian era. It is during this period that we can begin to trace the extraordinary complexity of the economic, political, artistic, and religious aspects of the Yoruba culture, which ranks among the most developed of West Africa.

One of the most outstanding characteristics of Yoruba culture was the formation of city-state kingdoms in a process of urbanization unique among primitive people. The center, both political and religious, of their civilization was the holy city of Ile-Ife.

All the various city-states or kingdoms formed a pyramidal socio-political structure at the apex of which was the city of Ife. The head of Ife was the Oni, or divine king, from whom all the other Yoruba kings or *obas* received the right to wear the beaded crown which was a symbol of their power. The Oni was said to be a direct descendant from Oddudúa, the founder of Ife, and one of the three deities sent to earth by the creator, Oloddumare, to oversee the destinies of humankind. Today, the Oni's dynasty is still very much in power in Nigeria, and he still traces his ancestry to Oddudúa.

The integral unity of Yoruba culture is directly related to the powerful religious beliefs that throughout the centuries have influenced and permeated their art and socio-political structures. Ife soon became a center of pilgrimage for all Yoruba people who came to consult the priests-chiefs who were dedicated to the cults of the principal deities or orishas. Ife became an oracle city, very much like Delphi in ancient Greece. And indeed, the complexity of the Yoruba pantheon of gods was not unlike that of Greek mythology. The legends that form the core of this book come to us from these early times, and indicate a sophistication of thought very close to that of the Greeks of sixth century B.C. There are definite parallels between the Yoruba deities and those of the Greeks. Like the Olympians, they were anthropomorphized and identified with natural forces. They were also invoked in times of need and propitiated through sacrifice. The one important difference between the Greek and the Yoruba gods is that while the worship of the Olympians was soon relegated to books on mythology and ancient history, that of the orishas or Yoruba gods is still very much alive today, not only in Nigeria but throughout the Western Hemisphere.

The Yoruba religion was and is based on the basic belief that energy—*ashé*—is the true nature of things. This energy is dynamic and malleable and can be used to alter, for good or for evil, our lives and those of all living things. The prime architect of *ashé*, which is the substance from which everything came into being, is Oloddumare, the supreme creator in Yoruba myth. The orishas are depositories of Oloddumare's *asheé* which they confer upon humankind by means of suitable ritual sacrifice—*ebbó*. The concepts of *ashé* and *ebbó* are at the root of Yoruba religious thought.

All material phenomena are explained by the Yoruba through the concept of *ashé* and the power of the orishas, identified with natural forces. This idea is closely related to modern scientific views which hold that our world, and indeed all things, are composed of energy in different manifestations. According to science, natural forces, embodied in physical laws, are what hold these energies together. In this context, scientific thought and Yoruba cosmology are not very far apart.

Although *ashé* is usually received directly from the orishas through propitiation and invocation, the Yorubas also believe that ritualistic dancing can increase and generate *ache* or life force in the individual. This generated power, which is tapped directly from the orisha to whom the individual is dedicating the dance, is said to be especially increased during the trance states of possession, when an orisha is said to take over the conscious personality of a believer. For this reason, many rituals of the Yorubas include ceremonial dances in honor of their gods, each of whom has their own special chants and drum rhythms. A ceremonial set of sacred drums, known as the *bataá*, is generally used during these rites.

During the slave trade, thousands of Yorubas were brought to the New World, where their powerful religious thought influenced deeply their new masters. Their influence was felt more in Cuba, Brazil, Trinidad, and Haiti where they were brought in large quantities. In Cuba, the Yoruba beliefs gave birth to a mixture of Catholic and Yoruba practices which became known as *Santería*, that is, the worship of saints. This was the result of the identification of some of the orishas with Catholic saints. A similar syncretism caused the birth of the *Shango* cult in Trinidad and *Candomble* and *Macumba* in Brazil. In Haiti, only a few of the orishas became popular, especially Oggún, the god of iron. But because there were other tribes involved in the Haitian syncretistic mixture, the resulting religion, known as *Voodoo* or *Vodoun*, had only traces of Yoruba beliefs. In Haiti, the African gods became known as *loas*, not orishas.

In the Americas, the cult of the orishas has become known in recent years as the Orisha Tradition, and includes the original Nigerian religion, African-Cuban Santería, Trinidadian Shango, and Brazilian Candomble. More than one hundred million people are estimated to be involved in the cult of the orishas in the New World.

The entire religious edifice of Santería is based on the legends known as patakis which explain the creation of the world and of humankind, and the interactions between human beings and nature, between human beings and the orishas, and between the orishas themselves. The resulting philosophy is rich in wisdom, understanding of the human condition, and spiritual insight.

The Orishas

The Yoruba religion is a magico-religious system that has its roots in nature and natural forces. Each orisha or deity is identified both with a natural force and a human interest or endeavor. In Yoruba tradition, the orishas were divided into two groups, the white orishas—*orisha fun fun*—and the dark orishas. The white orishas are cool and have life-giving powers. Among them are Obatalá, King of the White Cloth, symbol of peace and purity; Osain, god of herbs; Orisha-Oko, god of farming and agriculture; Oshún, goddess of river waters, love, and marriage; and Yemayá, goddess of the sea and maternity. On the other hand, the dark orishas are hot and their powers are present in war or when blood is shed, either in battle or in the hunt. Among them are Changó, god of fire, thunder, and lightning; Oggún, god of war and metals; Oyá, goddess of the lightning bolt and owner of the cemetery; and Chankpanna (Babalú-Ayé in the New World), who rules over disease, particularly smallpox.

The orishas are also seen as representations of human qualities or feelings. In many ways the orishas can be seen as archetypes of the collective unconscious.

Carl Gustav Jung believed that each archetype is an autonomous complex within the human personality which is independent from the rest of the conscious personality and often behaves as if it were a separate, supernatural entity. The archetypes have intensely individualistic characteristics and each one controls a different aspect of the personality and/or a different human interest. This definition of the archetypes could just as well describe the functions of the orishas. It is interesting to note in this respect that the Yorubas believe in the phenomenon of possession. Very often, during ritualistic invocations or during ritual dancing, the orishas descend and take possession of those initiated into their mysteries. During possession the individual displays all the characteristics ascribed to a particular orisha, as well as unusual precognitive abilities, strange powers, and superhuman strength, all natural attributes of an archetype formed of pure psychic energies directed into a specific channel.

According to Jung's views, each orisha may be seen as a representation of a human archetype which embodies both a natural and a spiritual force. Essentially they are natural forces of which we are an intrinsic part. We can then see that Yemayá is the Yorubas' supernal mother because the sea, which she represents, is a mystical symbol of motherhood, and all life on this planet came from the primordial seas.

The rivers are the sustenance of life because they are our source of water without which we would die. Oshún, as the river waters, sustains life and, as such, is also love, marriage, and the joy of living.

Changó is fire, thunder, lightning, and unbridled passion. His intense virility is the precursor of the life-giving rain that nurtures both rivers and oceans. But he's also fire, which evaporates water and destroys life if not controlled. Changó is a symbol of raw power without which nothing is possible, but which can only be of service if properly channeled. Changó's lesson is the control of passions and the wise distribution of energy.

Eshú or Eleggua is fate, the messenger of the gods, and is said to be standing in every corner zealously guarding the preservation of justice. He's the bitter enemy of all those things which thwart life—crime, hate, discrimination, abuse, vice, and corruption. He's also a trickster who tests people's strength and good will by causing trouble.

Obatalá is whiteness, purity, and perfection. He's the perfect human being, what we should all strive to become.

Oggún is war, a symbol of the struggles within the soul for betterment and perfection. He's the destroyer of evil. But he's also the iron worker and, as such, the hope of civilization. He gives us a choice—life or destruction.

Then there's Oyá, the lightning bolt, the scourge of the earth. But she's also the keeper of the cemetery, the guardian of the gateway to death and to another life on a spiritual plane. Her duty is to remind us constantly of the brevity of our human lives and the importance of using our time on earth wisely and productively. This productivity is emphasized by Orisha-Oko, the patron of agriculture, who is also a symbol of stability and success.

To the Yorubas, the orishas are not simply the grim reminders of our duties in this world. They are also conveyors of a far more important message: if we find harmony in nature and in each other, life can be a wonderful adventure, which is really what Oloddumare meant it to be.

The Cosmology

Although in Nigeria the Yorubas worship over six hundred orishas, in the New World their numbers have dwindled to a little over twenty. The diminishing numbers of orishas does not indicate a lessening in their worship. On the contrary, more people believe in the orishas' power in the Western Hemisphere than in Nigeria. The reason why less orishas are worshiped in the New World is that in Nigeria practically every village or town worships its own personal orisha. For example, Obatalá originated in the holy city of Ife, Changó is from Oyo, Oggún from Iré, Oshún from Oshogbo, Eleggua or Eshú from Ketu, and Yemayá from Abeokuta. During the slave trade, only some of the Yoruba villages were raided and their inhabitants brought to the Americas. The orishas they worshiped became part of the Orisha Tradition in the New World. But because the various Yoruba families inter-mingled during their exile, people began to worship various orishas instead of just one, as it is done in Nigeria. In some instances, like in the case of the orisha Ochosi—the divine hunter—an entire village with its corresponding orisha was brought over to the Americas. This ended the worship of that particular orisha in Nigeria, where no one remained who was familiar with his mysteries and his rites. But in Cuba and Brazil, the cult of Ochosi is very powerful.

The tales narrated in this book are a compilation of some of the legends of the orishas in the Cuban tradition of Santería. Most of them can be traced to Yoruba sources, but some are of purely Cuban origin. There seems to have been a fusion between the Yoruba myths and the Spanish and Christian beliefs, as well as with the legends of other African groups in the New World. The result was a brand-new crop of tales recounting the stories of the creation of the world and of the orishas. The tales have been purposely interwoven to create a sprawling saga of the lives and adventures of the orishas, in order to emphasize their intensely human qualities and their interrelations among themselves.

The Pantheon

Aganyú: The patron of volcanoes, he's said to melt stones with his breath; he's Changó's father; his colors are red and green and his number is six.

Babalú-Ayé: He's also known as Sonponno, Chankpanna, and Omolu; he's the patron of skin diseases, especially smallpox, and of paraplegics; he's very powerful and confers health, wealth, and prosperity to his followers; in anger he's swift and terrible; his colors are lavender, black, and beige; he dresses in sackcloth and in beggar's rags; his number is seventeen.

Changó: One of the most popular and powerful of the orishas; he's the the symbol of fire, thunder, and lightning and is one of the greatest warriors of the Yoruba pantheon; Changó represents lust and passion and control over enemies and obstacles; he's swift in anger and protects his followers fiercely against attack; his colors are red and white and his numbers are six and four.

Eleggua: He's the first orisha who must be honored in all ceremonies; he's also known as Eshú, Elegba, and Elegbara; Eleggua is the owner of the crossroads and is also said to stand in the corners to watch everything that is going on; he's the messenger of the gods and a trickster who tests the wills of humans by causing trouble; he's justice personified and hates evildoers; his punishment of evil is swift and characteristic of his personality; Eleggua is identified with fate and is often propitiated with candies which he loves; he has twenty-one aspects and his colors are red and black or black and white; his number is three and his day is Monday.

Ibeyi: The heavenly twins; in some legends, the Ibeyi are Changó's children by the goddess Oshún; they are represented as very young children and are the symbol of fertility and the duality of human nature; they are propitiated with twin dishes of candies; there are no specific colors or numbers assigned to them.

Obatalá: The first created orisha, a symbol of peace and purity; he controls the mind and all thought; the head, the bones of the body, and all white substances are his; he's the father of the orishas and of humankind; he has dozens of aspects in some of which he adopts a female form; in each aspect he has a different name; his color is white and his number is eight. He's known as King of the White Cloth.

Obba: Changó's wife and the patron of the home and of family life; another river deity, she's the patron of the Niger river; her color is pink; there's no specific number assigned to her.

Ochosi: The divine hunter; he walks often with Oggún and is identified with all wildlife and with hunters; his colors are blue and yellow and his numbers are three and seven.

Oddudúa: A female aspect of Obatalá and a symbol of maternity.

Oggún: The god of war and of metals; he's a powerful warrior who also provides employment and protection against wounds and all types of surgery; he's said to be responsible for all car and railroad accidents where blood is shed; his colors are green and black and his numbers are three and seven.

Oloddumare: God, the creative force of the universe.

Olokun: The original owner of the earth; she (or he, for this is an androgynous deity) is said to be an aspect of Yemayá, the sea goddess; Olokun represents the depths of the ocean and is sometimes identified with a mermaid; so awesome is her power that her followers invoke her only rarely; her colors are green and white; there's no specific number assigned to her.

Olofi/Olorun: Humankind's personal god; an aspect of Oloddumare.

Orisha-Oko: The symbol of agriculture and of the harvest; he also symbolizes prosperity and stability; his colors are pink and blue; there's no specific number assigned to him.

Orunla: The diviner among the orishas and a symbol of great wisdom; he's one of the most powerful of the orishas and is very trusted by Olofi himself; he's the patron of the babal-awo, the high priest of the Yorubas; his colors are green and yellow; there's no specific number assigned to him.

Oshún: The symbol of love, gold, and marriage and the patron of river waters; she's also a patron of the arts, especially of dance; her colors are white and yellow and her assigned number is five.

Oyá: A symbol of the wind and the lightning bolt; she's also the keeper of the cemetery and the guardian of the gates of death; her color is wine and flowery designs are also hers; her number is nine.

Yemayá: The symbol of motherhood and a representation of sea waters; she's the the protector of women and, according to one of the legends, she adopted Changó and raised him as her son; she's austere and immensely wealthy with all the riches of the seven seas; she has seven aspects and her colors are blue and white; her assigned number is seven.

Yemmu: A female aspect of Obatalá who is also said to be one of his wives; she's Changó's mother.

PART I

Creation of the World

In the beginning there was only Oloddumare, pure undefined energy, a being without beginning or end. Oloddumare's essence can never be comprehended by mortals
because his substance is beyond human ken. What Oloddumare is can best be understood by the Yoruba concept of *ase*
or *ashé*, that is, divine power. *Ashé* is the stuff of the universe,
the primordial atom, the breath of life. It is also intelligence,
movement, creativity, the impulse of being. In short, *ashé* is
Oloddumare. This undefined and indefinable entity is composed of three separate and equally indefinable spirits
known as Oloddumare Nzame, Olofi, and Baba Nkwa.

Oloddumare is the creative principle of this unknow-
able trinity. To give expression to his creativity, he brought
heaven and earth into being, and formed the sun, the moon,
the stars and all plant and animal life on this planet. When he
finished his work, he asked Olofi and Baba Nkwa what they
thought of what he had done. Both of his companions agreed
that Oloddumare Nzame had created great and marvelous
things, but pointed out the need for the creation of an intelli-
gent being to rule over the earth. At their suggestion, Oloddumare Nzame created from mud the first man in his own
image, giving him intelligence, beauty, and immortality. He
named his creation Omo Oba.

Very soon, Omo Oba became so conceited and so proud
of his great beauty and supernatural powers that he became
convinced that he was quite equal to Oloddumare. His arrogance grew to such proportions that Oloddumare, enraged at
Omo Oba's insolence, ordered Nzalam, the lightning bolt, to
destroy Omo and all life upon the earth. Unfortunately,
Oloddumare had forgotten that he had created Omo Oba
immortal, and therefore Nzalam could not destroy him.
Lightning bolt upon lightning bolt fell upon the earth, Nzalam in pursuit of Omo Oba. But the scourge of heaven left
Omo Oba quite unscathed, while destroying all other life on
the planet. Gone were the forests and the rivers, the seas

dried in rivulets of lava, all animal life lay in a gigantic steaming grave, the entire earth a lifeless desert. In the meantime, Omo Oba hid himself in the bowels of the earth, where he is still surrounded by the fire and brimstone caused by Nzalam's scourge. He changed his name to Olosi and comes periodically to the surface of the earth to incite humans to break Oloddumare's laws.

Soon after this unhappy incident, Oloddumare felt sad at the devastation caused by Nzalam, and decided to remedy the situation. The three spirits that form the deity descended upon the earth and mercifully covered it with new life. They created a new man to rule over the earth, but did not give him the gift of immortality. They named this new being Obatalá.

After this second creation, Olofi, one of the aspects of Oloddumare, was put in charge of the earth's affairs, and the other two spirits, Oloddumare Nzame and Baba Nkwa, left the planet to continue their work of creation elsewhere in the universe. Olofi is therefore the aspect of Oloddumare that is conceived in this mythology as humankind's personal god.

Creation of the Orishas

Olofi gave Obatalá a wife whom he named Oddudúa. After their creation, seeing how lonely they were, Olofi decided to provide them with adequate companions. He gathered together a number of flat, shiny stones which he called *ota*, and placed them in a circle around his feet. Then he poured some of his *ashé* into each stone, imbuing it with life and human form. From each *ota* was then born an orisha, some male and some female, but all with the creative power of Olofi's *ashé*

The first of the new orishas was Orunmila, also known as Orunla, who was given the power to foretell the future by means of sixteen kola nuts. This divination system, known as Ifa, also became one of the titles of Orunla.

After Orunla, the orisha Olokun came into being. This deity is considered to be androgynous in the Cuban tradition, and sometimes it is referred to as a male and others as a female. To Olokun, Olofi gave the domain of the sea waters which he placed below the sky.

Among the other orishas created from the *ota* were Aganyú, Orisha-Oko, Osain, and Babalú-Ayé. At first they did not receive any special powers from Olofi. But with time the Creator grew weary of his high office and stopped exercising his divine powers. When the orishas learned that Olofi was getting ready to retire they demanded that he divide his powers among them. Olofi agreed. He gave Aganyú the power to melt stones with his breath, thus creating the volcano. He gave Orisha-Oko the secrets of the harvests, thus creating the four seasons and all growing things. To Osain he gave the secrets of herbs and plants, thus creating the woods. And to Babalú-Ayé he gave the power to create and cure smallpox and other epidemics. Olofi had many other powers, but these he kept because he knew that with time other orishas would be created. He wanted to have some powers left to share with them.

Creation of the Ground

All the things Olofi had created were still the domain of the orishas who lived high up in the sky in a world of their own. Humankind had yet to be created.

Below the sky was the domain of the waters, and this belonged to the powerful orisha Olokun. This was a dark and dreary region, devoid of any kind of life. None of the orishas cared for the tenebrous depths below and did their best to ignore them. They all lived happily in the bright, happy realm of the sky and had no thoughts of Olokun and of the waters beneath them. All of them, that is, except Obatalá, who, being the owner of mind and thought, thought about everything. And it bothered him that there was no life in Olokun's domain. Finally, he decided to do something about it. Accordingly, he paid a visit to Olofi and explained his views to the deity. Olofi agreed immediately that Olokun's realm would be improved considerably by living things and told Obatalá to speak to Orunla about the problem.

Orunla is in charge of all the secrets of existence. He's the personification of total wisdom. He can discover the answer to any problem by means of his sixteen kola nuts. When Obatalá presented him with the problem of populating Olokun's domain, Orunla brought out his divining implements and set out to find an answer to Obatalá's question. After spending considerable time in the consultation of the oracle, he told Obatalá that what he wanted required a gold chain, a snail shell full of sand, a white hen, a black cat, and a palm nut.

Obatalá had an idea what the chain was for, but he was in the dark about the other things. Nevertheless, because he trusted Orunla's wisdom implicitly, he gathered all the objects together and set out on his self-imposed odyssey.

Obatalá had borrowed plenty of gold from the orishas to forge the chain, but when the goldsmith to whom he had entrusted the project presented him with the finished chain, it was clear that it would never reach the surface of the waters. Still, because he's stubborn and determined, he was unwilling to give up his plans, so he secured one end of the chain to one of the pillars of his house and let it fall down towards Olokun's realm. For a few seconds he stood poised above the abyss, and then with a courageous lunge he began the long descent.

Far above, standing next to Obatalá's house, Orunla watched in silence as his friend came closer to Olokun's domain. At last Obatalá reached the end of the chain and saw that, as he had foreseen, the chain did not reach the water. He hung over the darkness for a few minutes, clinging to the chain for dear life because he knew that unlike Omo Oba, he was not immortal. If he let go of the chain, he'd sink under the waters and drown.

Suddenly, from above, he heard Orunla's voice say to him, "Let the sand inside the snail shell fall into the water." Clinging to the chain with one hand, Obatalá dug inside his knapsack with the other and brought out the snail shell. With unsteady fingers, he tipped it towards the water and let the sand fall out. Again he heard Orunla's voice, "Release the hen now." Obediently, Obatalá brought out the hen and dropped it on the sand. Immediately the hen began to dig into the sand, dispersing it in all directions. Wherever the sand touched the water it became solid land. Soon there was a great expanse of dry ground over the water, and Obatalá let go of the chain and fell down on the new earth.

The new ground created by Obatalá with Orunla's help became known as the holy city of Ile-Ife, which is still to this day sacred to Obatalá. The palm nut he brought with him was planted immediately, and soon became a tall, shady palm tree. The cat was thoughtfully provided by Orunla to be Obatalá's companion until the city of Ile-Ife would become populated with other life.

Soon after Obatalá's descent from the sky, the other orishas became curious about the new land and one after the other they all came down to visit Obatalá.

Many of them returned to the sky after a while, but enough remained in Ile-Ife to give the city the beginning of the population it needed.

Creation of Humankind

Obatalá was happy in the city of Ile-Ife with Oddudúa and some of the orishas as his companions, but he still felt the place was too empty. Being of a gregarious nature, he missed the bustle of people around him, so he decided to create new life. He looked around for suitable building material, hoping to find some nice shiny stones, like the ones Olofi had used when he created the orishas, but there were no stones in the new land, only hard clay. Undaunted, Obatalá dug out some of the clay and began to shape human figures. As he finished each one, he laid it out on the ground to dry in the sun.

After he had been working for some time, Obatalá became very thirsty, and decided to drink some palm wine to quench his thirst. The sweet, sticky liquid made him even thirstier, so he drank some more. Very soon, his hands became clumsy through the effect of the liquid, and the figures which he then produced were malformed and twisted. Some had crooked backs, others had twisted legs and arms, and some had missing limbs.

Obatalá was too drunk to notice his mistakes and set these misshapen figures out to dry next to the well-formed ones. He then called out to Olofi to put the breath of life into the clay figures. Olofi, who had not seen the result of Obatalá's handiwork, and who trusted him implicitly, carried out his request and gave life to the figures. They immediately became living beings, full of human feelings and emotions.

When Obatalá's intoxication wore off and he saw what he had done, he was very unhappy and swore that from that moment onward he would never touch liquor again. He also became the protector of deformed people or those who are abnormal in some way.

This legend is the basis of the Yoruba belief that Obatalá shapes the newborn in their mothers' wombs.

Olokun

Obatalá's invasion of his domain for the creation of Ife had outraged Olokun, who had always been the supreme ruler of the waters. Obatalá's action had taken him at first by surprise, and he was not sure what he should do. For a while he roamed throughout his undersea palace, venting his anger at his retinue of tritons and mermaids. His mood grew blacker, until no one dared approach him for fear of his lashing fury. His anger was duly reflected in the ocean waters which grew more tempestuous each day. Finally, his seething rage exploded on the surface of the waters creating a gigantic tidal wave which burst upon the city of Ife, washing away half of the land and destroying many crops and human lives.

Obatalá was visiting Olofi and Orunla in the sky and was not present during Olokun's destruction. The people who still remained at Ife sent Eshú to bring the bad news to Obatalá and to warn him that Olokun's rage remained unabated and that soon all the land would be again covered by his waters.

Obatalá was naturally distressed by the news and immediately consulted his good friend Orunla on the best way to overcome Olokun. Orunla, calm as always, told Obatalá that he would descend to Ife and take care of Olokun his own way.

Olofi had conferred many powers on Orunla, including a great wisdom which made it possible for him to find solutions to almost unsolvable problems. It was therefore easy for him to control the waters and subdue Olokun. This he accomplished by presenting the enraged sea deity with the gold chain used by Obatalá to come down from the sky. Olokun, who is partial to fine jewelry, allowed Orunla to put the chain around him and did not realize his plight until he was unable to move. Orunla took advantage of his surprise to drop him thus chained into the water, where he sank immediately to the ocean floor. He still remains down there, bound by Obatalá's chains and unable to cover the earth with his waters. To the Yorubas, Olokun bound is the explanation for the law of gravity which keeps the ocean waters from covering the earth.

Yemayá

Yemayá

From Olokun, chained at the bottom of the sea, emanated the orisha Yemayá, who symbolizes the seven seas and all ocean waters. While Olokun is a male force, represented by a being half man and half fish, Yemayá is a female force and a symbol of motherhood. Because the seas are the source of all living things, Yemayá is seen as the mother of all that exists.

Olokun is Yemayá's most powerful aspect, the source of her existence. As long as he remains chained, she cannot cover the earth with her waters. And although occasionally she rages, and comes far inland destroying everything in her path, she must always return to her watery domain and respect the boundaries set by Obatalá and Orunla. But Yemayá does not enjoy destroying life. Her very essence is that of life giving. Only when she has been deeply offended by mankind's excesses does she punish by taking away that which she gives so freely.

Lovely, tender, warm and maternal, kind and forgiving, so is this most powerful orisha, whose blue mantle is trimmed with the foamy lace of the sea waves. She rides the waters in her silver boat, her long black hair covered with silver nets embroidered with pearls and seaweed, her turquoise tunic shimmering with the scales of a thousand silver fish. When she enters the waters in the high seas, she divests herself of her raiments and transforms herself into a mermaid. When she visits the earth she does so under the guise of a beautiful black woman whose unearthly beauty enraptures all men who see her.

Yemayá has seven aspects and in each one she has different characteristics. She's a powerful sorceress and sometimes when she dances, she wears a snake wrapped around her arm like a bracelet. Other times she hides her face behind a mask, a symbol of Olokun.

When Yemayá first walked the earth, wherever she placed her feet was born a fountain. From these fountains were created the rivers, symbols of her sister Oshún. But because all waters belong to the sea goddess, all rivers must return to the sea, a symbol of Oshún returning to her sister Yemayá.

One of Yemayá's first gifts to humankind was the sea shells, which are the mouthpieces of the orishas, through which they communicate to their priests the will of Olofi.

Yemayá's powers over the other orishas is explained in one of her many legends. One day Oloddumare-Olofi sent out a decree asking all the orishas to come to his *efín* (palace). Yemayá was in the earth at the time. When the news of the decree reached her she was sacrificing a ram, one of her favorite foods. Not wanting to come empty handed to see Olofi, and not having any other gift on hand, she placed the ram's head on a silver platter and brought it to the Creator. As it happened, she was the only one of the orishas who thought of bringing a present to Olofi. Touched by her thoughtfulness, the Creator rose from his throne and said, "*Awoyo Ori dori re.*" (A head you bring, a head shall you be.) And from that moment onwards, Yemayá was placed in rank above the other orishas.

According to another legend, Yemayá gave birth to the sun, moon, and stars after a brief dalliance with Olofi. As a gift for the magnificent children she had bore him, Olofi gave her Ochumare, the rainbow, to wear as her crown. That is why the rainbow only appears when Yemayá, as rain, has fallen upon the earth, and the sun, her child, shines through the clouds.

The Orishas in the World

After the land of Ile-Ife was created, other lands began to make their appearance throughout the planet. Now that Olokun was chained, Yemayá graciously acceded to surrender some of her territory to Obatalá. But as each continent sprang forth through the sea waters, Obatalá saw that the ground was wet and marshy. In order to dry the terrain he called forth the fiery orisha Aganyú whose breath can melt stones. With Aganyú's appearance upon the earth, the volcanoes were born, and from the ashes of the volcanoes the soil was created. The ruler of the soil was another deity, Orisha-Oko, who had the secret of the harvests. In those places where the ground was still damp with Yemayá's waters, Aganyú's ashes became muddy and swampy. These became the territory of still another orisha, Babalú-Ayé, who rules over illness and pestilence.

Finally the earth was dry and ready to spring new life. The orisha Osain now came forth and brought with him all the plants and the trees that are his domain. But because the earth had sprang from the sea it needed water to sustain life. Osain's woods and orchards and Orisha-Oko's crops needed Yemayá's blessing to grow rich and strong. As soon as she learned of the earth's needs, the gracious sea goddess came ashore and walked throughout the planet. And as we saw before, everywhere she placed her foot a water fountain was created. From these fountains, the rivers and the lakes rushed forth, ruled by Yemayá's sister Oshún, the goddess of love of the Yoruba pantheon.

Now the earth was covered with a green mantle of rich vegetation, the fields were ready to be tilled and planted, and most of the volcanoes had become mountains. Overjoyed with the results, Obatalá decided to create new forms of life to inhabit the planet. He created all manner of birds and beasts, many of which could be used by humankind to help in the tilling of the ground and for other tiresome chores. But the people living in Ile-Ife were not satisfied. They began to complain about the differences between themselves and the orishas. Why, they wanted to know, did they all look the same and had the same quantity of yams and money while the orishas all looked different and had different powers. It simply was not fair, they cried out. At first the orishas ignored the cries of the people, but after a while they became so vociferous that even the all-patient and peaceful Obatalá felt he had had enough. He traveled up to the sky and told Olofi of the people's complaints.

"Why do you allow yourself to be disturbed?" said Olofi. "Give them what they want. Assuredly they'll live to regret the day they asked to be different, but their ungratefulness deserves a punishment. Grant their wish." Obatalá saw the wisdom in the Creator's words and agreed to follow his instructions. Accordingly, he went back to Ile-lfe and called all the people to come and see him. When they had gathered around him, he told them he had decided to give them what they wanted thus making them different one from the other. The people were overjoyed by Obatalá's words and proceeded to express their desires. Those who wanted more land got it, those who desired more yams or money also got them. The ones who wanted lighter or darker skin also got their wish. And to make their differences more marked, Obatalá also gave them new languages so that they could not even communicate with each other.

At first the people were satisfied with the changes Obatalá had instituted. Then they began to grow suspicious of each other. Those with lighter skin felt superior to those with darker skin, those with more property began to look down their noses at their neighbors. Those who spoke the same language grouped together away from those who spoke different tongues. Slowly, they began to move away from Ile-Ife, seeking to put a safe distance between themselves and their old neighbors, whom they now distrusted. And eventually only the orishas were left in Ile-Ife.

Eleggua

As Olofi had foreseen, new orishas began to make their appearance on the earth. With the creation of the rivers, the orisha Oshún, who is the patron of all river waters and particularly of the river that bears her name, came into being. At the same time, the orishas Obba and Oyá made their appearances. Obba became the patron of the river that also bears her name, while Oyá became the patron of the Niger river (Odo-Oyá in Yoruba). Olofi conferred upon Oshún the ownership of gold and the patronage of love and marriage. Obba, he made the patron of the home, while upon Oyá he conferred the ownership of the winds. He also made her the keeper of the cemetery.

In the meantime, Obatalá, who is said to have twenty-four aspects, some of them female, got himself a new wife called Yemmu. (According to tradition, Yemmu is one of the feminine aspects of Obatalá.) Of the union between Obatalá and Yemmu was born a son whom they called Oggún. When he grew up he became the orisha who rules all metals, especially iron. He also became associated with the woods, where he is said to spend most of his time.

Also in the woods, of uncertain parentage, was born the orisha Ochosi, the patron of the hunt. He and Oggún became fast friends and had countless adventures together. Most of these adventures they shared with a third companion, the redoubtable Eleggua, also known as Eshú, who is one of the most important and colorful of the orishas.

There are many legends about Eleggua's origins. According to the most popular, he was at one time a young prince, whose parents were the *oba* (king) Oquiboru and his wife Anaqui. One day Eleggua decided to go on a hunting expedition with some of his friends. They had been riding for some time when suddenly the prince saw what seemed like three bright eyes shining in the distance. He stopped the cavalcade and bid them wait for him while he went to investigate the strange lights. When he approached closer he saw

Eleggua

that the three lights were emanating from a dry coconut (*obi*). He picked up the strange object and brought it back to his father's palace. But when he showed the coconut to his parents they were unimpressed by it. Eleggua himself soon lost interest in the coconut and threw it carelessly behind a door. Some time later the king gave a party and immediately after all the guests had arrived, the coconut began to emit the same strange lights that had caught Eleggua's attention. Terrified by the occurrence, the guests fled from the palace. Three days later, Eleggua died.

The coconut, still abandoned behind the door, continued to shine for some time, but after a while it stopped putting forth its strange lights. Almost at once Oquiboru's kingdom began to lose its former prosperity, and hunger and poverty soon covered the land with a mantle of despair. The *oba* ordered the priests to investigate the phenomenon and after many consultations with their oracles they concurred that their trouble was caused by the neglect of the coconut found by the dead prince. When they went in search of the *obi*, they found it had rotted away and was half eaten by insects. After some further consultations, the priests told the king that the coconut had to be replaced with a stone, a more durable and stable symbol of prosperity. Accordingly, the coconut was removed and a large stone put in its place behind the door. Soon afterwards the kingdom returned to its former glory. This story emphasizes the importance that stones (*ota*) have as symbols of the orishas.

In another legend on Eleggua's origin he is said to be the son of Alabwanna, identified in Cuban Santería with the tenebrous "Lonely Spirit," who is believed to be a lost soul in search of enlightenment. According to this story, soon after he was old enough to take care of himself, the mischievous Eleggua chained his mother hand and foot, and went off into the woods looking for adventures.

There are other stories concerning the birth of Eleggua, including one where he's said to be the son of Oyá, but in reality the origins of this formidable orisha are very vague. All that is known for sure is that he appeared one day, fully grown and ready for action, and that all the other orishas show him the greatest respect mixed with large doses of fear. For Eleggua, regardless of his uncertain origins, has the power to cross anybody's path, including that of the mighty Obatalá himself.

Among the Yorubas, Eleggua is known as Esu and Elegbara. According to their legends, he was one of the companions of Oddudúa when Ife was first created. Later on, he became an assistant to Orunmila in the divination system known as Ifa. He is said to have become the *oba* of the city of Ketu, where he is still revered by the inhabitants.

To the Yorubas, Esu has great phallic powers and can give or take away virility from any man. He is also a contradictory deity with many disparate qualities, sometimes beneficent and others openly malevolent. In Brazil, where he is better known as Exu, he has been syncretized with the devil.

In Cuban Santería, the orisha became known as Eleggua or Eshu. In contrast with his Brazilian counterpart, Cuba's Eleggua has been syncretized with several saints of the Catholic Church, such as the preeminent Saint Anthony, one of the purest and most miraculous of the Catholic saints. This curious identification may be due to the fact that Eleggua, like Saint Anthony, is also a miracle worker, capable of solving the most difficult problems. Of course in his negative aspects he can wreak havoc and disruption, and more often than not is busy causing trouble for the unwary. But these contradictory aspects of the orisha are seen in Santería as part of his ambivalent nature. For Eleggua in Cuba is identified with destiny, fate, sometimes bringing joy and other times bringing sorrow. He's above all a great champion of justice, delighting in punishing the guilty and rewarding the innocent.

There are innumerable legends about Eleggua. In fact, he often appears in the legends of the other orishas. That is because he is everywhere: in the woods, behind the doors, on the crossroads, in the sea, on the open fields. He is said to have twenty-one aspects and a different name for every aspect. In each of these aspects, he works with a different orisha. As Eshú Laroye, he works with Oshún; as Eshú Ayé, he works with Yemayá-Olokun; as Eshú Alabwanna, he works with Oggún and Ochosi. He's friendly with all the orishas because they value his friendship and for a very good reason, as will be seen in the following tale.

Soon after the earth's affairs had been more or less settled, Olofi became ill with a strange malady that depleted all his strength and weakened his powers. One by one he summoned all the orishas to see if they could use some of the *ashé* he had given them to cure him of his sickness. First came Orunla with the divination system of Ifa to try and determine what ailed the Creator. But even the divine oracle proved futile against the strange illness.

Obatalá tried next and after him Babalú-Ayé, followed by Yemayá and Oyá, but all to no avail. The stubborn illness continued to consume the Creator. Baffled by their inability to cure Olofi and saddened by his steadily worsening condition, the orishas sat down by the Creator's bedside to ponder what would be their next action. As they sat in consultation, there was a knock on the door. Obatalá rose to answer, but before he could get to the door it opened with a loud bang, and in strutted Eleggua. "I heard *Baba* (father) was ill and I came over to cure him," he said with a smile. "I know you think I'm too young and ignorant to be consulted when there are problems, but I want to show you how wrong you are." He flashed an insolent grin at the dumfounded orishas and swaggered across the room to the Creator's bedside.

Obatalá was the first of the orishas to recover from the surprise. Making a sign to the others to remain silent he went at once and stood by Eleggua's side. "Please *Baba*, forgive Eleggua's impetuosity," he said to the Creator. "He's only a youth, but he means well. I'll get him to leave right away."

Eleggua turned to him in a flash. "I don't need you to plead my case," he snapped at Obatalá. "And as for leaving, I won't until *Baba* is cured."

Olofi sat up with an effort and raised a hand. "Obatalá," he said, "you and the other orishas have tried to cure me and have failed. I appreciate your concern, but I believe in giving everyone a fair chance. Let the boy try. After all, he may have learned things roaming the woods that we don't know. Leave me with him. I'll call you if I need you."

Reluctantly, the elder orishas got up and left the room. As soon as he was alone with the Creator, Eleggua dug inside the shoulder bag he always carries and brought out a bunch of fresh herbs. "Here is your cure, *Baba*," he said. "I'll crush these in water and as soon as you've drunk the brew you'll be up and around, feeling better than before you got sick.

A few minutes later, the orishas who were hovering anxiously around the door heard Olofi calling. They went trooping into the room, expecting to find the Creator still sick and Eleggua chastised for his insolence. Instead, they saw Olofi standing proudly erect, radiating good health and majesty, his arm affectionately draped around Eleggua's shoulders. He beamed at them paternally. "My children," he said, "my old instinct did not fail me. Eleggua indeed had the cure for my illness. Obviously, unknown to all of us, he has acquired great wisdom. He may be young, but he has certainly come of age. I wish to reward him for his timely help. From now on he is to be the first orisha to be honored in all your ceremonies. He is the keeper of all doors and all ways. Without his permission no work, great or small, may be accomplished. Honor him now even as I myself honor him." He then took out a golden key and gave it to Eleggua to signify his guardianship of the doors. It is to Eleggua's credit that he did not gloat over his triumph nor attempt to humiliate the other orishas for their failure. Being wise beyond his years, he knew that it was to his best advantage to be friendly with his elders. And the other orishas, seeing his gracious and humble attitude, gladly accepted Olofi's command. There was much rejoicing in Olofi's palace over his recovery, and from that day onward, Eleggua took his rightful place among the orishas.

Changó

In the meantime, Obatalá's wife, Yemmu, had been away from Ife on some private matters. Having heard about Olofi's illness, she decided to cut her trip short and return to Ife. Unfortunately, since she had not been able to complete her business, she found herself without any money for the return journey. This did not worry her unduly, for the road back was straight and without danger, and she could walk and be home within a few days. The only impediment along the way was the crossing of a river, but she knew that the orisha Aganyú was in charge of ferrying people across, and she was certain he would agree to let her cross without having to pay the fee usually required of travelers.

The first part of the journey went on smoothly, and the next day Yemmu found herself by the riverside. As she had expected, Aganyú was in charge of the ferry boat. Very politely, Yemmu explained that she had no money for the fee and asked Aganyú to ferry her across free of charge. To her surprise, Aganyú refused. Almost in tears, Yemmu pleaded with the lord of volcanoes to let her cross, but Aganyú was adamant. A fee was required and without it, no one would be ferried across the river. Finally, in desperation, Yemmu offered Aganyú to lie with him in exchange for the trip across the river. The orisha considered the offer. Yemmu was beautiful and desirable, but she was also the wife of the powerful Obatalá. He might be risking the elder orisha's wrath if he found out. He debated between fear of Obatalá and desire for Yemmu for a few minutes, but Yemmu, seeing his indecision, continued to insist on her offer. And Aganyú, who had been without a woman for some time, succumbed to the temptation. He rushed with Yemmu to a wooded area by the riverside and for a long while the two orishas lay intertwined among the bushes, enjoying each other fully without thought of anything or anyone else.

Several days later, Obatalá was overjoyed to see his beautiful wife emerge from among the trees surrounding his yam farm. When he asked her why she had returned so soon, she explained she had heard about Olofi's illness and had wanted to be near him with the other orishas. Obatalá told her that Eleggua had already cured the Creator and all was well again in Ile-Ife. Yemmu rejoiced at the news and went back with Obatalá to their farm.

For a while everything went well with Yemmu and Obatalá, and she forgot all about her tryst with Aganyú at the river's edge. But several months later, she woke up with a familiar queasiness that made her remember Aganyú only too well. At first, she hoped that she was wrong about her fears, but very soon realized her fears were well founded. She was going to have a child and only Aganyú could be the father. Obatalá was so busy with the farm and overseeing the problems of humankind, he had not lain with her for a long time.

All gaiety seemed to abandon Yemmu all of a sudden. She was always tired and listless and never joined the other orishas in their frequent gatherings. Soon Obatalá, who is very observant, noticed the change in his wife. When he questioned her, he was surprised by Yemmu's reaction. She began to cry without a word and nothing Obatalá would say could calm her down. Finally, at Obatalá's insistence, Yemmu broke down and confessed what had happened with Aganyú. Obatalá was shocked and saddened by Yemmu's confession, but being the symbol of peace and magnanimity, he generously forgave the offense, and promised to raise her child as one of his own.

Apparently consoled by her husband's kindness, Yemmu continued her work in the farm and waited for the birth of her child. But deep within, her sorrow and shame were unabated. In due time, she gave birth to a beautiful boy whom she named Changó. Of all her children, he was the handsomest and the one she loved the most. Even Obatalá was captured by the child's vivaciousness and soon he was also his favorite. Thus Changó grew strong and secure, safe in the love of his parents. But unknown to Yemmu, her shameful secret was known to others. And one day, in the midst of play, one of his playmates, irked by Changó's growing arrogance, told the boy he was not really Obatalá's son. Crushed and humiliated, Changó ran to his mother and demanded to know the truth about his birth. This was the moment Yemmu had feared since Changó had been born. She knew he was a special child, one to whom she could never lie. So she sat down with her son, and fighting back her tears, told him he was not Obatalá's son. What she refused to tell him was the name of his real father.

Yemmu's confession went like a knife deep into Changó's proud heart. He felt he could no longer face his brethren and his friends, as long as he did not know the name of his father. His illegitimacy did not bother him, what gnawed at his mind was not knowing who his father was. Maybe his father was a rogue and a social outcast, and if so he would always have to walk with his proud head humbled to the ground. But if his father was a powerful orisha, then he would be able once more to walk among his friends with pride. Whatever the truth might be, he simply had to know.

As soon as Obatalá found out that Changó knew the truth, he endeavored to show the boy that he loved him as much as if Changó were his real son. Changó loved his adoptive father and now that he knew that Obatalá had accepted him knowing the truth, he loved him even more. But the obsession grew within him to find out the identity of his real father. Day after day, he tormented Yemmu with the same question, "Who is he, *iyá-mí* (my mother)? Who is my father?" Finally, unable to face the boy's questions anymore, Yemmu broke down and revealed the name of his father to Changó.

If Yemmu thought that her revelation would calm down her impetuous son, she was mistaken. On the contrary, the news that his father was the powerful orisha Aganyú so overjoyed Changó that he became determined to seek him out and tell him that he had a son. Yemmu, who suspected that Aganyú had long forgotten their brief encounter, tried to dissuade Changó from his plans. But all her pleas fell on deaf ears. Changó had made up his mind to find his father, and when Changó makes up his mind to do something, it is as good as done. So one fine day, a tearful Yemmu and a sad Obatalá bade goodbye to Changó as he set out to find the god of volcanoes. Yemmu cried all the more because somehow her mother's instinct told her that her son would never return home. And maternal instincts never fail, as she found out to her deep sorrow.

In the meantime Changó set out on his quest with the resolute determination that was to become one of his special attributes. For many long months he journeyed, braving bad weather, hunger, and the many dangers of the road, but Aganyú was nowhere to be found. Many years had passed since he had been ferrying people across the river, and he had moved away and no one could tell Changó where. But Changó is not one to give up easily.

One day he sat down by the side of the road and pondered where the mighty Aganyú could have gone. Suddenly a smile lit up his face. "Of course," he cried out loud. "Where else can he be?" He looked up with shining eyes and saw, among the tree fronds that shaded the road, the snowy peaks of a volcano.

Aganyú was busy melting stones when he saw a young boy, strongly built and of unusual beauty, approach his place of work. The boy was well dressed but his clothes were dusty and torn in places, as if he had been on the road for a long time. And there was something about his eyes and the soft curve of his lips that stirred a dim memory in the orisha's mind. He stopped what he was doing and stared at the boy curiously, but then he noticed the firm cut of the jaw and the faint air of defiance about the youth and the memory faded.

"What do you want, boy?" he asked brusquely. "I'm busy and haven't got time to waste." Changó stared at his father and said nothing. He had heard many stories about Aganyú but he was not prepared to find him in this fashion, dirty and dishevelled, working like a common mortal at the foot of the volcano. "Well, speak up, boy," snapped Aganyú. "I told you I'm busy. I haven't got all day."

"Are you ... the orisha Aganyú?" asked Changó shyly. For the first time in his young life he was face to face with someone who filled him with something close to fear.

Aganyú looked at his son with renewed curiosity. "I am indeed Aganyú," he said, not ungently. "What do you want with me?"

Changó hesitated, then the memory of his mother came rushing back to his young mind and his fear disappeared. "I am your son Changó, born of Yemmu, wife of Obatalá," he said proudly.

Changó's words were like a sudden torrent of clear water washing down a dam of deeply repressed memories. Aganyú suddenly remembered the encounter in the woods and the free ferry ride, and knew at once why Changó had looked so familiar when he first saw him. His first reaction was one of pride. So, he thought with masculine vanity, he had given something special to the beautiful Yemmu to remember him by. And the boy was strong and handsome, a source of pride to any father. But then a second, less pleasant thought came to his mind. If he admitted being the boy's father, he would also have to admit betraying Obatalá. And that might cost him dearly. Obatalá was the head of Ife and the chief of all the orishas. Aganyú was no coward, but he did not like the idea of having to face the rest of the orishas led by an enraged Obatalá. Because he was a warrior and an unforgiving foe, it did not occur to Aganyú that the peaceful and kind Obatalá might have forgiven him. So, very much against his inner wishes which were to embrace Changó and admit his paternity, Aganyú turned his back to the boy and resumed his work. "Your mother lied to you, boy," he said shortly. "I have never met her. I am not your father."

Of all the things Changó expected his father to say, this was the most shocking and unexpected. To be denied by Aganyú hurt and humiliated him, but the insult to his mother filled him with rage. "My mother did not lie," he cried, his voice trembling with fury. "You are the liar. You are a coward and a liar." Perhaps because Changó's words rang so true, Aganyú went blind with rage. Without thinking, he turned back to his young son and blasted him with a rushing stream of lava that went forth from his mouth in a single breath. The force of the blast blew Changó all the way up to the sky. Olofi, who had returned to his heavenly realm, was taking a walk around his garden when he saw the boy, enveloped in flames, land at his feet. And far below, Aganyú, repentant of his violent action and sure of Changó's death, sat down to mourn the son he had rejected.

But Changó was not dead. When the flames that covered him died out, he stood up on firm legs completely unscathed. And seeing Olofi, whom he immediately recognized, he dropped to the floor and paid *foribale* (homage) at his feet.

Olofi stared in amazement at the beautiful young boy that lay completely naked at his feet. Then he raised him up and gave him his blessing. At his orders, one of his servants brought new clothes for Changó, whose tattered rags had been burned off by the flames. Olofi, who could not understand why Changó had not been burned, sat the boy next to him and proceeded to interrogate him.

After he had heard Changó's story, Olofi understood why the young boy had not been harmed by Aganyú's flames. As his son, he had inherited Aganyú's immunity against fire. Won over by Changó's charming ways and his extraordinary valor, Olofi decided to reward him for all his troubles. He therefore decreed that from that day onward Changó would be the sole owner and master of fire, as well as thunder and lightning. A new orisha had been born, one of the most powerful and fearsome of the Yoruba pantheon.

But Olofi was still worried about Changó,who refused to be sent back to Yemmu.

The boy, ashamed by his father's rejection, did not want to humiliate his mother by telling her of his ordeal. So the Creator pondered the boy's situation, and finally thought of a happy solution. Far below the sky, in her watery domain, the orisha Yemayá cried constantly to him for the gift of a son. So far, Olofi had been too busy to answer her request. But now he had a son for Yemayá. And what a son!

Thus Changó's quest for identity had a happy ending. He spent the rest of his childhood and early youth in the loving care of the queen of the seas, who soon grew to love him as her own flesh and blood. And one day, when Changó finally returned to firm land, he found a humble and contrite giant waiting for him at the beach. It was his father Aganyú. Without a word, the god of the volcanoes started to kneel in front of his son. But Changó lifted him to his feet and did not let him reach the ground. Silently, the two orishas embraced while the waves sizzled at their feet. From that day forward their friendship has been so close that one cannot be without the other. That is why, in Santería, the person who receives the secrets of Changó must also receive those of Aganyú. And Aganyú cannot be received, except through his son Changó.

Changó

Changó Comes of Age

When Changó arrived on dry land, he settled in the city of Oyo, not too far from the holy city of Ile-Ife. And there, to this day, is a shrine in his honor and all the city's inhabitants worship him. The king (*oba*) claims to be a direct descendant from Changó, who, according to tradition, was at one time an actual living man.

One of Changó's first actions upon reaching solid ground was to visit his mother Yemmu and his adoptive father Obatalá. Because the orishas are archetypal forces that do not change once they have reached their full personalities, Changó found his parents just the same as when he had left. There was much rejoicing at Obatalá's farm and there were many festivities among the orishas to celebrate Changó's homecoming. But Changó had already decided that he wanted to settle down in Oyo, and one day, he embraced Yemmu and Obatalá and left Ile-Ife.

Changó had not been in Oyo for very long when the fame of his exploits as a warrior and his supernatural powers over fire and lightning won him the kingdom. Oyo had been without a king for a long time and the city's inhabitants were happy to have an orisha as powerful as Changó as their *oba*.

For a while, Changó settled down and gave all his attention to the business of ruling Oyo. He even decided, after much consideration, to get married. Finding a wife was not an easy task because Changó was a devastating womanizer. He loved women almost as much as he loved eating and dancing. And he was so handsome and charming there was no woman who could resist his advances. He had barely announced he had decided to put an end to his bachelorhood than there were hundreds of women banging at his palace doors wailing to be chosen as his mate. But Changó wanted to make the right decision. He knew that as the *oba* he could have many wives, but he only wanted one, the perfect woman to be his queen. This woman he found in Obba, goddess of the river that bears her name. Contrary to the beautiful women that constantly went through Changó's arms, Obba was rather plain and quiet. But she was stately and serene, both qualities that the fiery orisha found admirable in a woman. In short, Obba was a lady.

The wedding soon took place to the dismay of all of Changó's former paramours, and the happy new couple settled down to a long life together. For the first few months, Changó was a model husband. He was loving, tender, and attentive and his young wife was ecstatic. But soon Changó began to change. He still loved his wife, but he began to find her dull and unexciting. She offered him no challenge with her constant adoration. Worse still, he began to yearn for other women, for the thrill of other lips and the wild abandon of another body. In short, Changó was bored. As his boredom grew, his treatment of Obba worsened. Now he seldom came home to eat and spent most of his free time with wild women at wild parties. Of course Obba suffered, but being quiet and ladylike, she suffered in silence.

Watching this scenario from afar was another orisha, the fabulously beautiful and rich Oshún, goddess of the Oshún river and of love, gold, and marriage. For some time Oshún had been watching Changó, for whom she had developed a violent desire. She had carefully avoided meeting Changó face to face because she knew about his many dalliances with women and she did not want to be one more adventure in his life. She wanted to be special for him, and so she waited for the most opportune time to show herself. This time came one day when a great party was given in honor of one of the other orishas. Changó arrived early and immediately began to drink palm wine and play the *bataá* drums. Today these are the ritual drums in Santería which are played at parties honoring the orishas.

Halfway through the party Oshún made her triumphal appearance. She had decked herself in her most seductive clothes and looked more beautiful than ever. She slowly paraded herself in front of the drums, behind which Changó was pounding away tirelessly. Under other circumstances,

Changó would have noticed Oshún immediately and made an instant play for her. Unfortunately for the goddess of love, she had arrived a little too late. Changó had drunk so much palm wine and was so wrapped up in his drum playing that he did not even see her passing in front of him.

Undaunted by Changó's apparent indifference, Oshún circled the floor and passed once more in front of the drums. Once again Changó ignored her. At first Oshún could not understand the reason for Changó's lack of interest. She knew she was the most beautiful orisha in the room, so there had to be a strong reason for his attitude. She retreated to a corner of the chamber and studied the orisha from a distance. It soon became clear to her why Changó was paying her no attention. He was simply too drunk to notice. But Oshún has wiles other women envy, and she knew of an infallible way to attract Changó's attention. Hanging innocently from her golden belt, she had a small vial filled with the secret of her seductiveness: *oñi*, the substance commonly known as honey, which is a covert symbol of Oshún's sexuality.

Dipping her fingers lightly into the honey, Oshún approached Changó from behind and quickly smeared some of the cloying liquid over Changó's lips. The orisha's reaction was instantaneous. His drunken stupor lifted like a veil, and he was left as sober as if he had not drunk a drop of palm wine. He licked his lips and tasted Oshún's honey, and immediately turned around searching for the source of the sweet liquid. And there was Oshún, smiling invitingly at him, her eyes shining with unabashed lust. Changó needed no further invitation. The party, the drums, and the wine vanished from his mind as if they had never been there. He only had eyes for Oshún. Never had he seen a woman more beautiful and desirable. He simply had to have her.

Oshún, seeing her desire echoed in Changó's eyes, turned around and left the room. Changó followed her blindly. Once outside, she guided him to a wooded area where they fell into each other's arms without a word. Not that any words were needed. Their passion spoke for them both. For hours they lay on the ground in the throes of the most violent lust neither one of them had known. And for the first time, Changó found a woman who matched his ardor, beat by beat, never satiated, forever wanting more. Night came and gave way to day, and Changó and Oshún continued locked in each other's arms. When they finally separated, they both knew their passion had barely started. Oshún had succeeded in her plans, and she had become someone special to Changó, a woman he would love well and for all time. But her success would always be marred by the knowledge that Changó would never be totally hers. Because although love, symbolized by Oshún, cannot exist without passion, this passion, symbolized by Changó, can find other expressions, such as war, hatred, art, and inspiration. So Oshún continued to love Changó above all others, while he, still loving her, loved others better.

Oshún and Obba

While Changó continued to lead his frantic life of never ending pleasures, the faithful Obba languished in her palace, vir-
tually abandoned by her husband. But Oshún, whose passion
for the god of fire and lightning grew with each passing day,
begrudged Obba her rightful status as Changó's wife. Consumed by jealousy, Oshún conceived a plan to drive Changó
away from Obba's house. Changó still returned at night to
sleep with his wife, and even though he seldom made love to
her and Oshún knew it, the mere thought of Changó lying
next to Obba drove her wild with rage.

In order to execute her nefarious plan, Oshún pretended to make friends with Obba. She had been careful to
hide her illicit relations with Changó, and Obba was unaware
that her new friend was in reality one of her strongest rivals
for her husband's affection. As this false friendship grew
stronger, Obba confided to Oshún her problems with Changó
and her desire to regain his love. "Nothing could be simpler,
dear friend," said Oshún, placing a graceful arm around
Obba's unsuspecting shoulders. "You know how much
Changó loves food, and after all, everyone says that the way
to a man's heart is through his stomach. Feed him well and
he'll feel compelled to come home for supper every evening.
Once you have him in the house, you'll know what to do."
And she gave an affectionate hug to Obba.

"But Oshún," cried Obba, "I'm not a very good cook.
Neither do I have any of the supernatural powers Olofi
endowed you with. How can I cook for Changó and expect
him to come home every night?"

Oshún smiled and lowered her eyes modestly, but
through her long eyelashes she watched Obba with the same
ferocious concentration of a panther ready to jump its prey. It
pleased her to know that Obba was suffering, but she wanted
her to suffer more.

"Obba," she said finally. "I have never revealed to anyone any of my culinary secrets, but since you are my very

Oshún

best friend, I'm going to share one with you. Haven't you ever noticed how low I wear my headdress, making sure the cloth covers my ears?" And she adjusted the twisted turban usually worn by Yoruba women of high rank.

Obba stared at her curiously. "No, my friend," she answered innocently. "I never really noticed. And anyway, your headdresses are usually so beautiful one hardly notices how they are worn."

Oshún's smile deepened. "Well, there's a reason for it," she said, lowering her voice to a whisper. "You see, I haven't got any ears. I cut them off long ago to add them as a secret ingredient to my food. For some strange reason they act as an aphrodisiac. Men go wild with passion for the women who feed them their ears."

The innocent Obba gasped with horror. "Oshún, my dear, I never imagined," she cried. "Remove your headdress. Let me see what you look like without it." But Oshún moved quickly away from her and shook her head.

"No, my friend," she said, "Only my lovers can see me without my headdress. But as you well know, I have plenty of lovers, so having no ears has not detracted from my beauty. If anything, the unusual look makes me even more enticing."

Obba was well aware of men's fatal fascination for the beautiful Oshún, and since she had no reason to doubt her honesty, she readily believed the malicious lie. "Are you sure feeding Changó my ears will bring him back to me?" she asked her false friend. "What if it doesn't work for me?"

Oshún laughed. "Of course it will work for you," she said. "I tell you it's a secret ingredient. But don't tell anybody I told you about this. It's one of my most closely guarded secrets. Most especially, don't tell Changó. If you do, the charm won't work."

And with that, Oshún left Obba to ponder her advice.

Several days later Changó told Obba that he would be bringing a few friends for dinner the next day. And Obba, wanting to impress her husband with her cooking, decided to follow Oshún's advice. The friends were sitting with Changó, waiting for the food to be served, when in walked Obba with a large calabash full of Changó's favorite *cararu* (soup). None of them noticed that she was wearing her headdress very low, carefully covering her ears.

With bated breath, Obba set the *cararu* in front of her husband and sat down next to him. Changó lifted a ladle to spoon out the soup when he saw two strange objects floating on the soup's surface. He leaned forward to take a closer look and suddenly grimaced in disgust. He had recognized the floating objects as two neatly severed human ears. He turned at once to his wife, a look of horror in his face. "Obba, what have you done?" he cried. Obba, terrified by the look in her husband's face and the ominous tone of his voice, shrank away from him and covered her face with her hands. Changó's friends, sensing a marital dispute was in the air, left the room without a word. Changó, fearing the worst, leaped from his seat and tore the headdress from his wife's head. All at once he saw his fears confirmed, for there was only a horribly mutilated surface where Obba's ears should have been.

"Why, Obba? Why did you do such a dreadful thing?" he asked, looking at her with a mixture of pity and disgust. "How could you cut off your ears and serve them to me in a soup?"

The horror and loathing in her husband's eyes nearly broke poor Obba's heart. "It was Oshún," she wailed. "She told me to season the soup with my ears to make you pay more attention to me."

Changó sat down with a heavy sigh. "Poor Obba," he said softly. "You listened to such ill-intended advice out of love for me. I should have never married you. You're much too good for me. I should have married a woman like Oshún. She and I have a lot more in common."

Obba looked up with tearful eyes. "You marry Oshún? What are you saying, my husband?"

The pity in Changó's eyes intensified. "My poor Obba," he said sadly. "Don't you know why Oshún gave you such terrible advice? She has been my mistress for many months now. I thought you knew. I thought everybody knew."

Obba looked at Changó in dismay. "You and Oshún?" she whispered in disbelief. "But Oshún is my friend. She wouldn't hurt me on purpose. It can't be. I won't believe it."

"Suit yourself," said Changó impatiently. "You're my lawful wife. I will never humiliate you by taking another, but I can no longer live with you. Stay in the palace. I'll have another house built for myself, and you will always be provided for."

None of Obba's entreaties would make Changó change his mind. That same evening he left his wife, never to return. In due time Obba realized Oshún had indeed betrayed her. Ashamed by her naiveté and unable to exact revenge, she remained in her palace, forlorn and remote, wife only in name of the redoubtable Changó.

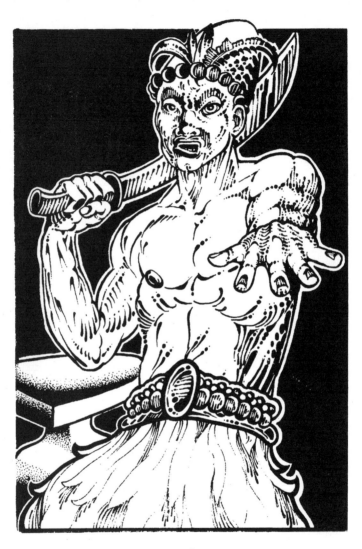

Oggún

Oggún

After he left Obba, Changó felt very sad and depressed. There was only one person he felt he could talk to who would understand his plight: his adoptive father Obatalá. Without a second thought, he saddled the huge hound he used as a horse and rode swiftly to Ile-Ife. When he arrived at Obatalá's yam farm, he found the place in disarray and the servants running to and fro in total confusion. His mother Yemmu was in her room crying, and although happy to see Changó, would not tell him what had happened. And Obatalá, usually so calm and serene, sat in a corner by himself, his face a quiet mask of despair. He looked up at Changó with sunken eyes, but shook his head when the orisha asked him to explain what was wrong.

Puzzled and distressed, Changó questioned the servants but they all fled from him in terror, refusing to speak. Changó wandered around the house for some time, looking for possible clues to the mystery, and finding none, decided to take a walk outside. He had barely taken a few steps when he saw his good friend Eleggua standing in the corner. The younger orisha was leaning against a fence, whistling softly and whittling away at a piece of wood. His cap was casually tilted at the back of his head. From time to time he dug into his shoulder bag, brought out a morsel of food and put it in his mouth. When he finished eating, he went back to his whistling.

Changó watched Eleggua in silence for a few minutes. He disliked discussing his family's affairs with the other orishas, but he knew Eleggua was a good friend. And Eleggua always knew everything that was happening among the orishas. It was his business to know. Undoubtedly he knew what was wrong at Obatalá's farm. Without any further hesitation, Changó crossed the road and walked over to Eleggua. The two orishas greeted each other warmly and after a few pleasantries had been exchanged, Changó asked Eleggua what was happening between Yemmu and Obatalá.

Eleggua went back to his whittling and was silent for a few minutes. Changó waited patiently. He knew Eleggua's ways. He'd talk only when he was good and ready. Finally Eleggua looked up. "I know you're quick tempered, my friend, and I don't know if I should tell you," he said. "But I think you have a right to know. It's your adoptive brother Oggún. It seems he offended Yemmu grievously and Obatalá threw him out of the house. There was a great fracas in there. You know how violent Oggún can be. But in the end he left and went back to his wife Oyá and their farm near the woods. He has set up a forge there and does all the metal work for the orishas."

Changó's eyes narrowed to slits, and behind those slits there was suddenly a red glow, like that of an open furnace. His nostrils flared and his upper lip lifted like a tiger when it snarls. A thin trail of smoke issued from his mouth as he glared at Eleggua. When he spoke, his voice trembled like a dull roll of thunder in the distance.

"What did Oggún do to offend my mother?" he roared. "What did he say to her? Tell me!" With each word he uttered, a small tongue of fire came out of his mouth. His hair bristled, his eyes sparkled, and there was a faint red glow all over his giant frame.

Eleggua seemed unmoved by the terrifying change in his friend. Undaunted, he continued to whittle and feed from his shoulder bag.

"I can't tell you what Oggún did to Yemmu or what he said to her," he said calmly.

"But you know everything," thundered Changó, trembling with rage. "You must know this also. Tell me or I'll …" As his voice trailed away, he moved menacingly toward Eleggua. The younger orisha, strong and wiry but of a slight build, did not flinch at the obvious menace in Changó's words.

Leaning back further against the fence, he looked up at Changó with clear, steady eyes. "Or you'll what?" he asked. Changó stared at his friend as if he were seeing him for the first time. His face relaxed and his eyes cleared. Eleggua's cool and calm demeanor seemed to pacify the fiery orisha. He took a deep breath and smiled ruefully.

"Forgive me, my friend," he said with an embarrassed grin. "My rage wasn't directed at you. I was blind with fury. Will you forgive me?"

Eleggua's face lit up with an impish grin. "What is there to forgive? Aren't we friends?" He came closer to Changó and put an affectionate arm around the wide shoulders of the god of thunder. "You think I don't know what you're feeling?" he asked kindly. "I know you're angry and want to avenge the offense to your mother. But violence is not always the answer. Sometimes it is better to use other methods."

"What do you mean?" asked Changó, puzzled."What methods are you talking about? I'm not interested in talking to Oggún if that's what you mean. All I want to do now is find him and break his neck. I don't even want to know what he did to my *iyá*. That he made her cry and Obatalá suffer is all I need to know."

"Talking wasn't what I meant," said Eleggua with a cagey smile. "After all, your brother Oggún is not much for talking either. But if what you want is to get even, there are better ways than fighting. Better … and more fun," he added maliciously.

"What do you mean, Eleggua?" asked Changó again. "You don't speak clearly."

"I never do," said the younger orisha going back to his whittling. "I like to make people think. It helps them see their problems in the proper perspective. You think of what I told you. You'll then see what I mean." He threw the carved piece of wood he had been whittling into his shoulder bag and straightened up. "I've got to go now," he said with a yawn. "I promised to run an errand for Orunla. See you around, my friend. If you need me, whistle." He flashed a grin at Changó and disappeared among the trees.

Changó went back to Obatalá's house in a pensive mood. The place had now been cleared and everything seemed to have returned to normal. Yemmu was back doing her household chores and Obatalá was sitting in a corner smoking a large cigar. He also seemed like his old, serene self. But there were shadows behind his eyes that Changó could clearly perceive.

As soon as Changó entered, Obatalá ordered one of his servants to prepare the god of thunder's favorite *cheketé*, a drink made with sour oranges and honey. He signaled his old favorite to come sit by his side, and soon the two orishas were smoking cigars and talking like old times. Changó carefully avoided the subject of Oggún's offense to his mother, and talked instead of his own marital problems. Obatalá seemed grateful for Changó's discretion and relaxed more. Soon he was busy counseling his adoptive son on the trials of married life, as if nothing had happened. The *cheketé* arrived, and for a long time the two orishas drank and talked companionably in the semi-darkness.

But all the time he was talking with Obatalá, Changó was going over in his head what Eleggua had told him. And suddenly it all seemed quite clear to him, Eleggua had been right. There was another way to get even with Oggún that was far better than a fight and, like Eleggua had maliciously suggested, far more fun.

The next day Changó woke up early and prepared to leave. Yemmu and Obatalá wanted him to stay longer, but he excused himself with the pretext that he could not stay away from Oyo very long. He kissed his mother and embraced his adoptive father, jumped on his dog and rode away.

But Changó had no intention to return to Oyo just then. As soon as he was out of sight from Obatalá's farm, he veered and rode in the direction of Oggún's house. When he was nearing his brother's forge, he alit from his dog and tied it by a tree where it could not be seen from the road. But instead of walking in the direction of the forge, where he could see Oggún busily working at his anvil, he turned and walked toward the field where Oggún's wife Oyá was tending the crops.

Oyá was bending down over a row of yams when a shadow came between herself and the sunlight. She looked up with a frown and saw Changó's towering figure standing before her. She rose at once from her squatting position and her hand flew automatically to her hair, covered modestly with a flowered bandanna. It was a reaction common among women when they first came face to face with the handsome orisha.

Oyá had seen Changó many times from afar, but she had never been in close contact with him. She thought him attractive but unbearably arrogant, and being a married woman, never gave much thought to the god of thunder, whose amorous exploits were legendary among the orishas.

Changó looked down at Oyá and a boyish grin curled his sensuous lips. "I salute my brother's wife," he said, and added gallantly, "even hard work and the blistering rays of the sun cannot detract from her beauty."

Oyá blushed and lowered her eyes. Her fingers, stained by the damp soil, self-consciously adjusted the top of her blouse. Changó's fiery eyes seem to burn holes in her clothes and she felt naked under his searching gaze.

"I salute my husband's brother," she answered conventionally. "We are honored by his presence."

"My brother asked me to come for you," said Changó, wasting no time. "He has been called away from his forge due to a peasant uprising in the north. He's worried about your safety and wants you to stay for the duration of the trouble in a small place he has near Oyo. He asked me to escort you there."

Oyá was puzzled but not disturbed by the news. Oggún went away to do battle very often. As the god of war and metals, his presence during armed conflicts was necessary. "But the north has been calm for many months," she said dubiously. "And why didn't he send for me before he left?"

"I came to bring him the news and there was no time to waste," said Changó convincingly. "Of course if you prefer to stay here alone I will not insist. I'm only conveying my brother's wishes."

"No, I'll go with you," said Oyá. "If that's what he wishes me to do, I'll have to obey his wishes. I'll just go to the house for a moment and pick up some things."

"There is no time for that, my sister," said Changó hurriedly. "My wife Obba will be glad to let you have some of her clothing. If you wish to go with me, we must leave at once."

As he spoke he looked worriedly in the direction of the forge. Catching the concern in his eyes, Oyá assumed he was worried about her safety. But Changó was more concerned to see Oggún come out into the fields. Under Changó's prodding, Oyá hurried from the fields and followed him to the place where he had left his dog. A few minutes later they were riding swiftly in the direction of Oyo.

Oggún, busy in his forge, did not notice Oyá's absence from the fields. It was not until he went into the house for supper that his servants told him his wife was gone. By that time Oyá was in one of the many houses that Changó kept in Oyo for his romantic adventures.

As soon as he and Oyá walked into the house, Changó called the few servants he kept in the place and ordered them to place sentinels around the small dwelling and not to let anyone come through. If someone approached he was to be told at once. Then he asked that food be prepared for him and his guest, and had some of the female attire that was in the house be brought to Oyá.

Changó's swift preparations to protect the house did not worry Oyá. She thought it natural that he would take proper precautions if there was unrest in the vicinity. She excused herself politely and went into one of the inner rooms to wash and change her work clothes. When she came back a few minutes later Changó was pacing up and down the floor, a worried frown creasing his forehead. He looked up when he heard Oyá approach and stopped in his tracks. Oyá had exchanged her stained clothes for a robe of purple damask embroidered with bronze-colored silk. Her long dark hair framed her beautiful proud face and hung far below her waist. She looked stately and majestic like a queen. Unlike

Oshún's classical beauty, Oyá's attraction was of a more earthy quality. Her features were not perfectly symmetrical, but they were alive with a magnetic intensity that made her overwhelmingly sensual. And her natural aloofness made her even more desirable in Changó's eyes.

Oyá saw Changó's searing glance and lowered her eyes. Her heart beat a little bit faster and she felt a strange excitement begin to creep inside her skin. She turned her back on the god of thunder and walked to the window. "Have you heard from my husband?" she asked. She could feel her hands trembling and her knees felt so weak they could hardly sustain her. She had never felt like this before. Never had any man awaken such feelings in her merely by looking at her.

Changó was silent for a few minutes, then he came closer to Oyá. "No, I haven't," he said, his voice hoarse and constrained. "I'm sure we will have news soon." He reached out a hand and touched Oyá's shoulder. "Oyá," he whispered.

Oyá jumped as if she had been burned. "No!" she cried, "No!" Blindly, she turned away from him and ran to the opposite side of the room. She cowered there, against the wall, her eyes wild with a mixture of terror and desire. She watched him approach her slowly, his eyes glowering like dull flames, his whole body trembling with passion. "No!" she moaned softly as his arms enveloped her and his mouth covered hers with frenzied kisses. Even as her hands pushed back helplessly against his chest, she found her lips responding to his. Soon she was fighting him no longer, her body, her instincts, and her will totally subjected to him and his desire. As if in a dream, she felt him pick her up and carry her inside. And all that night, as their passion roared, fed by Changó's voracious fires, the two orishas forged a link that would bind them forever.

For many days Oggún searched everywhere for the missing Oyá. The entire city of Iré, where Oggún lived and was the *oniire* (king), was turned literally upside down by Oggún in his search for his wife. Finally, the orisha realized Oyá had been taken outside his realm. And because people always talk, it was not long before Oggún was told that his wife Oyá was living in Oyo with Changó.

Oggún's reaction was predictable. Of all the orishas he is the only one whose violent strength and terrible temper can match Changó's. Blinded by rage and humiliation, the lord of iron jumped on the large ram he used as a steed and rode swiftly towards Oyo.

Changó's initial intention had been to seduce Oyá and then return her to his half brother, broken and humiliated. It was his way of avenging Oggún's offense to Yemmu and Obatalá. What he never expected was to fall in love with Oyá. He now knew he would do battle for her until death if necessary, but he would never surrender her to Oggún. With his usual blunt honesty, he had explained to Oyá what he had intended to do originally, and she, who was now enslaved by her love for him, accepted his explanation. It was to the united front made by Changó and Oyá that Oggún was now coming.

Changó's house was expectantly silent when Oggún arrived. All the guards and sentinels that had been surrounding the place had been removed. Oggún alit from his mount and approached the house.

"Changó!" he roared. "It is I, Oggún! Come out and bring my wife Oyá with you!"

Almost immediately Changó came out on the house's verandah. Oyá was by his side, her arm around his waist in a gesture of proud defiance.

"Here I am, my brother," said Changó with a mocking smile. "And here is your wife. Come and get her if you want."

Oggún's face went crimson with rage when he saw his wife and half brother brazenly and openly displaying their contempt for him and their passion for each other.

"You will surely die for this, Changó," he cried furiously. "But before I kill you, tell me why you have dishonored me. I thought you were my brother and my friend!"

"You dishonored yourself when you dishonored our mother and father," yelled back Changó. "I am no longer your brother or your friend!"

Oggún's face blanched at Changó's words, then he seemed to go mad with fury. With a loud yell he pulled out the large machete he always carries by his side, and lunged at Changó. But before he could reach his brother, Changó had leaped from the verandah to the opposite side of the courtyard. In his hand he brandished a huge *oshé*, the double-edged ax which is his traditional weapon.

The two orishas glared at each other and moved cautiously closer. Oggún growled deep in his throat like a wounded animal. Each time he moved, the huge muscles on his half naked body rippled sinuously. Changó watched him like a cat would a mouse, his eyes glittering red, his nostrils flaring, his mouth smiling in cruel anticipation of the first deadly blow. Faint tendrils of smoke issued from his mouth, nose, and ears.

With a loud snarl, Oggún jumped suddenly at Changó, swinging his machete at his brother's head. Changó roared and lifted his ax and the two blades met in midair with an echoing clang. From the verandah Oyá watched the two orishas do battle for her. She shook with excitement, her eyes shining. For Oyá, unlike the prim Obba, was also a warrior orisha. Though a female, her exploits in battle were already legendary. Goddess of the whirlwind, she fought like a raging storm, and men feared her as much as the male orishas. She watched now in silence, wanting desperately to join Changó in his battle against Oggún but not daring to intervene.

The two combatants were now locked in a deadly embrace, each trying to draw first blood. Desperately, Oggún made a supreme effort and freed his fighting arm. With the same movement, he brought down the machete against Changó's side. Unable to leap away in time, Changó felt Oggún's blade slash his thigh. The wound was superficial but it bled profusely.

The sight of his own blood maddened Changó. With a bloodcurdling scream he swung his ax and slashed Oggún across the chest. With the scream, flames poured out of Changó's mouth like a fountain. The fire leaped out and singed Oggún's hair. The orisha jumped back with a snarl and lunged once more at Changó. This time the machete made contact with Changó's left arm, cutting deeper. Changó roared and flames darted now from his nose and his ears. His entire body was emitting short burst of flames with every movement. His right arm swung once more, slashing Oggún's arm and thigh in the same motion.

The two orishas were now covered with blood. The smell of burnt flesh became sharper each time Changó came in contact with Oggún. The god of metals, unable to come too close to his brother, had to keep circling him, swinging the machete from a safe distance. But so great was his skill, that each time he swung, he cut Changó. The god of thunder knew then that he had met his equal in Oggún. Aware of the added help that his powers over fire could give him in the battle, he kept aiming mouthfuls of flames at the elusive Oggún, but the god of metals was fast and eluded the fire. One more swing of Changó's ax got Oggún on the shoulder, but he veered in time, and the cut was not deep.

From the verandah Oyá saw Changó's weakening position. She knew that if Changó's flames could reach Oggún, the god of thunder could win the battle. But Oggún was too fast and Changó had lost too much blood. His fire was not so powerful any more. She hesitated for a moment, torn between her desire to help Changó and her fear of his anger if she joined in the battle. But at that moment, she saw Oggún swing his machete and aim it at Changó's head. She hesitated no longer. Taking a deep breath she exhaled hard. A powerful gale wind issued from her mouth, aimed directly at Changó. And the flames that surrounded the god of thunder, which had grown steadily weaker, fed upon the wind, roared out and enveloped Oggún from head to foot. With a loud scream, the god of metals let go of his weapon and fell back away from Changó. He rolled on the ground in agony, trying to put out the flames.

Seeing his advantage, Changó lunged at his brother and raised the ax for the final blow. But at that moment, a strong hand closed around his wrist arresting the downward stroke. He turned his head and saw Oyá's clear eyes looking at him. "Let him go, Changó," she pleaded, "he has been punished enough."

Changó looked down at his brother, scorched and bleeding on the ground, and slowly the fires died out in his eyes and his body. "Get up, Oggún," he said. "Leave this place and never come back. My mother and my father have been avenged."

Without a word, the god of metals struggled to his feet. He swiftly looked at Oyá, then turned around and walked away. As he passed his machete, still lying on the ground, he bent down and picked it up. Changó stiffened, but Oggún replaced the weapon at his side and continued walking. He did not look back.

Oggún Meets Oshún

The humiliation experienced with Changó and Oyá so embittered Oggún that he left his forge and his iron works, and went to live in the woods. There he spent his time hunting and foraging around with his good friends Eleggua and Ochosi. Disenchanted with the world, he vowed never again to return to civilization.

Oggún's decision was very disturbing to the orishas and to humankind in general. Deprived of the god of metal's expertise with iron, civilization came to a standstill. There was no war, but there was no peace either because the struggle to survive made everyone bitter and unhappy. Finally, the orishas held a conclave and decided they had to have Oggún back. Accordingly, they brought their problem to Olofi and asked him to bring Oggún out of the woods.

After considering the situation, Olofi decreed that Oggún was free to spend his life wherever he chose, but that he would give permission to the other orishas to go into the woods to try and talk Oggún into returning. The orishas felt the decision was fair, and after discussing the matter among themselves, decided that Orunla should be their ambassador of good will in the matter.

Orunla meticulously prepared for the trip, rehearsing carefully what he would say to Oggún. He found the god of metals almost as soon as he entered the woods. He was standing by a tree, carefully baiting a trap for a wild hog. Oggún greeted Orunla in his usual gruff and distant manner, and listened in silence to what the elder orisha had to say. When Orunla finished speaking, Oggún told him that he could not care less about what was happening in the outside world. He had no interest in the affairs of the other orishas or in those of humans. Furthermore, he had made up his mind to stay in the woods forever and that decision was irrevocable.

Nothing that Orunla would say seemed to make any impression on the stubborn Oggún. All the carefully rehearsed words fell on deaf ears. Finally, saddened by the failure of his mission, Orunla bade farewell to Oggún and went back to the other orishas. Their distress and disappointment was great when they learned of Orunla's failure, but their determination to bring Oggún back did not diminish. After some further consideration, they decided that each in turn should try to talk to Oggún. They felt that sooner or later, one of them would wear down the will of the recalcitrant orisha.

After Orunla's failure, Babalú-Ayé decided to try his luck with Oggún. They had had some adventures together and Oggún liked and respected the orisha. But Oggún was just as cold to Babalú as he had been to Orunla. Orisha-Oko tried next, followed by Yemayá and Aganyú, but all to no avail. Oggún refused to come out of the woods. Perhaps Eleggua might have been successful, but Eleggua was happy with Oggún in the woods, and would not intervene. And Ochosi, whose life was spent entirely in the wilderness, would not even consider speaking to Oggún about leaving the woods. The ever-kind Obatalá would have gone, but he felt that his presence would antagonize Oggún even more. As to Changó and Oyá, they were so wrapped up in each other, they could not have cared less if Oggún never came back to the outside world. Not that any of the other orishas would have considered sending either one of them in search of Oggún.

The orishas had almost decided to give up and try to do without the power of metal altogether, when the orisha Oshún suddenly appeared among them. None of the orishas had considered sending Oshún as an emissary, being that she was only interested in love and games, but the goddess of love had not been her usual happy and carefree self of late. Changó's affair with Oyá was driving her wild with jealousy. And she now saw an opportunity to put a damper on their happiness. If she succeeded in bringing Oggún out of the woods, he would assuredly try to get Oyá back and he might be more successful the second time around.

The orishas were surprised, as well as dubious, when Oshún announced her intentions to try and bring Oggún out of the woods. If the wise Orunla had failed and the elder orishas, who were liked and respected by Oggún, had not been able to convince him to return to civilization, how could Oshún whom Oggún did not even know. But since they had exhausted all their possibilities, they felt they had nothing to lose by letting Oshún try. So they accepted her offer.

Oshún tied five yellow handkerchiefs around her slim waist, adjusted her vial of honey inside her girdle, and threw away her headdress. Her beautiful dark hair cascaded in wild curls around her back, and with a toss of her head, she started on her journey.

Contrary to the other orishas, Oshún did not set out to find Oggún. It was her intention that he should find her. As soon as she entered the woods, she began to sing softly in her melodious voice. As she sang, she pirouetted gracefully among the trees in a sinuous and sensuous dance that revealed every line of her lovely body. The many gold bracelets she wore on her slim wrists and ankles jingled together agreeably and made a charming accompaniment to her songs.

Oggún had been hunting alone among the trees when he heard Oshún's voice. Never had he heard anything as delightful as her song. Cautiously he peeked from among the bushes and saw a beautiful young girl, dressed in a delicate yellow robe and girdled with silken handkerchiefs, dancing and singing in a glade. Oshún's beauty was so astonishing and her voice so sweet that Oggún forgot his own resolve never to look at women again, and stood among the bushes transfixed, staring dumfoundedly at the lovely apparition.

Oshún had seen Oggún out of the corner of her eye, but she ignored his presence. Undaunted, she continued to sing and dance without making any effort to approach him.

And Oggún, seeing that she was paying no attention to him, forgot his shyness and moved a little closer. Oshún continued to dance, but now she gracefully undid her five handkerchiefs and tied them together into a long silken rope without missing a beat of her music. Her hand strayed casually inside her girdle and brought out her vial of honey. She still kept on singing and dancing.

Oggún came out from behind the bushes and approached Oshún. Her music and her beauty slowly intoxicated his senses until he became unware of his surroundings.

Oshún waited until he was within her reach, and then she quickly dipped her fingers into the honey. She swirled closer to him, and as she passed him, she brushed his lips with her honey.

Oggún licked the strange sweet substance and was enthralled. Blindly, he reached out for Oshún, but she was too fast for him and slipped between his fingers. With a taunting smile, she turned her back and fled between the trees. Oggún followed her. When she saw he was gaining on her, she stopped and let him come nearer. Once more she dipped her fingers in the honey and let him taste it. While he licked the honey, she slipped an end of the five handkerchiefs around his neck and tied it loosely. The other end she tied around her wrist. Smiling temptingly, she moved away from him, dragging him along by her silken rope. And the orisha, stunned by her beauty and the sweetness of the honey, let himself be led by Oshún. In this fashion she led him to the edge of the woods. Once there, she untied the handkerchiefs and let him loose. With a last enticing smile, she turned and ran away.

Oggún stood outside the woods, filled with contradictory emotions. A part of him wanted to turn around and return to the comparative safety of the trees, but another part cried for one more look at the beautiful woman who had enslaved his senses. He knew that once he left the woods he would have to return to his old life at the forge, a thought that he abhorred. But the thought of never seeing Oshún again was unbearable to him. And it was this desire to see Oshún again and to make her his forever that triumphed in the heart of the god of metals.

The other orishas, who had been watching the scene from a safe distance, saw Oggún hesitate and then come out of the woods. Overjoyed by his return, they all came forward and greeted him warmly. Oggún, touched by the loving reception, forgot his old bitterness and responded kindly to their greeting. That night a great feast was given in honor of Oggún's return and all the orishas were invited. Even Changó and Oyá made a cautious appearance. But Oggún, who only had eyes for Oshún, barely noticed their presence.

Oshún's plan to bring Oggún out of the woods so he would continue to pursue Oyá succeeded only in part. She did bring him out of the woods, but Oggún had no longer any interest in his former wife. His only interest now was Oshún herself. And Oshún, who will never let an opportunity escape her, decided to use Oggún's infatuation to make Changó jealous. During the entire evening, she flirted outrageously with Oggún, who was enchanted with her attention.

Oshún's plan succeeded to perfection. For the first time since their affair had started, Oyá saw Changó morose and distracted. His attention seemed to be elsewhere, and it wasn't very long until she noticed that the subject of his interest was the beautiful Oshún. Oyá knew that Changó and Oshún had been lovers, but she thought that the affair had long been over. Now she saw that the god of thunder had not entirely forgotten the goddess of love. Infuriated, Oyá got up from her seat and walked away. Changó barely noticed her absence. He was watching Oshún dance with Oggún, her eyes caressing the god of metal like they had caressed Changó at one time.

The god of thunder's great vanity was sorely bruised. He prided himself in being able to carry on several love affairs at the same time and to hold the interest of the women involved without any effort. His love affair with Oyá had not diminished his desire for Oshún. And although his affection and interest in Oyá grew steadily, it did not interfere in his feelings for Oshún, whom he considered his exclusive property. It did not occur to him that he had taken Oyá away from Oggún, thus inflicting a grievous wound upon his brother's male pride. What he saw was that Oggún had a penchant for interfering in his love life. First it was Oyá and now it was Oshún. In other words, Changó wanted both Oshún and Oyá as his women, and he was determined to have them both.

The Second Battle

Changó's jealousy was not unnoticed by Oshún, who was delighted to see her plan succeed so well. She was now determined to feed this jealousy until Changó left Oyá and returned to her. She therefore continued to accept Oggún's attentions until one day she finally gave in to him and let him make love to her. The news of Oggún's love affair with Oshún was soon common gossip among the orishas. And naturally, it wasn't very long until it came to Changó's ears.

The news hit Changó like one of his own lightning bolts. Now it was his turn to feel hurt and humiliated, not at all the sort of feeling generally associated with the proud god of thunder. The thought of Oshún in Oggún's arms drove Changó mad with jealousy. He thought of her lips, her exquisite body, and the violent passion they had so often shared, and he trembled with desire. No longer did Oyá's beauty appeal to him. He only had thoughts for Oshún. And like Obba before her, he began to neglect Oyá. But Oyá was not Obba. The goddess of the whirlwind and mistress of the cemetery was a warrior orisha. And she fought for what she wanted. Wise and wily, she decided to change her tactics. And instead of crying and remonstrating with Changó for his indifference, she endeavored to be more attractive and seductive than ever. She never complained or questioned him if he were late in coming home, nor pressed her attentions on him. And Changó, left alone to his brooding and resentment, began to feel the subtle effects of this clever maneuver. Soon he began to come home for dinner, and he once more made love to Oyá. But even though he paid her more attention, Oyá was still aware that a part of his mind was not with her. And sometimes in the middle of the night, while he made love to her, she could feel him far away from her, as if he were making love to somebody else. She knew that this somebody else was Oshún, and the thought pained her, but she was determined to hold him and never let him see that she knew what was going on inside him.

While Changó brooded over Oshún, Oggún became slowly obsessed by her. He followed her jealously everywhere until, finally, the beautiful orisha flared at him and demanded that he give her more freedom. She had no real interest in Oggún, other than making Changó jealous, and now that her scheme was succeeding, she grew impatient with the god of metal's fawning over her. She tried to escape him as often as she could, always in the hope that Changó would come to her, but Changó never did. He watched her from a distance, and she could see in his eyes the flame of desire, but he never came close enough for her to complete her snare.

One hot summer day, Oshún told Oggún that she wanted to go bathe in the river. Oshún is also the goddess of river waters, and she must periodically seek the coolness of the river to replenish her strength. Oggún immediately suggested that he go with her, but Oshún refused. She told him she wanted to be alone and stay in the water for as long as she wanted. Oggún then told her that he would accompany her as far as the river's edge and then he would go hunting in the woods. Oshún agreed and the two orishas left together for the river.

Changó saw them go by and immediately decided to follow from a distance. Once at the river, Oggún left Oshún alone as he had promised, and went to hunt in the nearby woods. Changó, hidden among the trees, saw him leave.

Oshún had not noticed Changó's presence. But if she had known he was watching her, she could not have been more alluring than she now was. With unconscious grace she undressed slowly, taking infinite care in the removal of each piece of clothing. Soon she stood completely naked by the water's edge, her smooth golden skin shimmering in the sunlight with a glow of its own.

Changó stood transfixed behind the trees, his heart hammering in his chest, as if he were seeing Oshún's body for the first time. He wanted to come forward and possess her wildly, as he had done so many times before. Instead, he stood there trembling like a shy young boy, and watched her step nimbly into the water and swim swiftly away.

Changó's burning eyes were not the only ones watching the beautiful Oshún. On the opposite side of the river, Oggún had also seen the unveiling of the ravishing orisha. And now, from both sides of the river, the two brothers watched and waited for Oshún to return to shore.

Oshún seemed to be in no hurry, and for many long hours the two brothers watched and waited. Finally Oshún came out of the river. Still unaware she was being watched, she walked to where she had left her clothes and proceeded to wash them in the river waters. She then stretched them out to dry, and laying down on the soft grass, fell fast asleep.

Changó, feeling that now was his chance to approach Oshún, started to move closer, but a sudden sound among the bushes made him retreat quickly to his place of hiding. And not a moment too soon, for the one who was approaching was Oggún.

Seeing Oshún naked by the water's edge, the god of metals quickly spread his hunting net over her. He then plucked some feathers from a brace of *acuaro* (pheasants) he had caught and strewed them over the net. Because of Oggún's action, Oshún became known as *Oshún Ibu Acuaro* (Oshún dressed like the acuaro by the river).

From his place of hiding, Changó had seen the entire scene. He waited for a few minutes to make sure Oggún had left the vicinity and then, unable to wait any longer, ran over to Oshún. For a while he watched her sleep, admiring the soft glow of her skin and the graceful curve of her cheek. He then reached down gently and lifted the net.

Oshún had been dreaming of Changó. In her dream they were in each other's arms and he was kissing her face passionately and softly calling out her name. She opened her eyes and she thought she was still dreaming. For there was Changó, kissing her and calling out her name as in her dream. Then she saw that she was not dreaming. With a cry of happiness, she opened her arms and embraced him, and all of a sudden there was nothing and no one in the whole world but him and the overwhelming passion of his love making. And that was how Oggún found them hours later when he returned from the hunt, locked in each other's arms and oblivious to everything around them.

Oggún's feelings were indescribable. For some moments he stood rooted to the ground as if unable to believe what he was seeing. Then he went mad with rage. Changó did not see Oggún until he felt the god of metals pull him up by the hair and hit him squarely on the jaw. The force of the impact made Changó reel and fall back to the ground.As he jumped to his feet, he saw Oggún reach for his belt and pull out the machete.

Changó was stark naked and his *oshe* lay some distance from where he stood. There was no way he could reach it in time. In a flash, Changó turned to Oggún and spewed out a volley of fire. Oggún jumped back to avoid the flames and Changó took the opportunity to grab his ax.

Once more the two orishas faced each other for the sake of a woman. All the old rancor bubbled up in both their breasts with renewed intensity. But now both knew each other's strengths and weaknesses. Oggún knew he had to avoid Changó's fire and Changó knew he could not let Oggún draw the first blood.

Within minutes the woods and the nearby mountains trembled and echoed with the violence of the struggle between the two rivals. This time Changó managed to wound Oggún first, and this gave him leverage over his brother. But very soon Oggún had retaliated and now both orishas were covered with blood and wild with fury.

Unlike Oyá, Oshún had no desire to join in the battle. Terrified, she ran screaming into the woods forgetting in her haste that she was naked. As usual, Eleggua was hunting in the vicinity and heard the sound of the battle and Oshún's screams. When he saw her emerge naked from among the trees, he looked away embarrassed and threw her his cassock so she could cover herself. Only then did Oshún realize that she was naked. Gratefully, she took Eleggua's cassock and put it on. Then she pleaded with him to go in search of Obatalá so that the elder orisha would stop the fight.

Obatalá was tending his fields when Eleggua arrived with the news of the battle between Changó and Oggún. Obatalá put down his hoe and shook his head sadly. "I knew this was coming," he said with a sigh. "I just didn't know when. Take me to them, *omo-mi* (my son)."

The battle was nearing an end when Obatalá arrived on the scene. Both Changó and Oggún were barely conscious through the loss of blood, but they still persisted in their ferocious struggle.

Suddenly a great white dove came flying from across the river and hovered over the combatants. In another moment, Obatalá's white mantle had fallen between the two brothers and their father stood by their side.

Obatalá's presence had an immediate effect. Not a word was uttered by the elder orisha. He simply stood there, tall and imposing, with all the majesty of his great age and authority.

With a muffled cry, Changó fell at his adoptive father's feet and paid him homage. Oggún stood by the side, his head fallen ashamedly on his chest, too afraid to speak or to move. And these two great warriors, who feared nothing and no one, were both humbled by the simple presence of Obatalá.

Bending down, the elder orisha tapped Changó's shoulders lightly and gave him his blessing. Then he helped Changó to his feet and embraced him tenderly. He turned and looked at Oggún.

"And you, my son," he said softly. "Don't you want to pay *foribale* to your old father?"

With a hoarse cry Oggún fell at Obatalá's feet. Like he had done with Changó before, Obatalá tapped Oggún's shoulders and blessed him. But when he tried to raise him to his feet, Oggún clung to Obatalá's knees.

"Forgive me, *baba-mi*," he sobbed. "Forgive me!"

Obatalá lifted him up and embraced him. "Of course I forgive you, my son," he said tenderly. "I forgave you a long time ago, and so has your mother."

He looked at Changó and motioned him to come closer. "Embrace your brother," he said, "and remember, no woman is worth the shedding of a brother's blood."

Under Obatalá's loving eyes, the two brothers embraced and swore friendship to each other. But each knew in his heart that the vow would be difficult to keep.

Yemayá and Oggún

After the uneasy truce he made with Changó, Oggún returned to his forge and did his best to forget the frivolous Oshún. He now knew she had never been interested in him, and that her old affair with Changó was as alive as ever. Fortunately for Oggún he was a very industrious orisha and enjoyed his work. So he did not pine very long over Oshún. He continued to carry on with his work for the other orishas and to tend his farm. From time to time he went off to war and his name as a mighty warrior grew with the passing of time.

Oggún's virility and his prowess in battle had impressed the mighty sea goddess Yemayá. Each time she came ashore to visit her adoptive son Changó and her sister Oshún, Yemayá endeavored to pass by Oggún's forge, dressed in her most beautiful clothes and arrayed with her best pearls and coral. But the god of metals, who had sworn never to look at women again, did not even raise his eyes to look at her. Gruff and unsociable, Oggún bent over his iron work, his mighty muscles rippling under his naked skin, a magnificent specimen of manhood in all its power and glory.

Yemayá's infatuation with Oggún grew steadily. She thought about him constantly and how she could seduce him and make him her lover. After much pondering of the matter she formed a plan. The next day, she called for her tritons and nereids to prepare her silver boat as she wanted to go ashore.

Oshún was in her *ile* (house), dressing her long dark hair with tortoise combs and tiny mirrors. That evening the orishas were giving a party and Changó was going to play the *bataá*(drums). She wanted to look especially seductive for him. Since the renewal of their affair at the river they had continued to meet occasionally, but he still lived with Oyá and that irked the river goddess, who wanted Changó all to herself.

Oshún had nearly finished her preparations when her sister Yemayá came into the room. The two orishas, who love each other tenderly, embraced warmly. Yemayá, strong-willed and masterful, wasted no time in subterfuges.

"My sister, I came to ask you for a very special favor."

"You know I'll do anything you say," said Oshún at once. "Everything I have, you have given me. I love you like I love myself. What do you want?"

"I want Oggún," said Yemayá.

Oshún stared at her sister. "Oggún? You want Oggún?" she asked incredulously. "Are you joking, my sister?"

"I never joke," said Yemayá haughtily. "I'm quite serious. I want Oggún and I want you to help me get him."

Oshún was dumfounded by her sister's request. "But what do you want with Oggún, my sister?" she asked.

"I desire him," said Yemayá bluntly. "He's the most magnificent male I have ever seen. You cannot see this because you're totally besotted for Changó, but Oggún has a raw, brutal sensuousness which I find utterly devastating."

"There's truth in what you say, my sister," agreed Oshún. "Oggún is very attractive. That's undeniable. But he's so … rude, so uncivilized. How can a woman like you, so beautiful and powerful, want Oggún as a lover?"

"Nevertheless I want him," insisted Yemayá, "and you can help me get him. All my efforts to attract his attention have failed. He's determined never to become involved with another woman. After what happened with you and with Oyá I can well understand his feelings. But I'm convinced that secretly he still wants you, and that's where you can help me."

"I'll do anything you want," said Oshún.

That evening all the orishas had a marvelous time at the party. Oyá was there, as cool and beautiful as ever, and so were Yemayá and Oshún, whose radiant charms had all the male orishas vying for her attention. Changó was behind the drums, intoxicated with the music and the palm wine, but not so drunk that he could not notice Oshún's splendid beauty. From time to time he winked at her, trying to figure out how he could escape Oyá's vigilance and spend the night in Oshún's house.

Eleggua, who was too busy eating to bother himself

with the wiles of women, shared a pipe from time to time with Orunla, whose wisdom he much admired. Obatalá and Yemmu chatted amiably with the benevolent Babalú-Ayé and the ascetic Orisha-Oko, who had never enjoyed himself with a woman. In a corner of the room, Oggún, Ochosi, and Osain smoked large cigars and got steadily drunk on palm wine. The three orishas shared a common love for the woods and for the hunt, and were good friends. Aganyú, who liked to mingle, went from one orisha to the other, studiously avoiding Yemmu.

Oshún danced with all the orishas. She particularly wanted to please her first dance partner Aganyú, as he was Changó's father. Then she danced with Orunla, Ochosi, and Obatalá. Babalú never danced but Eleggua pranced merrily with her around the floor. Even Orisha-Oko and the imposing Osain could not resist the temptation of dancing with the charming orisha. Only Oggún stood brooding in his corner, drinking and smoking and ignoring Oshún. But not for very long. Soon Oshún was standing by his side, smiling seductively and inviting him to dance. Oggún hesitated, but the goddess of love prodded him gently, and he finally gave in and moved with her to the dance floor.

While her sister danced with Oggún, Yemayá watched them with burning eyes.

She saw when Oshún whispered something in Oggún's ear and watched the orisha shake his head in angry denial. But Oshún insisted. Once more she whispered to him, pressing herself insinuatingly against his chest. Oggún hesitated. It was clear he was vacillating between his desire for Oshún and his resentment over her betrayal. Oshún pressed on and finally Oggún nodded his head in agreement. Yemayá relaxed and smiled faintly. Her beautiful eyes shone like jewels and her breath grew agitated with the intensity of her excitement.

Behind the *bataá*, Changó had also observed the exchange between Oshún and Oggún and his eyes narrowed. He started to get up when he saw Yemayá approaching.

"*Omo-mi,*" said the sea goddess, embracing her son, "I

bring you a message from Oshún. You are not to be angry over her apparent interest for your brother. She's only carrying out one of my orders. Tonight, after the party is over, you are to go directly to her *ile*. She'll meet you there shortly."

Yemayá's words appeased the god of thunder and he kissed her tenderly and went back to his drums. Across the room, Oyá had watched the conversation between Yemayá and Changó. She frowned furiously. There was no love lost between her and Yemayá. At one time it was Oyá who had owned the realm of the seas and Yemayá who had been mistress of the cemetery. But Yemayá had tricked Oyá into exchanging dwellings and now Oyá had to watch over graves while Yemayá lorded over the waters. The two orishas barely spoke to each other since that day, and Oyá knew that she could not expect much kindness from the sea goddess. The fact that Yemayá was Oshún's sister did not help alleviate the animosity between Yemayá and Oyá. She now felt sure that there was some kind of trickery at hand and that she could be on the receiving end of it.

Soothed by Yemayá's words, Changó saw Oggún leave the party with Oshún without batting an eye. Both Yemayá and Oyá were relieved to see the apparent reconciliation between Oggún and Oshún, although for completely different reasons. Oyá was relieved because she thought that now Oshún would leave Changó alone, while Yemayá ... Yemayá had her own special reasons to be pleased.

In the meantime, Oggún and Oshún had arrived at the house of the god of metals. Oggún had been drinking heavily at the party and was already a little drunk, but as soon as they entered the *ile*, Oshún asked the god of metals for some palm wine. When Oggún brought out the jug of wine, Oshún took it away from him with a saucy smile and poured two generous wine portions. She handed him one and kept the other. Watching him cagily from beneath her long lashes, she pretended to sip the wine, but at the first opportunity she poured out the liquid behind a chair. The unsuspecting Oggún emptied his calabash which was immediately refilled by Oshún. After this action had been repeated several times, the god of metals was thoroughly drunk. "Now, my lord and master," said Oshún, with her most enticing smile, "allow me to go into the inner chamber and make myself ready for you. Wait a few minutes and then come inside."

Oggún watched Oshún disappear into the bedroom with eyes full of lust. With an effort he struggled to his feet and swerving around the room, finally managed to reach the door to his sleeping quarters. It was dark inside, but from the door he could see the shape of Oshún's body among the animal skins that covered his bed. With a savage grunt, Oggún threw himself upon her. Her arms opened hungrily to receive him and within seconds they were locked in each other's arms. Not a word passed their lips. Oggún, thirsty for Oshún's kisses, spoke amply with his lips and his entire body. And she returned his caresses with wanton abandon and a wild frenzy she had never shown before.

The next day Oggún slept late into the morning, something unusual for him who was invariably up at dawn to begin his work at the forge. But the excesses of the previous night had taken their toll. He sat up in bed and sank his face between his hands. He was suffering from a terrible headache. Suddenly he felt the touch of cool fingers upon his forehead and a strange female voice whispered to him, "You'll feel better soon. Come, lay back next to me."

Startled, Oggún turned and saw Yemayá smiling at him. With a muffled oath, the god of thunder jumped off the bed and stared dumfounded at Yemayá. Then realizing he was naked, he picked up an animal skin and covered himself.

Yemayá laughed. "You weren't so bashful last night, my lord," she said teasingly. "Why do you hide your body from me now?"

"What do you mean?" asked Oggún, with a frown. "Last night I was with Oshún."

Yemayá laughed again. "No, my lord, last night you were with me. My sister knew I loved you and wanted to be with you. I asked her to let me replace her in your bed. She agreed. It was me you enjoyed last night, not my sister."

Oggún's face darkened with anger. "What are you saying?" he asked furiously. "Am I going to be forever the plaything of women? Can't I even choose my own bed partner? Are you so devoid of dignity you have to resort to trickery to bed a man?"

Yemayá drew herself up haughtily. "Take care, my lord," she said icily. "You forget to whom you are speaking. You should be proud and flattered to be desired by me. Last night you languished in my arms like the most devoted lover. Why the change today?"

"Last night I was drunk, madam," shouted Oggún angrily. "I would have made love to anybody thinking that woman was Oshún."

Yemayá's beautiful proud face paled at Oggún's stinging words. "And must you continue loving somebody who doesn't love you?" she asked spitefully. "A man as proud and strong-willed as you, the toy of my frivolous sister, who only has eyes for Changó. I thought a man of your strength and nobility deserved a more stable woman, a woman who would appreciate your values and cherish your love. But I guess I was mistaken." With a toss of her head, she threw away the bed covers and stood up. Naked and defiant, she walked across the room and picked up her clothes.

Oggún stared at her in silence. Yemayá's words had deeply hurt his male pride, but he knew in his heart that she was right. He watched her now as she began to dress with feline grace, the ample curves of her lovely body carelessly revealed with every move. Reluctantly, he admired the unashamed dignity of her movements, her unassuming loveliness, the spontaneous and natural ease of each of her actions. Supremely confident of herself, Yemayá continued to dress in haughty silence. And Oggún, touched by her openness and honesty, so different from Oshún's flighty and devious ways, began to regret his harsh words.

"Yemayá, I … I'm sorry," he stammered clumsily. "But this was so … unexpected. I never suspected …"

"That's quite all right, my lord," said Yemayá coldly. "I understand. As you said before, you have the right to choose your own bed partner. It was stupid of me to think I could make you forget my sister. I imagine once a man has made love to the irresistible Oshún, no other woman can take her place."

"That's not true," cried Oggún. "You are a beautiful and desirable woman. Perhaps no one but you could make a man forget Oshún."

The obvious sincerity in Oggún's words touched Yemayá against her will. Immensely proud and arrogant, she never suffered an offense lightly. But her passion for Oggún still raged in her heart. She hesitated, then turned to him.

"And what if you can't forget, my lord?" she asked, her voice still cold.

"I would like to try," said Oggún simply.

Yemayá smiled. "Now?" she asked softly.

"Now," answered Oggún.

Orisha-Oko

The news of the affair between Yemayá and Oggún aston-ished the orishas except Oshún, who was well familiar with her sister's determination. To her, the relationship between the god of metals and Yemayá was inevitable. It was also welcome because it freed her from Oggún's obsession and made her affair with Changó easier.

All went well with the lovers in the beginning. Yemayá was understanding and wise enough to accept Oggún's pas-sion for his work and for the hunt, and she never complained when he went to war for long periods. Similarly, Oggún was accommodating to Yemayá's responsibilities to her sea king-dom and did not balk when she left him from time to time to oversee her dominions.

When she was on land, Yemayá spent her free time helping Oggún in his fields which caused him constant worry because of his lack of expertise in farming matters. None of his efforts to till the soil seemed to be successful, and his lands languished, parched and barren, without bearing good fruit. His crops were always meager, and his failure to make his farm produce made him bitter and angry. And when Oggún was angry, he was a poor lover.

Yemayá worried about Oggún's brooding and suffered as a consequence his lack of interest in the bedroom. But Yemayá never allowed problems to get the best of her. She invariably found an answer. After much consideration, she came to a decision.

Orisha-Oko was the god of the harvests and the patron of agriculture. Naturally his fields were a joy to see. His crops were always bountiful and his yams were the envy of the other orishas. For a long time they had tried to pry the secrets of the earth from Orisha-Oko, but the god of harvests was stingy with his knowledge and guarded it zealously from others.

One day Orisha-Oko was in his fields plowing the soil when he saw Yemayá approaching. As usual, she was beau-tifully arrayed and her blue brocade robe shimmered with mother of pearl and aquamarine. Her lovely hair was braided with tiny seed pearls, and she fanned herself majestically with a blue *agbegbe* (fan).

Orisha-Oko greeted her politely, then returned to his work. Yemayá answered his greeting graciously and stayed there watching him work. After some minutes, she asked him some questions about the tilling of the soil, and listened attentively while he answered her. They chatted amiably for a while, then she bade him goodbye and walked away. Orisha-Oko watched her curiously for some time, admiring the graceful curve of her back and her stately figure. When she was lost in the distance, he went back to his work and forgot all about her.

The next day, Yemayá returned to the fields and once more spoke with Orisha-Oko for a long while. And the orisha, flattered by her attention, once more stopped his work and answered her questions.

Soon these agreeable morning chats became a pleasant habit that Orisha-Oko looked forward to in the midst of his busy day. One day Yemayá told the god of harvests she was feeling a bit faint and needed some rest. The day was unusually hot and Orisha-Oko did not find anything strange in Yemayá's behavior. Gallantly, he offered to bring her to his *ile* which was nearby, and she quickly assented.

Orisha-Oko's house was as simple and unpretentious as was to be expected of a man of the earth, particularly one who had never known or desired the company of a woman. But for all its simplicity, the place was cozy and impeccably clean.

Orisha-Oko led Yemayá inside and hurried away to bring her something cool to drink. When he returned, he found her lying languidly on his bed. Her eyes were closed and one graceful arm laid across her forehead.

"My lady," said Orisha-Oko anxiously, "are you feeling better?"

Yemayá opened her eyes and sighed. "No, my lord," she said faintly. "I am not well. The room keeps going round and round ... Please hold my hand ..."

Orisha-Oko immediately complied with this request and took Yemayá's hand in his own. The sea goddess pulled him gently to her and whispered softly, "Lay down by my side, my lord. Hold me gently. I'm so frightened. I don't feel well."

And Orisha-Oko, spurred by her soft words, laid by her side. His purity and innocence had kept him away from the world and the wiles of women. He therefore did not know how to defend himself. Yemayá's softness enveloped him like a blue mantle, and while his oxen waited patiently for the return of their master, he, who had never loved a woman, was craftily seduced by Yemayá.

Hours later, as he lay quietly in her arms, still enraptured by the passion she had awakened in him, Orisha-Oko found himself willingly revealing to his new mistress the secrets of the harvest.

As soon as she had learned Orisha-Oko's secrets, Yemayá arose and dressed quickly.

"Are you leaving so soon, my lady?" asked the unsuspecting Orisha-Oko. "Are you fully recovered from your fainting spell?"

"Yes, my lord," said Yemayá, with a seductive smile. "Your love has worked wonders. I feel marvelously well."

"Will I see you tomorrow?" asked Orisha-Oko.

"No, my lord," said Yemayá sadly. "My lord Oggún returns today from the wars. I don't know when I will see you again. It would be dangerous to incur his wrath. But I want you to know today will be forever engraved in my heart as one of the most beautiful experiences of my life."

"It will be the same for me," said Orisha-Oko. "I have never loved a woman until today and I shall never love another."

The two lovers embraced gently and then Yemayá left Orisha-Oko's *ile*. That night, when Oggún came home after a long time at battle, he found Yemayá waiting for him with a happy smile.

"I have a wonderful surprise, beloved," said Yemayá. And she proceeded to tell him the secrets of the harvest.

Oggún was thrilled by the knowledge, but puzzled as to how Yemayá had unraveled the mystery. "That is something you must never ask me," said Yemayá quietly. "You must trust me in this, and you must also promise me that you will never tell anyone you know this secret. Orisha-Oko must think he's still the only one who possesses this knowledge."

Oggún agreed readily to do as Yemayá asked. It was not his intention to divulge the secret anyway. And he was too happy to possess it to worry for too long as to how Yemayá had discovered it.

From that moment onward, Oggún's crops were every bit as plenteous as Orisha-Oko's. And everything he touched in the fields or in his garden flourished marvelously. In time, he became known as the master of the woods and Orisha-Oko never suspected that he had been betrayed by Yemayá.

The Third Battle

Oggún's affair with his adoptive mother Yemayá irked Changó, whose resentment for his brother was unabated. The friendship pact they had made by the river under Obatalá's prodding had not changed Changó's feelings about Oggún. And day after day he pondered how he could finally get even with his brother.

One day a great party was announced in a nearby city, and Changó decided to use the occasion to play a trick on Oggún. That evening he went to his brother's house in his most friendly attitude. Yemayá was away in her sea kingdom and the god of metals was alone.

Oggún's reception of Changó was cordial but guarded. Changó wasted no time and told Oggún at once the reason for his visit.

"Oggún, my brother," he said, putting on his best smile, "I need your help. As you may have heard there's an important feast in Ketu and I would like to go. The party is in honor of our mutual friend Eleggua, who is now the ruler of the region. Unfortunately the hound I use for long trips is ailing and none of my other steeds is fast enough to make the journey on time. Aside from that, all my best clothes are still in my palace, and I don't want to go there and risk meeting Obba. I wonder if you would lend me your ram and your clothes for the occasion."

Oggún had no affection for Changó and desired no contact with him. He disliked and distrusted him, and was as deeply resentful of Changó as Changó was of him. But he wanted to avoid trouble with him for the sake of Yemayá, and since he had no plans to go the party, he saw no reason to turn his brother down.

"Of course," he said immediately. "The ram is in the barn. You can take it when you leave. As for the clothes, you can also have them. I will replace them with *mariwó*."

Oggún's real clothes were the *eyé*, that is, the blood that is shed in battle and other tragic occurrences. When he was not at war or causing mayhem, he usually wore a pair of tight breeches surmounted by a red shirt, a color sacred to him because it is the color of blood. But sometimes, when the weather was specially warm and he was working hard at his forge, he took off his clothes and wore instead a skirt of *mariwó*, a kind of thick palm leaf, that hung to his knees and gave him freedom of action. It was with this skirt that he now replaced the clothes that he lent Changó.

Changó thanked his brother and went back to his house with the ram and Oggún's clothes. The following day, to the astonishment of the other orishas, he arrived in Ketu mounted on Oggún's steed and wearing his red shirt. But when they asked him why he was using Oggún's shirt and his ram, Changó simply smiled and winked at them.

The festivities lasted several days, and as usual Changó spent the time drinking, eating, dancing, and cavorting with women. When it was over, he said goodbye to all his friends, Eleggua in particular, mounted the ram and returned to Oyo.

Nearing his kingdom, he saw a beggar in rags standing by the side of the road. In a flash, Changó climbed off the ram, took off Oggún's shirt, and gave it to the beggar. He then slew the ram, made a bonfire, and roasted the meat which he shared with the beggar. When he finished eating, he continued the journey on foot and arrived in Oyo that same evening.

Several weeks went by and Oggún, who knew that Changó had long returned from Ketu, waited in vain for his brother to return his clothes and his ram. Finally he decided to pay him a visit.

Changó was in his courtyard, saddling his hound, when Oggún arrived.

"Greetings, my brother," he said with a smile. "Why do you honor my humble *ile* with your presence?"

"I have waited for you for some time," said Oggún, "but you never came. I would like you to return my clothes and my ram."

"I would like to, my brother," said Changó, with his most ingenious smile. "But I can't."

"What do you mean you can't?" said Oggún. "I loaned you my ram and my clothes because you said you needed them to go to Ketu. You're back from Ketu now, so give me back my property."

"But I can't, my brother," insisted Changó. "You see, when I was nearing Oyo I found a poor derelict by the road. The miserable creature was dressed in rags and hadn't eaten for days. He broke my heart, truly he did. I couldn't just leave him there, naked and hungry, could I? So I did the only thing I could do. I gave him your clothes and killed the ram and shared it with him. I thought you wouldn't mind, you who are always so generous and kind. By the way, the ram's meat was delicious. You ought to try it some time."

Oggún's eyes narrowed to slits. "You are lying," he said, "you could not have done this. I gave you the clothes off my back and my prized ram. You must be lying."

"But I never lie, my brother," said Changó, still smiling. "Everyone knows that. Changó doesn't have to lie because Changó fears no one, including you."

Oggún stared at Changó venomously and a low growl rumbled deep in his throat. He knew now his brother was telling the truth just as he knew that Changó had planned the whole thing to humiliate him. He did not mind so much the loss of his clothes as he did that of the ram, which had been his symbol since his early beginnings. More than fighting Changó he wanted retaliation for his insolence and effrontery. Wildly he searched his mind for something which Changó loved and which he would hate losing. Suddenly his eyes rested on the hound which Changó had been saddling.

With a triumphant snarl Oggún lunged at the dog, and before Changó could stop him, sank his teeth into the animal's neck. The hound gave a shrill yelp which died out in a whimper as blood started to gush out of its severed jugular vein.

Throwing the dead hound at Changó's feet, Oggún stood up and said to his brother, "Now we're even."

Changó stared in shocked horror at the mutilated throat of his prized steed, still unable to believe Oggún's ferocious act. Oggún, knowing that Changó would surely jump on him, backed away slowly and brought out his machete. Changó looked up at his brother and his eyes glowed red. His huge frame shook uncontrollably. Slowly his mouth opened in a loud bloodcurdling scream that echoed through the mountains. At the same time a large ball of fire issued from his mouth enveloping Oggún from head to foot. Instantly, the *mariwó* skirt that Oggún was wearing became a living furnace. The orisha screamed in agony and tried to put out the fire with his hands, but the dried palm leaves were the perfect fuel for the flames and burned quickly. In desperation, Oggún took off the flaming skirt and threw it far from him. Badly scorched and trembling with rage, he grabbed his machete and jumped at Changó.

Changó was unarmed but his double-edged ax was within easy reach. The god of thunder, however, made no effort to get his weapon. Instead he reached his fist out to the sky and brought it back down, aiming it directly at Oggún. And from his tightly clenched fingers came forth a bolt of lightning that caught Oggún squarely on the chest. Oggún reeled under the terrible impact and fell back, his chest smoking. Once again Changó repeated the same gesture and a second lightning bolt hit Oggún's hand making him drop the machete. Quickly the god of metals rolled over and tried to retrieve his weapon, but a third lightning bolt blew it out of his reach.

Oggún stood on trembling legs, dazed and badly burned. All around him the grass and the trees were covered with flames. In the midst of the inferno, legs wide apart, arms akimbo, stood the god of thunder, eyes aflame, roaring his rage and his power.

Oggún stared at his brother, his eyes full of venom. There was no fear in his heart, only the most consuming hatred.

"Why don't you fight like a man?" he screamed at Changó. "Why don't you pick up your ax and battle with me and my machete? I'll tell you why you don't. Because you know I'll beat you."

"You'll never beat me," roared back Changó. "The *oshe* is not my only weapon. I saved my best weapon for last. A warrior uses whatever weapon he wants to defeat an enemy. I've defeated you with fire and lightning, not because I had to, but because I so chose. And from this moment onward I will strike you with lightning whenever and wherever I feel like it."

This was the last of the great battles between Changó and Oggún, but Changó kept his vow and to this day the lightning bolt continues to strike metal. The ram, which had been Oggún's steed, became Changó's traditional offering, while the dog, which had belonged to Changó, became Oggún's property. And while Oggún continued to wear his *mariwó* skirt, Changó wore nothing but red from that day forward.

Obatalá's Gift to Changó

After his defeat of Oggún, Changó returned to his happy and carefree life of partying and womanizing. Oggún, silent and morose, went back to his forge and his work at the farm. The two brothers avoided each other, but whenever they came close there was a rumble of thunder in the sky and a sudden flash of lightning. Obatalá, who had heard of the renewed feud between the two brothers, summoned Changó to his presence.

"*Omo-mi*," he said to the god of thunder, "your continued battles with Oggún sadden me. You must make an effort to control your violent temper."

"He started it all, *baba-mi*," said Changó. "First he offended my *iyá*, then he came after Oyá, and later on he tried to interfere between Oshún and me."

"He was wrong in offending his mother," said the elder orisha, "but Oyá was his wife and Oshún tempted him. Besides, don't you think he has suffered enough? For his offense to his mother he has been condemned to work without rest during his entire life. That is a strong punishment. Besides that, he has lost both his wife and his mistress. Then you took away his ram and his color."

"He got even, didn't he?" answered Changó bitterly. "He killed my hound. Now he can claim dogs for his own."

"*Omo-mi*, I understand your resentment," said Obatalá kindly, "but you must remember that power uncontrolled can be destructive. Your power is great, but it needs direction. That is why I've decided to give you this."

Obatalá took off the necklace of white beads he always wore and removed one of the beads and gave it to Changó.

"Now," he said, "you can wear this white bead, which is a symbol of peace and wisdom, among the red beads of your own necklace. With the bead I confer upon you the ability to channel and direct your power and to control it wisely. Justice, rather than vengeance, shall be your aim. And nothing and no one shall ever overcome you."

All of the orishas wore necklaces with their own specific colors. Oshún wore a necklace of yellow beads, Yemayá, a necklace of white and blue beads, Eleggua a necklace of red and black beads, and so on. Since his defeat of Oggún, Changó wore a necklace of red beads as a symbol of his virility, his passion, and his raw power. Obatalá's gift implied that Changó could now claim white as well as red as his colors. This was a great distinction and an invaluable gift.

Changó fell down to his knees and paid homage at Obatalá's feet. With a loving smile, Obatalá blessed him and raised him to his feet.

"*Modupué, baba-mi*," said Changó humbly. "You honor your unworthy servant."

"You're not unworthy, *omo-mi*," said Obatalá. "Your nobility is great. That is why I know you'll do honor to my color."

From that day onward Changó's necklace was composed of red and white beads, and although Changó's power remained intact, he now knew how to use it wisely and with justice.

Oshún and Oyá

Changó's persistent affair with Oshún humiliated and enraged Oyá. At first, she had tried ignoring the situation in the hope that Changó would soon tire of his philandering and return to her. But Changó gave no sign that he had any intention to stop seeing Oshún, or any of his many other women. And Oyá, who was a determined woman, decided to put an end to his unfaithfulness in her own way.

Very few people knew that the mighty god of thunder, who claimed to fear nothing, lived in dread of one thing: the *iku*, that is, the dead. Changó could not stand the sight or the presence of the *iku* around him, and Oyá knew this very well. Since she was the mistress of the cemetery and all the dead were at her command, she commanded a slew of them to leave their graves and post themselves around Changó's house.

The next morning, when Changó tried to leave his *ile*, he found himself surrounded by an army of *iku*, who swiftly cut off all exits from the place. Changó's face blanched with horror. In two leaps he was back inside the house, where he quickly barricaded himself against the ghastly invaders. When he questioned Oyá about the siege, she coolly admitted having set up the dreadful guards to stop him from leaving the house.

"Are you crazy?" thundered Changó. "I have to attend to the affairs of my kingdom. I can't stay locked in here forever. What if there is an attack from neighboring tribes? What am I going to do to protect my people?"

Oyá laughed. "The only affairs you're concerned about are your affairs with women, particularly the one you've been having with Oshún. As to your kingdom, it is at peace and there's no danger of attack from anyone. Your ministers will come here to get your orders and your advice in courtly matters. And I'll see to it that you're duly informed if anything should go wrong."

"But it is humiliating for the king of Oyo to be held captive by a woman," said Changó, infuriated. "I won't stand for it. You'll regret this action."

"I'd like to see what you're going to do about it," countered Oyá, with a mocking laugh. "If you're so determined to leave, why don't you do so? The doors were locked by you, not by me."

With that, she turned her back on him and left the room. For several days, Changó languished in his self-imposed prison, cursing Oyá and raging about women's domineering ways. He roamed his *ile* like a caged tiger, thundering and spouting flames from every pore. But Oyá turned a deaf ear on all his ravings, and busied herself around the house as if she did not hear him.

The news of Changó's humiliating situation soon reached the ears of his good friend Eleggua, who came to pay him a visit. Oyá, like all the orishas, had a healthy respect for the impish Eleggua, and did not dare to deny him entrance to the house.

As soon as Eleggua was alone with Changó, he said to his friend, "Don't despair. I have a plan to get you out of here, but we need Oshún's cooperation. Remain calm while I go get her. In the meantime, try to get Oyá to leave the house."

Eleggua's words soothed Changó's mounting impatience. As soon as the orisha had left, he called Oyá.

"Eleggua told me there is talk of rebellion in the eastern part of the kingdom," he said to her. "I need the immediate presence of my ministers. Please get them for me."

Oyá, who had no reason to doubt this false piece of news, agreed to run the errand for Changó. Hidden among the bushes behind the house, Eleggua and Oshún were waiting to see Oyá leave. As soon as she disappeared from view they approached the house. The *iku*, who had only orders to detain Changó from leaving, did not try to stop Eleggua and Oshún from entering the *ile*.

As soon as they were inside the house, Eleggua and Oshún busied themselves with the execution of their plan. While Eleggua hunted around for some of Oyá's clothes, Oshún painted Changó's face with powdered eggshell. Then she made a supreme sacrifice that spoke clearly about the depths of her love for Changó. She cut her long hair, braided it, and pinned it to Changó's head. Eleggua had found one of Oyá's robes and one of her headdresses. With these, Oshún finished Changó's disguise.

A few minutes later Oshún emerged from the *ile*, and motioned to the *iku* to come near. At first they hesitated to leave their posts, but her charm and beauty soon won them over. When the first *iku* came close to her, Oshún dipped her fingers into her honey gourd and passed them over the skeleton's mouth. Even the dead felt the magic of Oshún's love potion. Ecstatically, the *iku* begged for more and his companions, curious about the honey, also came closer. And while the dead were distracted in this fashion by the goddess of love, Changó, disguised as a woman, left the house with Eleggua. The *iku* gave the two orishas a passing glance, but were too enthralled by Oshún to pay too much attention to Changó and his disguise.

As soon as she saw that Changó and Eleggua were safely out of sight, Oshún said goodbye to the *iku*, and left the house. Unwilling to let her go, they followed her to the edge of the woods, begging her to stay. But Oshún cagily reminded them of their duty to guard Changó, and they returned reluctantly to their posts.

When Oyá returned with Changó's ministers and found that he had escaped her prison, she was furious. She vented her anger against the poor *iku*, who could not understand how Changó could have escaped their vigilance. But after she had questioned them for hours, Oyá was able to piece together the careful plot that had freed Changó. Her anger and frustration so terrified the *iku* that they did not wait to be dismissed by her, and went back to their graves as swiftly as their bones could carry them. As for Oyá, she vowed swift vengeance on Changó and Oshún. Only her fear and respect for Eleggua kept her from uttering the same oath about him.

Oyá

The Secret of the Thunderbolt

For several days after Changó's escape Oyá roamed her *ile*, pacing the floor like a tigress, muttering to herself, and ruminating her vengeance. She knew that now that the god of thunder was free from her vigilance, it would be nearly impossible to pin him down. Any physical attack against him was doomed to failure because of his power over fire and the thunderbolt. If only she knew how he had acquired those powers she might be able to get them herself and meet him on equal grounds. Oyá was a warrior orisha and few men could best her in battle, the exception of course being Changó and his supernatural powers. If only she could learn his secret. Suddenly she stopped her pacing and a look of cunning flashed in her beautiful eyes. She had remembered that all the time he had lived with her, Changó had kept one of the rooms in her house constantly locked. He had told her that several secrets of state concerning his kingdom were in the room, and that for that reason no one, including her, could enter inside. At the time she had not found anything strange in his request and had dutifully stayed away from the chamber. But now, looking back in retrospect, she remembered that the only things he had brought with him when he arrived at her *ile* had been his ax, his mortar, and the gourd he sometimes carried with him. It was unlikely, considering the haste in which he had left, that he had taken all these implements with him. Maybe among them she would find an answer to her questions.

Her cheeks aflame with excitement, she rushed to the forbidden chamber and tried the door. It was locked as she had expected, but closed doors have never posed a problem for the goddess of winds. Taking a deep breath, Oyá blew hard on the door which burst inward in a shower of splinters. Panting with anticipation, Oyá rushed into the room, but no sooner was she inside than she gasped and retreated in horror. In the middle of the room, staring at her with baleful eyes, was the decapitated head of a ram, an object which had always filled her with unaccountable terror. Paralyzed with horror and repulsion, Oyá stared at the loathsome object. Her knees were trembling and her legs refused to move. With a supreme effort, the orisha forced herself to move backward. A step at a time she retreated slowly from the ram's head, cursing inwardly at Changó who knew her one weakness and who had obviously placed it there to keep her away from his secret. As she moved, her eyes caught sight of the mortar and the gourd which had been placed near the window some distance away from the ram's head. An idea came suddenly into Oyá's fertile brain. Regaining the rest of her composure, she turned around and bolted from the room. A few minutes later she was out of the house and standing outside the room's window. With a swift puff from her powerful lungs, she blew in the window and quickly climbed inside the room. This time the ram's head posed no fear for her as it was looking toward the room's door. With a satisfied smile, Oyá took the mortar and the gourd and went out the same way she had come in.

Carefully carrying her two prizes, Oyá reentered her *ile*. She placed both objects in the center of her sleeping chamber and secured the door. She then sat on the floor and contemplated the mortar and the gourd. For a long time she stared at them and considered their use. After a while, she reached for the gourd and looked curiously inside. There was a thick herbal mixture inside that exuded a peculiarly musky smell. She remembered having seen Changó dip his hand into the gourd once and lick his fingers. When she had questioned him about it he had seemed enraged and flames spouted from his mouth. Frightened by his violent reaction, she had never dared question him again about the gourd. Now that he was not present and that her resentment towards him churned inside her, she no longer feared him or his reprisal. With a toss of her proud head, she dipped a finger inside the gourd, scooped out some of the mixture, and ate it. All at once she let the gourd fall to the floor and stood up gasping for air. Her tongue and the inside of her mouth burned horribly, as if she had eaten a mouthful of live coals. She blew out air in an effort to cool her blistering tongue and instantly a volley of flames came out of her mouth. Terrified, she kept on blowing more air in a vain effort to put out the fire that was further inflamed by the gale issuing from her lungs. But it did not take long for Oyá to realize that the flames were not burning her mouth and that with some effort she could control their flow and their intensity. If she closed her mouth they would die out and only burst out again if she blew air or tried to speak. After some experimenting, she found that she could hold back the fire at will and shut it out when she so chose. This realization filled her with great elation, and she sat again on the floor with a satisfied smile. At last, she thought to herself, I know one of your secrets, my lord Changó. But the mystery of the thunderbolt still remained to be solved, and Oyá was convinced that the solution was in the mortar.

Carefully, she pulled the mortar over and looked inside. Unlike the gourd, the mortar was empty, with the exception of the pestle which rested on its bottom. Oyá lifted the pestle, inspected it carefully and finding nothing unusual in its composition, put it back inside the mortar. She could not imagine what Changó wanted with it, but she still felt sure that in its usage lay the secret of the thunderbolt. She looked at the mortar for some time. Maybe Changó put some magical ingredient inside the mortar and ground it with the pestle. After all, mortars were used for grinding. As if to underline her thoughts, she picked up the pestle once more and thrust it hard into the mortar with a swiftly grinding motion. A sudden flash of lightning illuminated the room and Oyá found herself surrounded by a fiery energy which was quickly absorbed by her body. She stood in the middle of the room, transfigured by the experience, her entire body permeated with the power of the lightning within it. This time Oyá was not afraid, but felt instead wildly triumphant. She knew she could control the force that coursed throughout her body, but how to use it was another matter. She suddenly remembered Changó's gesture whenever he wanted to bring down lightning. He lifted a fist to heaven and when he brought it down, lightning came down with it. Quickly she ran out of the house and without wasting any time repeated Changó's gesture. A sudden bolt of lightning flashed across the sky and crashed with a powerful explosion at her feet. But unlike Changó's thunderbolt, which was always straight as an arrow, the trajectory followed by Oyá's zigzagged across the heavens as if reluctant to come down to earth. The crash sound it made was also different and crackled like a new fire.

Far away in Oshún's house, Changó saw the thunderbolt zigzag across the sky and come down with a crash in the vicinity of Oyá's house. Instantly, he knew what Oyá had done. In one leap he was out of Oshún's bed and putting on his clothes. In vain, the goddess of love tried to detain him. "Don't leave now, my lord," she besieged him, hanging onto his sleeve. "We had just begun ..."

But Changó pushed her away impatiently. "I must leave," he said savagely. "That witch Oyá has found out the secret of my thunderbolt. If I don't hurry, she'll find out about the fire as well, if she doesn't know by now." And he left the beautiful Oshún open-mouthed by her front door while he hurried away on his ram in the direction of Oyá's house.

As soon as she saw her crooked thunderbolt hurtling to the ground Oyá knew that wherever he was Changó had also seen it. And once he saw it he would know she had his secret. Suddenly the thought of Changó's anger filled Oyá with the old, familiar dread. No one knew better than she how devastating her lover's rages could be and how cold and pitiless he could be to an adversary. An adversary, had it really come down to that? Was she really Changó's adversary? Oyá's thoughts turned to Changó's passionate lovemaking and her fear grew, but this time what she feared was losing his love forever. If she could only stay away from him until his anger abated then she might find his judgment less severe and his heart more prone to forgiveness. But where could she go that he would not find her, where could she hide that he would not think of searching? All at once she thought of the palm tree, one of Changó's favorite haunts and one of his magical attributes. Surely he would not think of looking for her in his own hunting grounds, especially if she hid beneath the ground.

No sooner had she thought of this plan than she made the decision to follow it through. Quick as the lightning which she now possessed, Oyá took to the air in a whirlwind of fire and a few minutes later was standing at the foot of Changó's favorite palm tree. She looked swiftly around to see if anyone was watching her, and seeing no one she began spinning rapidly upon herself. As her spinning motion grew in speed she began to sink into the ground. In no time she had disappeared from view and the earth above her had resumed its original form. No one could have possibly imagined that Oyá was hiding among the tangled roots of the palm tree. No one, that is, except the shadowy form that suddenly darted behind a tree with a mischievous grin on his impish features. No one, except Eleggua.

Changó arrived at Oyá's place to find the house in utter confusion. The few servants that had not run away after the thunderbolt had fallen on the courtyard were standing around with frightened faces, staring at the smoking hole the lightning had made on the ground. Changó's presence brought them out of their state of shock and they all disbanded in terror, without waiting to be questioned by the thunder god.

Changó surveyed the scene for a few minutes with a grim face. He then turned around and walked to the house. As soon as he saw the broken door and window, he realized what had happened. The ram's head had frightened Oyá but she had still kept enough of her wits to know how to get into the room and steal his mortar and his gourd. Changó's face darkened with fury and small tendrils of smoke began to issue from his ears and nostrils. He turned around to leave the room when suddenly a familiar voice stopped him in his tracks.

"Are you going to leave the ram's head behind my friend?" said the voice. "You may need it later."

Changó quickly whirled around and saw Eleggua emerge silently from behind the door.

"You startled me, Eshú," said the god of thunder. "I wasn't expecting to find you here."

"You know I always show up where I'm least expected," said Eleggua with a grin. "I enjoy surprises."

Changó did not answer him. His eyes narrowed and followed the younger orisha as he bent over, picked up the ram's head and offered it to the god of thunder.

"You know where she is, don't you?" asked Changó finally, taking the ram's head.

Eleggua smiled and nodded his head. "I always know everything," he said lightly. "It's my business to know things."

"So where is she?" asked Changó impatiently. "I've got to get to her before she reveals my secret to anybody else."

Eleggua shook his head and his smile deepened. "Come on, my friend," he said reprovingly, "for someone so well versed in women you show a surprising ignorance of their true character. Oyá does not intend to reveal your secret. All she wants to do is meet you on an equal level so she may better secure your affections. Other than that she's completely devoted to you. And knowing your secrets won't turn her into an adversary, but rather into a potentially powerful ally."

"I don't need a woman to help me in battle," said Changó loudly. "What I want to do now is find Oyá and punish her as she deserves. So please tell me. Where is she?"

"Very well," said Eleggua, shrugging his slim shoulders. "She's where she's never found and where you always are."

Changó frowned. "You speak in riddles, my friend," he said. "Can't you be more specific?"

"It's really quite clear," said Eleggua. "Where do you usually go that Oyá doesn't follow?"

My *ile*?" asked Changó incredulously. Eleggua shook his head but said nothing. Suddenly Changó's eyes lit up and his mouth curved in a knowing smile. "Of course," he whispered hoarsely. "The palm tree. She's at the palm tree."

"Or beneath it …" added Eleggua with a malicious smile.

"Beneath it …" mused Changó, smiling back. "Thank you again, my friend."

"Always glad to oblige," countered Eleggua. "I'll see you around, *oba Kosso*." Just as swiftly and unexpectedly as he had appeared, the mischievous orisha vanished from view.

Changó stared down at the ram's head that he still held in his hands, and with a deepening smile secured it to the back of his belt. He then went out to the courtyard where he had left his ram and rode away towards the forest.

Oyá was beginning to make herself at home in the huge underground cave that lay beneath the palm tree when a sudden violent tremor shook the earth and the ground above her opened up with a strepitous sound. Poised over the opening stood the thunder god, arms akimbo, his eyes glittering like live coals.

Oyá cowered behind a rock, paralyzed with fear. She could not understand how Changó had been able to find her so quickly, but she was determined to escape him somehow.

"Oyá," bellowed Changó from above. "I know you're down there. Hiding won't help. If you don't come out at once I'll come in after you and it will be worse for you. I know what you have done, but it will be of no use to you. Such powers are not meant for the feeble hands of a woman. They would eventually destroy you. So come forth and return my mortar and my gourd."

Changó's words had a completely opposite effect on Oyá than the one intended by the thunder god. Her fear gave way to such an overpowering indignation that Oyá forgot Changó's fiery temper and came rushing and swirling out of the ground like a tornado.

Oyá's sudden appearance took Changó totally by surprise. The wind goddess stood face to face with her lover, her eyes burning with defiance.

"I heard you calling, my lord," she said with a proud toss of her head. "Here are your mortar and your gourd," she added, placing them at the feet of Changó. "I had no intention of keeping them. I was simply curious about their use. But now that I have discovered their secret, I have no regrets. And I strongly disagree with you that they are not meant for the hands of a woman. In fact they are so easy to use that even a child could avail himself of their powers."

Oyá's arrogant attitude and her disparaging words filled Changó with a blinding rage.

"Insolent witch!" he cried, moving menacingly towards her. "How dare you defy me!" His huge frame shook with each word and small tongues of fire issued from every pore of his body.

Oyá stared at him impassibly, all her former fears gone with the strength of her anger. "You don't intimidate me, Changó," she cried out with a loud voice. "What you can do I can now do as well." And she exhaled a large volley of flames that quickly enveloped the thunder god.

Changó saw the fire sent by Oyá blend with the flames surrounding his own body and he trembled with impotent rage. His hand flew automatically to the double ax he always carried at his side, but he did not bring out the weapon. He knew he could never use the *ose* against a woman. Suddenly he remembered the ram's head he had secured to his belt and which he knew never failed to terrify Oyá. He started to unhook the head from his belt but as he felt the head become loose his hand hesitated. Across from him, Oyá stood her ground proudly, her beautiful head thrown back in angry defiance. As he looked at her, Eleggua's words seemed to echo in Changó's ears. And suddenly he knew Eleggua was right. Oyá was devoted to him. She would never betray him. What she did, she did out of love for him.

Oyá saw the sudden change in Changó's face. She saw the softening of his eyes and the flames die out as if extinguished from within. Her eyes filled with expectation and her heart in her breast beat rapidly.

Changó said nothing. His hand let go of the ram's head which fell unnoticed to the ground. He took one step toward Oyá and suddenly she was in his arms, crying and laughing and covering his face with kisses. "My lord, my lord, forgive me, my lord," she whispered breathlessly between kisses, until his own passion caught with hers and words were no longer necessary.

A corollary to the reconciliation between the two lovers underlines Eleggua's unerring vision. For many times after this, Oyá joined Changó in battle against his many enemies, helping him vanquish them through her acquired power over fire and lightning.

Yemayá and Orunla

In the meantime Yemayá, whose love affair with Oggún had been souring for some time, decided to leave the irascible god of metals. The parting was more or less amicable because both orishas share a mutual respect for each other and neither wanted to incur the other one's wrath. Therefore one day a large retinue of Yemayá's servants showed up at Oggún's *ile* and moved all of their mistress' belongings out of the house and back to her undersea palace.

For a while Yemayá lived in comparative peace at the bottom of the ocean, returning to earth only to visit her sister Oshún and her beloved adopted son Changó. Occasionally she attended one of the reunions given by Obatalá to discuss with the other orishas the affairs of humankind, or one of the parties given by Olofi in his palace in the sky. Yemayá's beauty, which remained untouched by the years, did not go unnoticed among the male orishas, particularly the divine seer and diviner Orunla, better known among his peers as Ifá. Regarded by the other orishas as Olofi's secretary, Orunla held a very high position in the divine hierarchy headed by Obatalá, and all major decisions undertaken by the orishas were first consulted with him. In those early days, Orunla used sixteen cowrie shells to divine the future and to decide matters of importance.

Orunla's interest in her flattered Yemayá, who held the older orisha in the highest esteem, and who found his wise ways very appealing, perhaps because they contrasted so strongly with Oggún's rough materialism. Since she did not want to appear too flighty in his eyes, she surrounded herself with an almost impenetrable haughtiness, but always left enough room for hope so that Orunla would not give up the chase too readily. So it was that one day, finally judging that she had made Orunla wait long enough, Yemayá acceded to accept his proposal to become his wife.

Yemayá's union with Orunla delighted the orishas, particularly Changó who loved and respected the seer with whom he shared strong bonds of friendship. The marriage seemed to have been made in heaven, as indeed it had been, and the harmony between Yemayá and Orunla was a joy to see. Yemayá's periodic absences to oversee her undersea kingdom did not disturb Orunla, who was also away often on his own mysterious endeavors.

For a very long time everything went marvelously well between Yemayá and Orunla, and it might have gone on in such a way forever if it had not been for Yemayá's curiosity. For some time she had been observing her divine husband's uncanny gift for divination, and it did not take her very long to learn the secrets of the cowrie shells. Yemayá's superior intelligence and resourcefulness is one of her strongest attributes, and she used it to best advantage in piecing together the mysteries of the oracle from her careful observation of her husband while he used the cowrie shells.

One day, while Orunla was away on business, Yemayá decided to try her own hand at divining. One of the orishas, not knowing that Orunla was not at home, came to see him for a consultation. This was Yemayá's opportunity to test her skill with the cowrie shells. After telling her husband's client that Orunla was away, she offered to read the oracle for him. And the orisha, who was pressed for an answer and who had no reason to say no, agreed to let her read the shells for him. Yemayá read the oracle with consummate expertise and marked an *ebbó*, that is, a remedy, for the orisha's problem. And so exact were her predictions and so perfect her recommendations that the orisha solved his problem within days. Elated with the results, he spread the word that Yemayá was every bit as good if not better than Orunla with the cowrie shells, and very soon a steady stream of Orunla's clients began to go to Yemayá for a reading. Her predictions were so accurate and her *ebbós* so miraculous that her fame as a diviner grew steadily until it eclipsed that of Orunla.

Several months later, Orunla, whose business had kept him away longer than expected, returned to his *ile*. Outside his house stood a long line of people, all waiting to be seen by

Yemayá. Piqued by curiosity, Orunla went inside his house and followed the line straight into his divining chamber where he found Yemayá, seated on a straw mat on the floor, reading the cowrie shells for one of his former clients.

Yemayá looked up and saw Orunla staring at her in silence. Unlike Changó, whose patience has a short fuse, Orunla never loses his self-control. His anger is always quiet and self-contained. This time he simply looked at Yemayá icily, then turned around and walked away.

Fully aware of the seriousness of her actions, Yemayá wasted no time in sending away all the people who had come for a consultation, and turned a deaf ear on their complaints. Then she began searching for her husband. She found him some distance away from the house, moodily staring at the distant woods. She approached him quietly and sat down by his side on the grass. Orunla did not look at her. Yemayá was silent for a while, then finally reached out and touched Orunla.

"Are you very angry, my husband?" she asked softly. "I did not mean to offend you. I thought you wouldn't mind if I tried the oracle. In fact, I thought you might be pleased. After all, if we both work at divining, we could double our income."

He did not answer. Although Orunla was sitting close to her, Yemayá felt as if he were many miles away. His silence and stillness disturbed her more than if he had raged and cursed at her. She suddenly realized that he was beyond her reach and that very possibly she had lost her husband.

"Orunla, my love, please answer me," she said humbly. "Do not chastise me with your silence. I can bear anything but that. I must know what you are thinking."

Orunla turned to look at her. Never had Yemayá seen such cold depths in her husband's eyes. The iciness flicked at her with the stinging impact of a horse whip. She recoiled from him instinctively, as if indeed she had been stung, and her eyes looked suddenly upon a stranger. When Orunla finally spoke, his voice was sad and distant, as if he were speaking to one of the people who came to consult his oracle.

"The most important aspect of the relationship between a man and his wife is mutual trust and respect," he said quietly. "Without these two things there can be no marriage. Your actions tell me you have no respect for me and, therefore, I cannot trust you. As love is built upon these strong foundations, the love that we shared is lost forever. From this day onward you are free from any allegiance to me and I'm free from any allegiance to you. You are no longer my wife."

Yemayá stared at him unbelievingly. "But I did nothing wrong," she cried. "All I did was share in my husband's interests."

"But you did so without my permission," countered Orunla. "Maybe if you had asked me I would have said yes, but you didn't. That shows you have no respect for me or my opinion. My work as diviner was a right conferred upon me by Olofi. You usurped that right without consulting him or me. Since the cowrie shells mean more to you than my love, I give them to you. From now on, you or anyone else who so desires can read them. I will no longer use them as a divining tool. With Olofi's help I will devise a new oracle that only I or my priests can read. And I will ensure that no woman will ever have access to it."

"But I don't want the oracle," said Yemayá, almost in tears. "I only want you."

"But you have already lost me," said Orunla coldly. "If you give up the oracle you will have a double loss."

Without another word, he stood up and walked away from his wife. Yemayá watched in silent grief as he went back into the house. A few minutes later he came out again, carrying a few of his belongings. Without looking back, he threw the knapsack over his shoulders and walked away in the direction of the woods. Yemayá did not try to stop him. She knew in her heart that she had lost him forever.

Orunla

The Table of Ifá

True to his word as usual, Orunla never again touched the cowrie shells. Disenchanted with humankind, specifically women, he went to live in the woods where he eked out a meager living from the rare game he found, for he was a poor hunter. A thinker and philosopher at heart, he spent most of his free time roaming the woods and pondering the mysteries of nature, few of which were closed to him. But deep within he missed his true calling, which was predicting the future and helping others find a solution to their problems. For a long time he considered the creation of a new oracle with which to exercise his gifts as a diviner, but even he, who could find the answer to practically any question, found himself at a loss in his quest.

One day, while he roamed the woods searching for game, he met Eleggua, who was one of his oldest and closest friends. The two orishas greeted each other warmly and then Eleggua asked Orunla why he had decided to stop divining with the cowrie shells. Considering Eleggua's ability to find out everybody's business it is dubious that he did not know the reasons for Orunla's decision. But if he did, he kept the knowledge to himself and pretended he did not know.

Orunla felt no qualms in telling his friend the truth. He liked and trusted Eleggua, whom he knew was a good ally.

"What troubles me the most," he said, after finishing the story, "is that now I don't have an oracle that I can use, and I hesitate to ask Olofi for help. At first I had planned to tell him what happened, but then I decided against it. He has enough work to do, considering the state of humankind, for me to burden him any further with my personal problems."

"If that's all that's worrying you, I may have the solution to your problem," said Eleggua, draping an arm around Orunla's shoulders. "I happen to know that many years ago Olofi presented Changó with a divining table that is said to be a wondrous thing. It is reputed to be the most exact of all oracles, one that can never be wrong."

"But I never knew Changó was a diviner," said Orunla with a frown. "We have always been close friends and he never mentioned he owned such a table."

Eleggua laughed.

"You know Changó as well as I do," he said, digging in his knapsack for some candy. "All he cares about is having fun and cavorting with women. As soon as his work is finished, his mind turns to women as ducks turn to water. He has no interest in such things as divining tables."

He took several pieces of coconut candy from the knapsack and offered them to Orunla who shook his head. Eleggua stuffed two in his mouth and put the rest in the shoulder bag.

"But why did Olofi make such a present to Changó?" insisted Orunla.

"Maybe he thought that would sober Changó a little," said Eleggua with a wink. "But whatever his reasons, the truth is that Changó thanked our heavenly father for the gift, then put it down somewhere in his *ile* and promptly forgot all about it. I happen to know that he'd like to get rid of it and you have something he might exchange it for."

"What could I possibly have that a man like Changó may want?" countered Orunla. "Changó has everything. He's handsome, talented, rich—even if he throws away his money—and has more women than a regiment. Besides that, he has power over fire and lightning and is undoubtedly one of the best, if not the best, warrior that has ever been known."

"That may very well be true," said Eleggua, "but it is also true that Changó is very fond of partying and dancing. And I happen to know that it secretly irks him that you are a better dancer than he. Somehow he feels that if he had your gift for the dance he'd be totally irresistible to women."

"More than he already is?" asked Orunla unbelievingly.

"It's his vanity," said Eleggua with a smile, "his one weakness. And after all, it hurts no one except an occasional enraged husband."

"But the gift of the dance was Olofi's present to me," said Orunla. "It is true I seldom make use of it, but I treasure it because he gave it to me. I don't want to risk offending him by exchanging it for something else, especially when that something else also happens to be a present of his to another."

"I happen to know he wouldn't mind one bit," said Eleggua.

"You always happen to know," shot back Orunla. "How come you always happen to know? Where do you get your knowledge? If I had your sources of information I wouldn't need an oracle to divine the future."

Eleggua leaned back against a tree and his laughter echoed through the woods.

"Ah, my friend," he said, still laughing, "excuse my laughter. But so many people have asked me the same thing. And really, it is very simple. It is my business to know." His face grew suddenly serious, making him look strange, like an old, precocious child. "You may call it another one of Olofi's presents," he added with a smile, and it was as if a curtain had fallen over his face, the smile hiding the truth within.

Orunla looked at him curiously, but wisely refrained from questioning him further.

"If what you say is true," he said, "and I have no reason to doubt it," he hastened to add, "how can the exchange be made?"

"You leave that up to me," answered Eleggua. "As I told you before, Changó will be eager to make the exchange The one we have to convince is Olofi."

"But I thought you said Olofi wouldn't mind one bit," said Orunla.

"And he won't," answered Eleggua, with an impish smile, "if he can be convinced you know how to work the divining table."

"But I don't know how to work it," argued Orunla.

"You will in time," said Eleggua, "but time is the one thing you haven't got. You cannot gain knowledge of the table unless you own it, and you can't own it until Olofi agrees to the exchange. So we must trick Olofi into thinking you know how to work the table on your own. That will make him think you are indeed the greatest of all diviners and he will then insist you own the table."

"But that is dishonest," said Orunla with a frown. "I don't like tricking Olofi."

"It is not dishonest," countered Eleggua. "It is fair. It is the right thing to do. You want the divining table and Changó wants the gift of the dance. By making the exchange we are making both of you happy. Therefore that must be the right thing to do. Doing the right thing is what matters. How you do it does not count."

"But how are we going to convince Olofi I know how to work the table when I don't?" insisted Orunla.

"Simple," said Eleggua. "You and Changó will come to the fields in front of Olofi's palace. Changó will bring the table and you will bring the gift of the dance. I will get Olofi to set up a test for you. The test will be to determine which half of the field will yield a corn crop, the right or the left half. On the left, I'll get Olofi to sow toasted corn and on the right, healthy corn seed. Naturally, only the right side of the field will yield a corn harvest. Remember, that must be your answer. At a given moment, Olofi will hand you the table and you must make believe you are using it to determine where the corn will grow. When you give the correct answer Olofi will be convinced you truly deserve the table as a divining tool."

"I still don't like tricking Olofi," said Orunla.

"Don't worry about it," grinned Eleggua. "I'll take care of everything."

The two friends parted and several days later they met again as planned, in front of Olofi's palace. Changó was there as expected with the divining table, and so was Olofi, sitting under a parasol and surrounded by all the orishas.

At a sign from Olofi, Changó handed the table to Orunla who took it from him, carefully avoiding his old friend's eyes. He knew the laughter he would find there and he was too mortified to share Changó's sense of mischief.

The test went as well as it had been planned by Eleg-

table with the full blessing of Olofi, who congratulated him on his uncanny gifts of divination. All the orishas then came forward and shook his hand and joined the Creator in congratulating Orunla.

Neither Changó nor Orunla, both flushed with the excitement of their new possessions, saw Eleggua wink at Olofi and Olofi wink back.

Several days later Eleggua visited Orunla.

"How are you doing with the table, my friend?" he asked.

"Wonderfully," said Orunla, "I am already in full possession of all its secrets. It is truly my very own oracle, which only I can read. And from this moment onward it shall be known as the Table of Ifá. In time I will teach its secrets to my own priests who will henceforth be known as *babalawos*. No woman will ever know its secrets. That is my vow."

"Are you happy?" asked Eleggua.

"Yes, I'm happy," answered Orunla, "except for one thing. It still bothers me that we tricked Olofi."

Once more Eleggua's laughter rang strong and clear throughout the woods.

"Don't worry, my friend," he said, still laughing. "I happen to know Olofi cannot be tricked."

He dug out a few pieces of candy from his knapsack and stuffed a couple into his mouth. He waved a hand at Orunla.

"See you around, friend," he said, and disappeared quickly among the trees.

Orunla and Death

Orunla's proficiency with the table grew with time until his fame as a diviner became legendary. People would come from all parts of the world to consult him and his priests, the *babalawos*. The cowrie shells continued to be read by Yemayá and the other orishas, but there came a point in the reading of the shells where the diviner could no go any further. At that point, he was forced to consult the Table of Ifá. Even Yemayá herself had to consult her former husband on more than one occasion. The first time she had gone to him with great misgivings, but he had received her so affably that she soon relaxed in his presence. It was soon obvious to her that although their former relationship was over, a new friendship could now flourish. It was not what she wanted, but it was something.

Orunla continued to work his oracle, and his priests and his following continued to grow. Every day hundreds of people came to be consulted, most of whom had to be turned away due to a lack of time. Then suddenly and inexplicably, the number of consultants began to diminish. Even the *babalawos* began to thin out. Worried about his business prospects, Orunla consulted his oracle. The answer he received filled him with dismay. The table informed him that Ikú—Death— had decided to take over the earth and to that end was killing everyone in sight. Orunla, being an orisha and therefore immortal, had no reason to worry. But his priests—the *babalawos*—and the vast majority of his clients were ordinary human beings. If something was not done soon, Orunla would lose not only his priests but most of his clientele.

After some consideration, Orunla thought of a solution to the problem. Without further ado, he sent a message to Ikú, telling her he wanted to speak to her. The Grim Reaper, flattered by Orunla's attention, sent back word to the diviner that she would soon pay him a visit. And true to her word, she came by his house in the woods, dressed in widow's weeds and leaning on her scythe.

After the usual pleasantries were exchanged, Orunla asked Ikú to sit down and take some refreshments.

"You do look exhausted, dear lady," he said solicitously. "You must not overexert yourself. Your work, unlike that of others, can be done at your own leisure. After all," he added with a discreet smile, "no one but you can do it."

"That is so true, my lord," answered Ikú, arranging her bones in what she considered her most seductive pose. "But as you very well know, being your own boss has its disadvantages. One tends to drive oneself too hard."

"May I offer you something to replenish your strength?" asked Orunla with a gallant bow.

"Thank you, my lord, but I never eat, or drink for that matter," answered Ikú with a girlish smile. "Wouldn't know where to put it," she giggled.

"You really don't need it," answered Orunla softly. "You have a most enchanting form. It would be a pity if you lost it. But if you will not take any nourishment, at least rest a while. My own bedroom is at your disposal if you desire."

Ikú looked at the handsome Orunla with libidinous eyes. "Your own bedroom, my lord," she said with an enticing smile. "Does that also include your own bed?"

"But of course," said Orunla. "Allow me to take you in."

He took her gently by the arm and led her into his sleeping chamber. Being a bachelor and a hunter, Orunla had not taken the trouble to turn his bedroom into a showcase. His bed was a large pile of animal skins arranged cozily in a corner, and there was little else in the room other than a few hunting trophies. But Ikú made a great show of how deliciously intimate and masculine the place was. Orunla simply smiled his very special private smile and made every effort to make Death as comfortable as a bundle of bones can be.

"And how about you, my lord?" said Ikú with a saucy smile. "Wouldn't you like to rest by my side?"

"I would love to, my lady," said Orunla, "but I have several pressing things to do. I will be back as soon as I am free, however, and then we can both rest together."

"How promising!" said Ikú, rattling her bones in excitement. "I'll be waiting for you with breathless anticipation."

"You honor me, dear lady," said Orunla, looking at her with admiring eyes. "But I do hope you rest while I'm gone. Rest does wonders for a woman's beauty."

All at once Ikú lay back on the furs and closed her eyes. "How tender and considerate you are!" she said dreamily. "I'll do as you say and wait for you to wake me up with a caress."

By the time Orunla reached the bedroom door she was already snoring. Orunla did not waste any time. As soon as he was out of the bedroom he searched for Ikú's scythe and when he found it, he took it to the back of the house and hid it under a pile of logs. He then took his hunting implements and spent the entire night hunting in the woods.

It was close to noon when Orunla returned to his *ile*. His hands were empty and he felt mildly frustrated. In his rush to get away from Ikú he had forgotten that as long as she was resting nothing could die. At first he had thought he was having unusual bad luck in locating and pinning down his prey. But when he saw one of his arrows go straight through a hart's neck and the animal shake off the arrow as if it had been a wheat stalk, he suddenly realized what was happening. By that time the sun was up, and it was time to go back home.

When Orunla entered the house he found Death sitting in a corner, wearing an angry pout.

"So, my lord," she exclaimed indignantly as soon as she saw Orunla. "Is this the gallant way you treat your female guests? By letting them sleep alone all night in your house while you go gallivanting Olofi knows where?"

"A thousand apologies, dear lady," said Orunla. "I spent all night in the woods searching for game and I forgot that hunting was a hopeless pursuit while you rested. I'm sorry if I neglected you. It was not my intention."

Ikú was too angry to listen to apologies.

"Your reputation seems vastly exaggerated," she said, standing up. "Someone as wise as you are supposed to be should never forget things, especially how to treat a woman who has the powers I have. Such clumsy blunders may be expected of common mortals, not of orishas, particularly the wise and ever-knowing Orunla, owner of the Table of Ifá."

Orunla had the grace to blush.

"Even Ifá can fail to perceive things, my lady," he said stiffly. "Only Olofi is ever-knowing."

Ikú gathered her black robes around her and straightened her gaunt shoulders.

"I have no further time to lose, my lord," she said. "I must return to my work. Kindly find the scythe I left by the door and give it to me so I may relieve you of my presence."

"I'm afraid that's impossible," said Orunla with a cold smile. "If you wish to leave I cannot detain you, but the scythe remains with me."

Ikú swept him with a contemptuous smile.

"So," she said sardonically, "now I see this has been a farce from the beginning. All your gallantry and your concern over my well-being was simply a despicable plan to despoil me of the scythe. What is your game, Orunla? Are you tired of divining and want to take my place?"

"No one would ever want to take your place, Ikú," said Orunla sadly. "Yours is the most hateful and thankless of all occupations."

"You are lying," cried Death angrily. "I'm respected and admired by everyone. My position is exalted and enviable. My power is awesome. I could destroy all life on earth with a single sweep of my scythe if I so desired."

"And you think that's enviable?" said Orunla. "Do you really believe people respect and admire you? You are wrong, Ikú. It is not respect and admiration that you awaken in everyone. It is fear and hatred. Yours is the power that takes a young child away from his loving mother, the stinking breath that withers a rose in bloom, a bird in flight, the leaves on the trees. Yours is the power that strangles a warrior's cry of triumph, that covers the earth with a mantle of gloom and despair. No, Ikú. I don't envy your power and I have neither respect nor admiration for your work."

Ikú's shoulders sagged visibly under her somber robes. "You are right," she said sadly. "I've known this all along. I try to maintain the pretense that my work is respected and that I receive the recognition that I feel I deserve. But I can feel the hatred and the fear that surrounds me. It is oppressive in its magnitude. Some days I feel I can no longer go on. That's why I've decided to take over the earth and destroy everything in my path. When no living thing exists I will no longer be feared. My ghastly work will no longer be needed."

"And you think that's the answer?" asked Orunla gently.

"Is there any other?" said Ikú bitterly. "My work may not be pleasant, but it is vital to human and natural evolution. If it is true I sometimes take children away from their mothers, it is also true I often relieve the pain of the terminally ill, and take away the things that are wasted and have long lost the desire to live. I clear away the refuse of the past to make way for the hope of the future and the reality of the present. Surely that must have some value."

"And it has," said Orunla with a kind smile. "But the living don't like to be reminded of the brevity of their days on earth. Neither do they like to be separated from the ones they love. That is why your work is thankless, even if it is necessary for evolution. Olofi created you for a purpose. In his infinite wisdom he knew only *you* could do this heavy task. What you have to remember is that you are beyond blame or praise. Neither the respect nor the hatred of the living should touch you. Accept your fate and your duty with stoic resignation. Above all, don't abuse your power. Those who do promptly lose it."

"So what I should I do?" asked Death.

"Just do your work," answered Orunla. "Stop this wild rampage that's causing so much terror and destruction and simply take that which Olofi has commanded. I will return your scythe at once if you promise to do that."

"I will," said Ikú, standing up once more. "I have much to thank you for, Ifá. You have shown me my true path. I guess your reputation was not exaggerated after all."

"Reputations are false fronts, Ikú," said Orunla gravely. "Anyone can hide behind them. It is actions that really matter."

He went back to the courtyard behind the house and returned with the scythe. "Here," he said, handing it to Ikú. "Use it wisely and never too soon."

"Isn't there something I can do to show my appreciation, Ifá?" said Death with a smile.

Orunla looked at her for a few minutes and suddenly nodded his head. "There is one thing," he said softly. "You know my colors are green and yellow. They are in fact my banner. I would like you to spare the life of anyone wearing an *idé* (a bracelet) made of green and yellow beads. When you encounter such an individual you will know he's either one of my priests or one of my followers."

"But I cannot spare anybody's life indefinitely, Ifá," said Ikú. "Not even for you."

"I know," said Orunla. "When you meet someone wearing the *idé* whom you want to take, come see me and we will agree whether or not I can let you take him. Each time you meet that person you must return to me until I tell you his time has come to accompany you. Some people you will take right away, but for others you may have to wait a long time."

"That may require our meeting very often, Ifá," said Death with a sudden return to her former flirtatious manner. "Would you mind that very much?"

"On the contrary," said Orunla gallantly. "It would be my greatest pleasure."

The pact ratified between Orunla and Death was so successful that to this day his priests and all of Orunla's followers wear an *idé* of green and yellow beads around their wrists to keep Ikú away.

Orunla Battles Osain

After his separation from Yemayá, Orunla established his home in the woods. At first as a hunter and later on as the oracle of Ifá. The woods and all they contained had always belonged to the orisha Osain, a morose and saturnine individual with a short temper and a penchant for solitude. The other orishas always tried to be on good terms with Osain because they needed the *ewe* (the plants, herbs, and trees that grew in the woods) to prepare their *ebbós* or magical works. But it wasn't always easy to be on good terms with Osain, and only a few of the orishas—notably Eleggua, Oggún, Ochosi, and Changó—could call themselves friends of the antisocial Osain.

Orunla's presence in the woods and the constant parade of visitors who came to consult the Table of Ifá bothered Osain, who felt that his privacy was being violated. He especially resented the fact that Orunla never asked his permission before establishing his residence in the woods.

As time went on, Osain's anger and resentment toward Orunla continued to grow. Finally it erupted into a grave altercation between the two orishas during which Orunla, being a pacific and gentle person, suffered the most damage. Osain challenged Orunla to battle and when Orunla refused, calling such an action barbaric, Osain lost what little patience he had left and jumped on the diviner, leaving him badly bruised and half-conscious by the door of his *ile* in full view of his priests and clients.

Osain's violent actions deeply humiliated Orunla, who although being a quiet man, was also stubborn and determined to the extreme. He therefore made the firm decision to oppose Osain's bellicose attitude and remain in the woods for as long as he felt like it. So he built a tall fence around his *ile*, posted some of his servants around it, and continued to carry on with his business as if nothing at all had happened.

When Osain saw that Orunla seemed determined to stay in the woods and that he was not intimidated by Osain's threats and aggressiveness, he decided to use other methods to oust the diviner from the woods. These methods called for the use of the powerful herbal magic for which Osain was famous.

As soon as Osain started to work his magic *ebbós* on Orunla, the diviner began to feel listless and depressed, and his prognostications lost most of their brilliant accuracy. The *ebbós* or magic remedies he prescribed for his clients also began to fail. Naturally this reflected adversely on Ifá's reputation, and as a result, his clientele began to diminish. No longer did lines for consultations form in front of Orunla's house, and his priests, the *babalawos*, started to go hungry.

At first Orunla thought the situation was caused by his natural anxiety over Osain's attitude, and that it would soon change for the better. But after a while, when he saw that things grew from bad to worse, and that he was forced to close his business through lack of customers, he began to suspect that an evil force was at work and that if he did not do something about it, he would go out of business for good. He knew that consulting his own oracle would do him no good because his precognitive powers were at a low ebb due to the negative influences around him, but he was sure that Osain was behind his problems. There was only one person he knew whose magic was stronger than Osain, and that person was Changó. He therefore decided to pay the god of thunder a visit.

Changó was in the courtyard of his palace, sitting on his throne under a red and white parasol. He was holding audience and for that reason he was wearing an elaborate crown from which hung long strings of beads in the shape of a veil. The beads hid Changó's handsome face from view, but his shrewd eyes were visible from behind the veil, glittering more than the colored beads that hid him. He was surrounded by the high officers of his court and by the women of his household, all wearing his colors and fancy headdresses.

Orunla waited until Changó had heard several of his subjects and had settled their problems. Then he came forward and paid *foribale* (homage) at his feet. Changó stood up immediately.

"Ifá, my friend," he exclaimed, coming forward and helping Orunla to his feet. "you don't have to salute at my feet."

"In the house of the king," said Orunla with a smile, "all must pay homage."

"Not all, my friend," said Changó, embracing him warmly, "and especially, not you."

He turned to one of his aides and said to him, "The audience is over for today. I'll be inside with Ifá. Inform the people of my decision, then see to it that refreshments are brought to my chambers."

The official nodded, and Changó, his arm wrapped around Orunla's shoulders, led him to the palace.

After the two orishas had chatted amiably for a while and Orunla had partaken in full of Changó's hospitality, the god of thunder smiled at his friend and said, "Well, Ifá, I think it is now time for you to tell me the real reason you came to see me."

Orunla laughed and leaned back further on his straw mat.

"You're a shrewd observer, my friend," he said. "I'm not going to waste your time or mine by denying a truth which is self-evident. I did come to you for a special reason. I imagine you must have heard the trouble I've been having with Osain …"

"I've heard something to that effect," said Changó helping himself to another portion of his favorite cornmeal and okra. "But I thought you had overcome that problem by building a fence around your *ile*."

"News and Eleggua travel fast," said Orunla. "But what he didn't tell you is that I have reason to suspect that Osain is working magic against me. He hasn't attacked me bodily again, but he has been attacking me in other ways. As a result my work with the oracle has been failing, and I may have to stop divining permanently. You know I'm a peaceful man. I'm not very well versed in the magical arts, so I can't defend myself very well against Osain. I thought you, with your profound knowledge of these matters, might be able to help me with this problem."

Changó finished eating and lay back with a contented sigh. "So Osain is giving you trouble with his *ewe* magic," he said, stretching himself like a sleek, lazy cat. "He's very handy with his magical gourd and can do wonders with an herb or two. But don't worry. I'll tell you what to do. Just promise me you'll do what I tell you and that you'll do it as soon as you get home."

"Of course," said Orunla immediately. "That's why I came to see you."

"Very well," said Changó, standing up. "Come with me and I'll prepare an *ebbó* for you that will solve your problem. It will also bring grief to Osain, but that's something that can't be helped. After all, he started the whole thing."

The two orishas went to Changó's sleeping chamber, where he kept his magic gourd and the mortar where he mixed his thunder and lightning. Under Orunla's curious eyes, Changó began to prepare the *ebbó*. He moved quickly around the room, gathering ingredients from several closed containers scattered throughout the place. A few minutes later he handed Orunla a large vessel containing twelve *odduaras* (flint stones) and twelve cotton wicks soaked in palm oil.

"As soon as you get home, light the twelve wicks and watch what happens," he said. "But remember what I told you before. It must be done at once, without wasting a single minute. This stuff is volatile and will go off by itself if you don't hurry. Then Osain won't have to worry about you anymore. There won't be any more you to worry about."

"I'll do exactly as you say," said Orunla, gingerly taking the vessel. "I'll let you know what happens."

"You don't have to," said Changó with one of his loud, infectious laughs. "I'll find out as soon as it happens."

The two friends embraced warmly, and after thanking Changó profusely, Orunla left the palace and returned home.

While Orunla had been consulting Changó, Osain had been busy in the woods searching for herbs with which to harm the diviner. By now he was so consumed by hatred for Orunla that he was determined to destroy him completely.

As soon as Orunla reached his *ile*, he secured all the doors and went into his consulting chamber. Placing the vessel on the floor, he immediately proceeded to light the twelve cotton wicks as Changó had instructed him to do.

The moment the fire touched the cotton, Changó's powerful magic went into effect and from the twelve flint stones rose a roll of thunder that shook Orunla's house to its foundations. All at once a huge thunderbolt sprang from the vessel, burst with a roar through an open window and went rushing through the air into the middle of the woods, exactly where Osain was looking for *ewe*. Within seconds the entire area was covered with flames, trapping Osain in their midst. If Osain had not been so intent in his task of destruction, he would have seen the bolt of lightning crashing through the air and might have escaped intact. But he was so absorbed in his search, he was not aware of what was happening until the lightning fell and the woods surrounding him caught fire. By that time it was too late to evade the flames.

From his *ile* on the edge of the woods, Orunla watched aghast as the blast hit the center of the woods, kindling it like a giant bonfire. And his nobility was such that he prayed from the bottom of his heart that Osain would not be hurt by the inferno. But his prayers were of no avail. Immortal as he was, Osain could not be killed by the flames, but he was left lame and blind for all eternity, losing an arm, a leg, and an eye in the conflagration.

After this terrifying experience, Osain did not trouble Orunla any more. And in time, realizing the error of his actions, and his own part in the tragedy that befell him, he nobly forgave Orunla and offered him his friendship. The two orishas became such inseparable friends that they worked together from that time onward.

Oyá and Osain

For some time after Osain's encounter with Changó's magic, the woods remained partly scorched and devoid of life. But nature has remarkable healing powers, and so it was that one day new life grew where only charred trees had been, and the woods again became a source of joy for all living things. A green mantle covered the scars of the old battleground and hunters returned to look for game. The orishas also returned to look for *ewe*, without which their *ebbós* would come to naught. Among them came Changó. But Osain had not forgotten that it was Changó's thunderbolt which had caused his humiliating defeat at the hands of Orunla and the loss of his limbs. And when Changó asked him for some *ewe* to prepare his magical works, Osain denied him the necessary herbs.

Changó returned to his palace, angry and frustrated. He knew that neither threats nor pleas would change the irascible Osain's mind, and he was unable to use his magic against him through lack of *ewe*. It was in this somber frame of mind that Oyá found him when she came to visit him one day.

"What ails you, my lord?" she asked him, when she saw that all her caresses failed to awake any response in him. "You are not yourself today. Have I angered you in any way?"

"It's not you," said Changó, turning his face to the wall. "It's Osain. He has obviously decided to get even with me for the magic I gave Orunla against him and now he refuses to let me have any of his *ewe*. There are several herbs I need to complete a work I'm doing and if he doesn't give them to me I stand to lose a great deal."

Oyá was silent for some time.

"If that's all that's bothering you," she said at length, "maybe there's something I can do about it."

Changó turned to look at her with a condescending smile.

"I know you mean well," he said. "But what could you possibly do to change Osain's mind? Your magic is not stronger than mine."

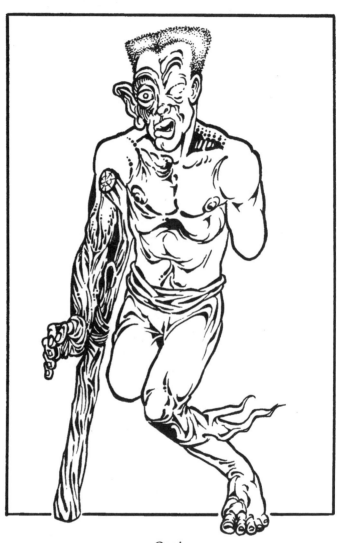

Osain

Oyá looked at him and her eyes twinkled mischievously.

"Maybe not," she said with the faintest trace of irony in her voice, "but I believe there's still something I can do."

Changó leaned on one elbow and stared at her curiously.

"What do you have in mind, my love?" he asked, a gleam of interest in his eyes.

"Come with me and I will show you," answered Oyá.

The two orishas left Changó's sleeping chamber and walked out into the courtyard. Once outside, Oyá raised a great wind that carried them swiftly into the center of the woods. As the two orishas touched solid ground, Changó saw that they were standing by a large ebony tree.

"Look up there at that high branch," said Oyá, pointing upwards. "What do you see?"

Changó strained his eyes against the glare of the sun which seeped through the branches of the tree. After some initial effort, he saw the object Oyá was pointing at.

"It looks like a giant gourd," he said finally. "What is it?"

"That is the gourd where Osain keeps the essence of each plant, herb, flower, and tree that exists in the woods," said Oyá. "It also contains the secret of his power over the *ewe* we all need."

"I had heard about this," said Changó, looking at Oyá with undisguised admiration in his eyes. "But I did not know where he kept it. You are truly a witch, my lady. I bow to your ingenuity."

Oyá flushed with pleasure at the flattering words from her lover.

"I have known about this place for a very long time," she said with a saucy smile. "The wind goes places where fire can't reach."

Changó was faintly annoyed by Oyá's statement, but he was so thrilled by the discovery of the gourd that he decided to let it pass without comment.

"If we could only reach the gourd," he said, staring at it with hungry eyes. "Imagine the power that's in there. But it is far too high to be reached from the ground and the trunk of the tree is too smooth to climb. Even the lower branches are beyond our reach. Osain could not have picked a better place to keep his secret," he ended bitterly.

"I agree it cannot be reached from the ground," said Oyá with a malicious smile. "But that doesn't mean it is completely out of reach."

"What do you mean?" said Changó, tiny flames of excitement dancing in his eyes. "What are you planning to do?"

"This," answered Oyá with a stentorious laugh. Picking up her wide skirts, she began fanning them rapidly until she created a gale wind of such proportions that all the branches of the huge tree bent wildly under the impact. Each new motion of her skirt made the branches bend faster, first forward then backward until the gourd began to sway violently atop the tree. Suddenly, from within the gourd, there came a shrill, earsplitting whistle that echoed throughout the woods.

"The gourd!" exclaimed Changó, his ears still ringing from the sound. "It's warning Osain it's about to fall!"

Almost instantaneously Osain burst through the bushes, hopping on his one leg with the aid of a crooked branch.

"*Ewe O!*" he screamed frantically, "*Ewe O!* My herbs! My herbs!"

But Oyá was not intimidated by his presence. Faster and faster she continued to fan her skirts, and faster and faster the branches and the gourd continued to swing until finally, with a terrified whistle that died in a whimper, the gourd fell from the tree. Immediately all the *ewe* within spilled in all directions strewing the ground with its wealth of power.

Changó and Oyá fell at once to the ground and began to pick up as many of the *ewe* as they could find. The other orishas, informed by the ever-present Eleggua of what had happened, also rushed to the scene and began to pick up the scattered herbs.

In the midst of this frantic scavenging, Osain went hopping around on one leg, unsuccessfully trying to prevent the taking of his beloved *ewe*. He begged and he threatened alternately, but the orishas did not seem to hear him. The treasure hunt was far too exciting.

When it was finally all over, each orisha had picked up a share of the *ewe*, some more, some less than others. And from that moment onward all the herbs that each one picked became his or her property. Some, who had grabbed the same herb at the same moment that it was being picked by another orisha, had to share it with that individual. But for the most part, each herb became the property of a specific orisha.

As for Osain, although he now was forced to share the *ewe* with the other orishas, he still kept his power over herbs and plants, and he remained the master of the woods to whom due homage had to be paid before using the *ewe*.

Babalú-Ayé

Babalú-Ayé

The orishas held periodic festivals to celebrate harvesting times. When they came down from the sky and settled on earth, they began tilling and planting the fields to show human beings the importance of living and working together. They also taught humankind the arts of singing and dancing, and invented the first drums which were to be used both as musical instruments and for the purpose of invoking the orishas.

During the time of the yam harvest, they celebrated one of their festivals, as they usually did. The celebration was held in the center of town where they brought all sorts of food and drink, especially their favorite palm wine. Also present was a set of *batas*, the sacred drums they used for their ritual dancing.

All the orishas were present, eating, drinking, singing and dancing, and generally having a marvelous time. The palm wine was in a large calabash in the center of the courtyard where the dance was being held. Everyone came from time to time to the calabash and dipped his or her gourd into the liquid and drank some of the wine. After a while everybody became slightly drunk, some more than others, but all enjoying themselves royally.

Babalú-Ayé, sometimes known as Chankpanna, the patron of disease and infirmity, and particularly of smallpox, was also present at the festival, but he was the only one of the orishas who wasn't dancing. Babalú had a reason for staying away from the dance floor. Unknown to the other orishas, he had a wooden leg which he carefully hid under his long robes. He was afraid that his secret would be discovered during the movements of the dance. Therefore he wisely refrained from joining the other orishas on the dance floor, and contented himself by watching the festivities and dipping his gourd in the palm wine with slightly more frequency than the rest of his companions.

Babalú 's abstention from dancing did not go unnoticed by his friends, who began to murmur amongst themselves, judging his reluctance to join them as a planned slight on the part of Babalú. Perhaps if they had not been drinking so heavily, they would not have reacted so strongly against his apparently antisocial behavior, but they had all drunk beyond their limits, and their powers of judgment were considerably diminished.

"Look at Babalú," cried one in aggrieved tones. "He refuses to join us on the dance floor. He must think himself too important to mix in with the rest of us."

"That's right," said another, looking at Babalú with resentful eyes.

"Maybe he does think he's better than the rest of us. If that's what you think, why don't you leave Babalú, and find yourself more agreeable company?"

Babalú felt mortified by all this harassment. The last thing he wanted to do was call attention to himself and possibly risk revealing his infirmity.

"You are wrong, my brothers," he cried, standing up with an effort. "I am honored to be in your company. It is simply that I'm too old and tired for dancing. Besides, I've been drinking a little more than I should. But to prove to you that I don't mean to hurt your feelings, I will join you in the dance."

With the aid of his staff, he hobbled to the middle of the dance floor and began to sway to the rhythmic beating of the drums. The other orishas, delighted with his company, began jostling him around with much laughter and clapping of hands. Babalú tried valiantly to keep his balance, holding on to his staff for dear life, and hopping around frantically on his one good leg. But he had been drinking too heavily and was unable to stand for very long. With a cry of dismay, he felt his knee give way, and with a great flourish of his wide robe he fell headlong to the floor, exposing his wooden leg for all to see.

For one heart-stopping minute there was a sudden, shocked silence among the orishas. Then they all began to laugh. The laughter grew in huge, terrible waves around the humiliated god of smallpox, who struggled painfully to his feet with the aid of his staff. This was not an easy task because he kept slipping back to the floor each time he attempted to straighten up, causing a new explosion of laughter from his companions. But at last, Babalú-Ayé was standing firmly, leaning on his staff with both hands, all traces of drunkenness gone from his enraged mind.

For several minutes, he stood among the other orishas, his cold, pale face a mask of stern anger. Slowly, the laughter died away and the suddenly sober orishas lowered their ashamed faces to the ground. Babalú said nothing. With grim determination, he raised his staff and began to strike at the orishas. Everywhere the staff fell it left an angry, painful welt. Amidst cries of dismay, the orishas scattered throughout the courtyard, trying to escape the inexorable staff. But not before each and everyone had been hit at least once. That was the end of the festivities. A few minutes later, the dancing floor was empty and the drums were silent. Babalú-Ayé looked around with a grim, satisfied smile, and then turned and left the courtyard.

The following day, all the orishas woke up sick and feverish, their bodies covered with the stinging pustules typical of the dreaded smallpox. They understood at once the terrible power hidden in Babalú's staff and sorely regretted having incurred his wrath.

Far away on his farm, Obatalá heard of the orishas' predicament and of Babalú's violent actions. Donning his white robes and brandishing the ox tail switch that is a symbol of his authority, he presented himself at Babalú's *ile*. But as soon as the god of smallpox heard that Obatalá was on his way, he hid himself in the woods. He knew he had acted rashly and that he should have waited for Obatalá to pass judgment on the orishas instead of exacting his own revenge. For that reason he feared facing the elder orisha.

When Obatalá saw that Babalú-Ayé had flown from his house, he was filled with indignation.

"While the other orishas acted shamefully in casting scorn upon Babalú for his infirmity," he exclaimed, raising the hair switch in the air, "it was equally shameful of Babalú to punish them without waiting for my judgment. Therefore, because of his impulsive act, he shall be banished from our society and be condemned to roam throughout the woods from this day onward!"

He brought down the switch with a final gesture, thus sealing Babalú's fate.

The unfortunate god of smallpox, saddened by Obatalá's judgment, but incapable of defying its authority, left his home in the city where he had long been revered, and began his long exile. Everywhere he went people shunned and despised him. Many threw water at him to cleanse away the evil influences that he was supposed to carry with him.

It seemed that Babalú-Ayé had reached the depths of the most abject misery and despair. Feared and despised by all, he lost himself in the woods, hungry and destitute, his clothes in rags, his body covered by the same sores with which he afflicted others.

There was only one among the orishas who felt compassion for Babalú-Ayé. That was the usually merry and carefree Eleggua. Babalú's unhappy situation deeply disturbed Eleggua, and he finally decided to do something about it.

One day, Orunla, who had returned to Ile-Ife, looked up from his divining table and saw his old friend Eleggua approaching in the company of a ragged beggar, covered with sores and leaning on a crooked staff.

"Greetings, my brother!" said Eleggua cheerfully, upon reaching Orunla's side. "I trust you're happy and enjoying the greatest of success."

"Greetings, Eshú," said Orunla guardedly. "What brings you to my humble *ile*?"

"I need a favor from you, Ifá," said Eleggua with a genial smile. "I'm sure you won't deny it."

"There's little I can deny you, my honored friend," said Orunla, still guarded. "What favor do you want from me?"

"Actually, the favor is not for me," said Eleggua, making himself comfortable in a leather cassock and digging inside his knapsack for something to eat. "It's for my friend here, Babalú-Ayé. I'm sure you know him well." He brought out a few corn fritters which he shared with Babalú. Orunla turned him down politely, explaining he did not eat during working hours.

"Naturally, I know, Babalú," said the diviner after a moment of silence. "I'm sorry I did not greet you sooner, Chankpanna," he added, addressing himself to Babalú. "I just did not recognize you."

Babalú, who had been silent since his arrival, shifted his weight painfully with the aid of his staff and lowered his head in shame.

"You don't have to apologize, Ifá," he said sadly. "No one would recognize me in my present condition."

"That is why we're here," said Eleggua, still munching on a corn fritter. "Only you can help Babalú now. With the help of the table you can find out what he can do to overcome the curse that's come upon him. I'm sure you'll agree he has suffered enough. No one should be condemned to his kind of fate forever. Please say you'll help him."

Orunla looked at Eleggua with a rueful smile.

"You sure get yourself into some problems, my friend," he said, shaking his head. "And the worst part is, this time you're determined to drag me in with you."

"What do you mean?" said Eleggua with feigned innocence.

"You know very well what I mean," retorted Orunla. "Obatalá decreed Babalú's fate. It is unthinkable to go over his head. To do so entails risking Olofi's displeasure. Then all three of us will be in trouble."

"Please don't take any risks on my account," interposed Babalú-Ayé. "I'm used to my life now. I don't want to cause any further trouble."

Orunla smiled and shook his head.

"Trouble has always been my middle name," he said, pointing to the straw mat in front of him. "Sit down, Chankpanna. Let's see what the table has to say to you."

With a satisfied grin, Eleggua helped Babalú sit down and took a seat right behind him. Orunla brought out his divining implements and proceeded to interpret the oracle.

The first thing Orunla did was spread some of the sacred *yefa* or yam powder on the divining table. Then he began a series of ritualistic chants. When these were finished he started to mark a series of vertical lines with two fingers in the *yefa* powder. He drew four rows of the lines before beginning to interpret the meaning of the oracle.

When he was finished, he leaned back with a sigh of relief and said to Babalú, "You are lucky, Chankpanna. Olofi has forgiven you. But now you must promise to do exactly what I tell you."

"Absolutely," said Babalú immediately. "I'll follow your advice to the last detail."

"Good," said Orunla. "This is what you have to do. First, you must gather together all sorts of grain, such as beans, wheat, oats, corn, and so on. You will then mix all of them together and rub them in handfuls over your body. That *ebbó* will cleanse you of the sores that cover your body. When you finish doing that, you must find yourself a dog, which must always accompany you. Then you must leave Yoruba and go to the neighboring land of Dahomey. There you will be worshiped in your true nature as an orisha."

"Must I leave this land?" said Babalú in dismay. "I don't know the strange land you mentioned. And the people there don't know me. Why should they honor me there, unknown to them as I am?"

"Nevertheless, they will," answered Orunla gravely. "And you must not question the oracle. You said you'd do as I told you. Why are you hesitant now?"

"I'm not hesitant," said Babalú anxiously. "But leaving here for an unknown place …"

"Why should you want to stay here?" asked Eleggua, who had been following the conversation closely as usual. "All you have gotten from the people in this place is scorn and derision. I would imagine you should be glad to leave."

"You are both right, of course," said Babalú dubiously. "Any place would be better than this one, after all I've endured. I'll do it," he added, with sudden determination. "I'll do the *ebbó* and leave at once. The only problem is finding a dog."

"That's no problem," said Eleggua, jumping to his feet with his usual agility. "Oggún will give you one of his hounds. I'll speak to him about it."

He helped Babalú get up and they both thanked Orunla for his help.

"It was a pleasure," said the diviner kindly. "But next time, Eshú, let me know ahead of time what you plan so that I may be prepared."

"Even I don't know what I'm going to do ahead of time," grinned Eleggua. "You are asking for the impossible, Ifá."

The three orishas embraced warmly and Orunla watched with thoughtful eyes as Eleggua and Babalú disappeared into the nearby woods.

Soon afterward, all the orishas in Ile-Ife were commenting amongst themselves how a healed Babalú, dressed once more in his princely robes and accompanied by a large hound, had left the city for good. In due time, news came in from nearby Dahomey, where the god of smallpox had been received with great honors and where his worship soon equalled that of Obatalá himself.

Olofi, well pleased with Babalú's obedience to Orunla's mandate, had sent a healing rain on the god of smallpox, cleansing him of his disease and of all his sins. Then he ordered the earth to open up at Chankpanna's feet, burying all of Babalú's past miseries therein forever. Orunla remained the keeper of Babalú's secret and his staunch friend for all eternity. As for Eleggua, he became Babalú's closest ally and the guardian of his palace.

Ochosi's Curse

Ochosi, the divine hunter, always lived in the woods, where he often roamed in search of game with his good friends, Oggún, Eleggua, and sometimes, the redoubtable Osain. His skill in hunting was legendary, for the animals he caught were the most beautiful and the most admired.

Ochosi's hunting weapons had always been the crossbow or the bow and arrow, but one day, tired of hunting with the same implements, he decided to try something new. He borrowed a rifle from his friend Oggún and some gun powder from his friend Changó and went back to the woods looking for game. After some time he came across two of the most beautiful pheasants he had ever seen. Walking so lightly that even the ground could not feel his footsteps, he took careful aim and pulled the trigger. The two birds rose in the air with the force of the impact, then fell down at his feet with a muffled cry. So perfect had been Ochosi's aim that both had been killed with the same blast, yet neither showed signs of the gun wounds. It was undoubtedly one of Ochosi's finest hunting feats.

Carrying the two beautiful birds crisscrossed over his shoulders, Ochosi went to the town market in search of Orunla. He knew that the diviner was looking for a pair of *acuaro* to present to Olofi, and he wanted the finest birds for the Creator. Not finding Orunla in the market, Ochosi returned to his house in the woods, where he carefully hid the pheasants behind some animal skins. He then returned to town to look for Orunla.

Shortly after Ochosi left his *ilé,* his mother arrived there. She came to visit her son periodically to help with his housekeeping. Being a confirmed bachelor, Ochosi's house was always in great disarray and he welcomed his mother's help in keeping things in order.

The good woman arrived at the house and immediately began to straighten the place. She diligently swept the floors and put Ochosi's clothes away, and while she was cleaning, she came across the brace of *acuaro* in the corner behind the pile of animal skins. She had never seen such beautiful birds before and after admiring them for some time, she decided to take one. She was sure her son would not mind. Ochosi was a thoughtful and generous son, and he shared all he possessed with his mother. Therefore, she finished her work at the hut and, tying one of the birds in a piece of cloth, she took it home with her. She promised herself that tomorrow she would tell Ochosi she had taken the pheasant.

In the meantime, Ochosi had searched everywhere for Orunla without finding a trace of the diviner. It was late in the day when he finally came across Eleggua on a street corner, whittling a piece of wood while munching on an orange. Ochosi asked his friend if he had seen the diviner.

"Sure," said Eleggua with a grin. "He's been at Oshun's house all day. He's consoling her while Changó is out of town with Oyá. But he must be ready to leave by now. He told me he had an early appointment to see Olofi. If you hurry, you may catch him on his way out."

Ochosi thanked Eleggua, turned around and walked quickly towards Oshun's house. Halfway there, he saw Orunla come from the opposite direction, walking sprightly with a satisfied smile on his face.

The two orishas greeted each other and then Ochosi told Ifá about the two beautiful pheasants he had caught earlier in the day.

"This is pleasant news indeed," said a beaming Orunla. "I am on my way now to visit Olofi to whom I had promised a brace of *acuaro*. Let us go to your house first and I will purchase the birds from you. Then I can bring them to Olofi this same evening."

Gratified by Orunla's interest in his game, Ochosi happily led the way to his hut in the wood. But when he went to look for the birds, he found to his dismay that there was only one where two had been. Unable to understand the bird's disappearance, Ochosi searched all over the house. But his search was to no avail. The pheasant was nowhere to be seen.

"I can't understand it," said Ochosi, mortified by the embarrassing situation. "I left the two birds here, behind these furs. I would not have made you come all the way from town under false pretenses."

"Don't upset yourself," said Orunla kindly. "I know your integrity. If you brought me here it is because you had two pheasants to show me. What has happened is obvious. Someone has stolen the bird."

"Stolen?" said Ochosi indignantly. "Nobody steals from me. No one would dare!"

"Somebody has dared, my friend," said Orunla gravely. "Don't fret about it. Tomorrow you can hunt for a new brace of birds. Judging from the one I see here, no one can get what I want but you."

"No!" cried Ochosi fiercely. "If what you say is true, the thief must pay with his life! *Beni otitu kigbamu aiye kan fi ofa mi lokua!* If it is true that someone stole the pheasant, let my arrow kill the thief!"

Blind with rage, he took his crossbow and shot an arrow high into the sky. The arrow, impelled by the force of Ochosi's curse, came rushing to the earth and imbedded itself in the heart of Ochosi's mother. With a shrill cry, she clasped her breast and fell dead to the ground.

Far away in his *ilé*, the god of the hunt followed with his mind's eye the trajectory of his arrow and cried out in horror when it pierced his mother's heart. Her cry found an echo in his own and something irreplaceable died in him in that terrible moment.

"You have sealed your fate, Ochosi," said Orunla sadly. "Your judgment was so true it would not even spare your own mother. From this moment onward, you shall represent justice."

The Birth of the Ibeyi

The tragic occurrences that had befallen some of his friends saddened Changó, but not for very long. Sadness was a sentiment incompatible with the god of thunder's perennial optimism and joy of living. He commiserated with Ochosi and Osain (for whose loss he was largely responsible), and commented on Babalú's departure for Dahomey. But if truth be served, it must be acknowledged that he did not lose any sleep over these happenings. It's not that he was unsympathetic, it was simply that he was too busy living his very exciting life to have time to spend in mourning.

Changó divided his time equally between work and pleasure, and he gave all his ferocious energy to each endeavor with equal intensity. When he worked, he worked. When he enjoyed, he enjoyed. Going to war was for Changó both work and pleasure. Nothing outside of womanizing gave him more joy than the heat of battle. Of all the warriors of the Yoruba pantheon, he was the most fierce and indomitable. Only his brother Oggún could rival his valor and dexterity in war. But not even Oggún could stand up to Changó when the god of thunder went into one of his raging furies. When Changó lost his temper, he invariably lost his self-control. At such times he often did things he later regretted. During one of these temperamental occasions, he lived to regret his actions for a very long time, for the person he lost his temper with was his adoptive mother Yemayá, and nobody, not even Changó, offends Yemayá with impunity.

What happened was this. Several years earlier Changó had returned from a very long time at war to find himself the father of a beautiful set of twins (Ibeyi). Nobody knew for sure who was the mother of the children. Some said it was Oshún, others claimed it was Oyá, but since neither of the two goddesses was talking, the mystery around the birth of the Ibeyi remained unsolved. All that was known was that one morning Yemayá found them at her doorstep with a terse message to the effect that they were Changó's sons and that the mother, although loving them dearly, was incapable of caring for them properly. Yemayá was still married to Orunla at the time and had plenty to do, as she had to divide herself between the diviner and her undersea kingdom. But she was still overjoyed with the babies, and promptly took them under her protection.

When Changó came home from the war and found the children with Yemayá, he was immediately taken with them. As a father, he was loving and tender and fiercely protective. His sons simply could do no wrong in his eyes. Everything they wanted was theirs just for the asking. This worried Yemayá who was a strict disciplinarian, and she soon told Changó in no uncertain terms that while the children were his, she would be the one to raise them. She intended to make sure that they be taught better self-control than their father was wont to exhibit at times. And Changó, who knew he would have great troubles raising two small boys on his own, agreed to let her take charge of the Ibeyi. As to the real mother of the children, no one ever found out for sure who she was. And if Changó knew, and Yemayá suspected he did, he wasn't saying. Not that it mattered to Yemayá. On the contrary, her one consuming fear was that the children's mother would come forth one day to claim them.

Several years went by and the Ibeyi grew strong and handsome, and each day Yemayá loved them more, until they became her all-consuming passion. The children had been walking for some time when Yemayá decided to give a party in their honor. It was a glittering affair and all the orishas were present, including Oshún and Oyá, both of whom were suspected by two contending groups of people of being the Ibeyi's mother. Naturally Changó was also there, drinking and eating to his heart's content, and showing to everyone present his recently acquired gift of the dance, the famed transaction he had conducted with Orunla through Eleggua's help.

Everything was going splendidly when Changó, who had been drinking more than his usual share of palm wine, saw a large bunch of *oguede* (bananas) that one of the orishas had brought as a present for the Ibeyi. Changó, whose passion for *oguede* is well known, dropped the *bata* drums he had been playing, and directed his uneven steps toward the bananas. His voracious appetite is legendary, and when Yemayá saw him grab the bunch of *oguede* and head for a corner, her eyes narrowed to slits. She knew that within a matter of minutes Changó would decimate the bananas and there wouldn't be any left for her precious Ibeyi.

Without wasting any time, she began to cross the dance floor. The room was large and packed with swaying people, and it was with some effort that she wove her way through the enthusiastic dancers and reached Changó. But by the time she got to him, most of the bananas had disappeared.

"*Omo-mi, fumi oguede!*"she said severely, her eyes shining ominously. "There's hardly any left for your *omokenkere!*"

Changó looked up at her, his mind still befuddled by the palm wine he had consumed, and hugged the bananas to his chest.

"Why should I give you the *oguede*?" he said crossly. "Everything you get is for the Ibeyi. I love them too, but you are still my mother. Something you seem to have forgotten!"

"*Daque!*" cried Yemayá imperiously. "How dare you speak that way to me! Give me the *oguede* and get out of here! *Iwolo!*"

The altercation between mother and son brought a halt to the dancing and the other orishas surrounded them with concerned faces. They all knew Changó's temper and Yemayá's terrible powers.

"Yemayá, *cuele, cuele!*" they muttered soothingly. "Calm yourself, Yemayá!"

But Yemayá was beyond soothing.

"Did you hear me?" she screamed at Changó, her nostrils flaring with rage. "*Iwolo! Iwolo!*"

Humiliated by being ousted from the party by his own mother, Changó stood up furiously, eyes aflame, his huge frame trembling with anger.

"*Emi ti!*" he said contemptuously, and with a toss of his proud head threw the *oguede* at Yemayá.

The bunch of bananas, thrown with all the strength of the god of thunder, hit Yemayá squarely on the chest. The force of the impact was such that it made Yemayá lose her balance and career back against the wall.

Yemayá regained her balance with the help of some of those present, and turned to her son like a fury.

"*Motimoti!* *Eletán!* Drunkard! Thief!" she screamed at the top of her lungs. "I'll teach you how to respect your *iyá!*"

She grabbed her wide skirt angrily and began to fan it rapidly. All of a sudden a giant wall of water stood where Yemayá had been. Changó, the essence of fire, is terrified of water and ran away screaming, "*Onón komí!* Don't touch me!"

All the orishas dispersed quickly, fearing the unleashed fury of Yemayá's waters, but as soon as Changó left the room the sea goddess resumed her normal form. Her face was darkened by anger and she refused to answer each time someone tried to talk to her. Only when her sister Oshún approached her did Yemayá deign to speak, but when she did, her words were ominous.

"*Aburomi,*" she said in severe tones, "tell your *oko* Changó that I don't ever want to see him again. As far as I'm concerned, he's dead and gone to Ikú. He's no longer my *omokeke.*"

Oshún lowered her eyes respectfully and nodded her head sadly. From that day onward Changó's easy life took a turn for the worse. Some neighboring tribes crossed the borders of his kingdom, destroying everything in their path, and there was nothing Changó could do to stop the onslaught—he who had always been triumphant against all foes. The fire seemed to have gone from his life and he lay around all day in his *ilé*, morose and ill-tempered, refusing to see anyone, including his two favorite *obini* Oshún and Oyá.

Eleggua, who came to see him one day, found him in the courtyard of his palace, listlessly grooming one of his steeds.

"Greetings, Alafia," said Eleggua with an infectious grin. "I haven t seen you for a very long time. How have you been?"

"Sorry, Eshú," said Changó without raising his head. "I don't want to see anybody, not even you."

"I know what's ailing you, my friend," said Eleggua, ignoring Changó's cold attitude. "You are sorry you were disrespectful to Yemayá, but are too proud to apologize to her."

"Apologies have nothing to do with it," said Changó. "I know my *iyá*. She doesn't accept apologies. Once you've offended her, that's it. She'll never forgive me. I know she won't. What's worse is that she won't let me see the Ibeyi. She's determined to ostracize me for good. And I'm beginning to get so tired of it all, I'm seriously thinking of leaving Oyo."

"That would be a very unwise thing to do," said Eleggua gravely. "I have a better solution. If you do what I tell you, I'm sure Yemayá will forgive you and everything will be fine again."

Changó looked at Eleggua curiously.

"You do have a knack for solving problems," he said with a smile. "What do you have in mind?"

Eleggua looked around cautiously to ensure that no one was watching, then he bent down his head and whispered a few words in Changó's ears.

Changó looked at his friend in shock and shook his head.

"I couldn't do that, Eshú," he said with a worried frown. "It's so cruel. Besides, it will probably make matters worse."

"No, it won't," insisted Eleggua. "It will solve all your problems."

Changó hesitated, still dubious.

"What's the matter? Don't you trust me?" asked Eleggua indignantly. "Have I ever let you down?"

"No," said Changó, patting his shoulder affectionately. "No, you haven't. Maybe you're right. Things couldn't get any worse than they already are. I'll do it tomorrow."

As if Eleggua's suggestion had lifted the dark cloud that had been hovering over him for so long, he put his arms around his friend's shoulders and called out to one of his servants to bring them food and drink in the courtyard. The two orishas spent the rest of the day in close camaraderie, drinking and eating and exchanging jokes like old times.

The very next day, Changó showed up at the empty lot where his children used to play and plied them with toys and candies. The Ibeyi, delighted to see their father, jumped around him full of joy. Changó played with them for some time, then picked up one of them.

"*Omo-mi*," he said to the other child. "Tell my *iyá* that I took your *aburomi* and that I'm going to bring him to Yewá, the mistress of the graves and overseer of the cemetery."

His son nodded innocently and ran away immediately to inform Yemayá of what Changó had said. The god of thunder turned around swiftly and ran into the woods where he hid the child among some bushes.

When Yemayá heard what Changó had done she went mad with grief. She ran outside her *ilé*, screaming in anguish, and asking everyone she met if they had seen Changó with the Ibeyi. But no one had seen the god of thunder, and when Yemayá returned to her house, trembling with rage and fear, she found to her double dismay that Changó had abducted the second boy. She nearly fainted at the shock of the discovery, but Eleggua, who had planned the entire thing, managed to calm her down.

"*Acuele, acuele*, Yemayá," he said soothingly. "I know where Changó has taken the children. He doesn't want to make you suffer. All he wants is for you to forgive him."

"Fine way to ask for forgiveness," said Yemayá indignantly. "I'll deal with him later. Take me to the children now."

On her way to the woods, she invoked all the other orishas and everyone else in sight and made them accompany her to the place where Changó was waiting.

When Changó saw his mother approaching surrounded by all the inhabitants of the town, he brought out the Ibeyi who promptly ran to meet her.

Yemayá embraced the children wild with joy and the Ibeyi, who had been carefully instructed by Changó, immediately interceded with Yemayá to forgive their father. Their pleas, echoed by the rest of the orishas, moved Yemayá, who had already been planning to forgive Changó, and she turned to him with a stern look.

"Are you going to offend your *iyá* again?" she asked severely.

Changó fell to the floor and paid *forivale* at his mother's feet.

"*Toto jún!*" he begged humbly. "Forgive me, *iyá-mí*. I was a beast to offend you."

Yemayá tapped his shoulders lightly, signifying that she blessed and forgave him, and then the two orishas embraced amidst the rejoicing of all those present.

Obatalá

Obatalá Tests the Warriors

The land of the orishas had always been fertile and rich in crops and game, but suddenly everything changed and the crops and the game began to diminish. Olofi had decided to teach humankind the meaning of self-sacrifice and deprivation and the orishas, as usual, had to give the prime example. The idea was to teach humankind the importance of sharing and working together in order to survive.

Obatalá convoked all the orishas and informed them of Olofi's decision. From that day onward, he said, they had to pool together all their resources. Oggún, Ochosi, and Changó, who were the mightiest warriors and hunters of the Yoruba pantheon, agreed to hunt for Obatalá in exchange for their daily fare. Obatalá accepted, and the three warriors sat at his table and ate until they were satisfied. Then they separated and each went his own way in search of game.

As Olofi had decreed, animals were scarce and after a while the hunters saw that it would be difficult to keep their promise to Obatalá without going hungry. After some difficulties, Oggún, who had started first, found a goat. He immediately killed the animal, skinned and salted it and turned his steps back to the city of Ile-Ife, where Obatalá was waiting. But halfway to Obatalá's *efin*, he became so hungry that he stopped and sat down by the roadside, roasted the goat and ate it. He was sure he would be able to find some thing else to bring Obatalá. Although he searched the woods with the greatest skill, he was unable to find any other game. It doesn't matter, he consoled himself, I'm sure Ochosi and Changó will be able to catch some game for Babá. With this thought in mind, he returned to Ile-Ife.

In the meantime, Ochosi had found an opossum, and following Oggún's same line of reasoning, he had roasted the animal and eaten it. Like Oggún, he had also failed to find any other game and had to return to Ile-Ife empty handed.

Of the three orishas, Changó had fared the worst. Being more a warrior than a hunter, he was not as well versed in the art of the chase as his two companions, so he searched for a very long time in the woods without finding any game.

By the third day he was so hungry his strength began to fail him. He sat down by the roadside to rest a while when he suddenly saw a mouse dart from a hole in the ground. With his remaining strength, Changó picked up a stone and threw it at the mouse. So unerring was his aim that the mouse, caught in midair, dropped to the ground without a sound.

Changó grimaced with distaste at the sight of the dead mouse, but he felt so weak he knew he would not be able to return to Ile-Ife unless he had some nourishment. Grimly putting aside his queasiness, he, who had always feasted like a king, roasted the mouse and ate it.

Several days later, feeling very tired and covered with grime, the three orishas arrived late at Obatalá's palace. Each expected the others to have brought back some game, and they were all filled with dismay to find out that they had all returned with empty hands to face Obatalá.

Obatalá was disappointed to see the three warriors arrive empty handed and questioned them as to what had happened.

"I hunted for weeks, Babá," said Oggún, his eyes lowered to the ground. "But I was unable to find any game. The woods are depleted of animals. There is not one to be found. I sustained myself by eating berries and tree bark. I'm so famished I'm nearly fainting. That is the absolute truth."

In reality he was the one who had eaten better and felt the strongest, but he sat down on a straw mat as if he really had no strength left. Obatalá looked at him thoughtfully but said nothing.

"How about you, *omo-mi*? "he said to Ochosi. "How did you fare?"

"Not much better than Oggún, *baba-mi*," said Ochosi, also lowering his eyes. "It is true that the woods are empty of game. You know how swift my feet are and how deadly my arrows. Yet I was unable to find any game. I am also exhausted and terribly hungry."

With a sigh, he sank by Oggún's side and made himself comfortable on the straw mat.

Obatalá turned to Changó with inquiring eyes.

"And what is your story, *omo-mi*?" he asked, a twinkle in his wise, old eyes. "Were you also unable to find any game?"

Changó stood up to his full stature and looked straight into Obatalá's eyes.

"I found no game, *baba-mi*," he said quietly. "But I did find a mouse after a long time of searching. I was so hungry, however, and so weak that I had to eat it. I thought that if I didn't eat it, I might not find the strength to return to Ile-Ife."

"Do you still feel weak, *omo-mi*, like your two companions?" asked Obatalá kindly. "Or do you feel better after your scanty meal?"

"I feel better, *baba-mi*," said Changó with a smile, "but I'm still hungry. A mouse is not much of a feast for a grown man."

Obatalá stood up from his throne.

"My sons," he said gravely. "I don't believe in accusing anyone unjustly or without proof. Therefore I am not going to say that you are lying. But these are dire times for us and we have to be able to trust each other implicitly. That is why I'm sure you won't mind if I ask you to submit to a test."

Oggún and Ochosi stood up.

"What test do you mean, Babá?" asked Oggún, his eyes wide with alarm. Next to him, Ochosi shuffled his feet nervously.

"A simple test of truth, *omo-mi*," said Obatalá gently. He suddenly pointed his cowrie-studded tail switch at the three orishas and cried,"*KPO YADE!*"

The magical power of those words was such that the palace walls shook to their foundation, and their echoes were still reverberating in the distance when suddenly Oggún, Ochosi, and Changó were overtaken by such convulsions that they regurgitated the animals they had eaten in the woods. There, by Obatalá's throne lay the goat, the opossum, and the mouse, all in one piece as if they had not been eaten.

"That is the truth I was speaking about," said Obatalá angrily. "I could understand that you were so hungry you had to eat the game you found. What I find unforgivable is that you would lie about it and expect to fool me."

"Forgive me, *baba-mi*," cried Oggún and Ochosi in unison. Full of shame they fell at the feet of the orisha to pay him *forivale* and ask his forgiveness.

"You may stand," said Obatalá gravely, tapping their shoulders with his tail switch to indicate that he forgave them. "But your deed will not go unpunished. From now on, it will be known to all posterity as one of the parables of the cowrie shells. As long as the *diloggún* is read, it will be known to all humankind how Oggún and Ochosi lied to Obatalá. Neither one of you will ever wear a king's crown, for kings are supposed to be truthful at all times."

"As for you, my son," he added, turning to Changó, "your veracity will not go unrewarded. Because you did not lie and honestly declared your fault, you will always wear a king's crown and you will be forever revered and honored, both among humans and among your own kind."

Obatalá's Visit to Changó

After Obatalá's test, the three warriors returned to their respective cities. Changó went back to his *efin* in Oyo, Oggún to his iron forge in Iré, and Ochosi to his hut in the woods. Olofi, considering that the orishas had fulfilled their duty and shown humankind the importance of society living, returned the fields to their former fertile splendor and the game was once more plentiful in the woods.

Some time went by and then one day Obatalá decided to pay a visit to Changó in his palace at Oyo. He had always been especially fond of his adopted son, and now that he had once more proven his intrinsic nobility and honesty, he had grown closer to him than ever. Changó had now become known as the Stone Thrower—Takata—a title he may have earned as a result of his prowess of killing the mouse with one stone.

Obatalá told his wife Yemmu to prepare his white robes for the trip. He never traveled with an escort, as his spotless white clothing identified him wherever he went. But Yemmu was unhappy about her husband's coming trip.

"Please do not go to Oyo, my lord," she told Obatalá almost in tears. "I had a dream last night where your white clothing was so badly spotted that no matter how hard I washed it, the spots would keep reappearing. I think it is a bad omen. You should not travel now."

"A dream is just a dream, Yemmu," answered Obatalá. "My robes are spotless now. What could possibly soil them so badly that the spots would keep coming back?"

"I don't know, my lord," said Yemmu. "But I still wish you would not go to Oyo."

"If it makes you feel better I'll ask Orunla to check his oracle for me," said Obatalá kindly.

When Orunla consulted the Table of Ifá, he shook his head and looked at Obatalá with worried eyes.

"I fear Yemmu's dream was prophetical, dear friend," he said. "There are grave dangers surrounding this trip. If you want my advice, I think you should postpone it for a while."

But Obatalá, whose obstinate determination is legendary, was not to be so easily dissuaded.

"I have already made plans for this trip and if I don't go now I may not be able to go for a long time," he said. "Besides I'm Obatalá, King of the White Cloth and ruler of the orishas. My person is inviolate. Who would dare attack me?"

"One who doesn't know who you are," answered Ifá.

"But everyone knows who I am," retorted Obatalá haughtily. "My white clothes are my insignia."

Orunla shook his head again but did not answer. Obatalá, more determined than ever to make the trip, stood up and nodding his head stiffly, took his leave of Orunla and returned to his palace. The very next day, without any further ado, he started on his trip to Oyo.

He had not walked very far when he came across Eleggua, who was standing in the middle of the road trying to lift a large vessel filled with palm oil.

"Greetings, Babá," said Eleggua when he saw Obatalá approaching. "It is most opportune that you should chance to come by when I so desperately need some help. Will you help me lift this oil vessel and put it on my head so I may carry it with greater ease?"

Obatalá, who will never deny his help to anyone in trouble, immediately set his staff and tail switch aside and helped Eleggua lift the vessel and place it on his head. But a sudden movement by Eleggua tilted the vessel a little, and some of the bright orange oil spilled over Obatalá's robe.

"Oh Babá, how clumsy of me," cried Eleggua. "I'm desolated that your robe has been soiled. Please forgive me!"

"It is not your fault, my son," said Obatalá, looking down with unhappy eyes at his spotted clothes. "I'm still close to my house. I'll go back and change clothes."

"You still plan to make the trip after this?" asked Eleggua incredulously.

"Of course, why shouldn't I?" said Obatalá, looking at him suspiciously. "Did you do this on purpose? Are you also trying to keep me from my trip?"

"No, Babá, " said Eleggua, shaking his head vigorously. "Why should I do such a terrible thing? I just thought …"

"Well, keep your thoughts to yourself," snapped Obatalá in a rare flare of temper. "And next time be more careful!"

Without waiting for Eleggua's answer, he turned around and went back to his palace. A few moments later he emerged, dressed again in his immaculate white robes.

He walked for some time without any further mishaps, and very soon his long and firm footsteps had taken him across the frontiers of Ile-Ife, each time further away from his palace. In spite of his old age and apparent frailty, when Obatalá set out to do something, he did it and did it well. He was beginning to consider stopping for a rest when he suddenly saw a young boy on the road ahead. The boy was standing on a wooden board that had been stretched over a large mud hole and he seemed afraid to walk across it.

Obatalá came closer and addressed the boy with his usual kindness. "Let me help you, *omo-mi*," he said, taking the boy by the arm. "There's really nothing to fear."

He stepped gingerly onto the board and began to move across it, pulling the boy behind him. The child, who had never said a word, clung to Obatalá for dear life. They were halfway across the board when a sudden movement from the boy tipped their frail gangway, and they both toppled head-first into the mud. When they finally waded across to the other side, Obatalá's immaculate clothes were covered with mud stains. The boy, without even a word of thanks, jumped to his feet and ran away into the nearby woods.

Obatalá sat down by the side of the road and contemplated his ruined clothes. He remembered Yemmu's dream and Orunla's oracle, and for the first time since he started his trip, he wondered if he should not have stayed home. Surely now he would be unrecognizable as the usually impeccable Obatalá. In fact, his clothes were in such a disreputable state he might be confused with a common derelict. He pondered whether or not he should return home, then he decided against it. He was now closer to Oyo than to his palace in Ile-

Ife, and he felt safer going to Changó's land than turning back on his tracks. It was beginning to get dark, so he stood up once more and resumed his steady pace.

He was nearing Oyo when he saw a beautiful white horse grazing peacefully by the side of the road. He immediately recognized the animal as one Changó had acquired recently. Worried lest someone steal the priceless steed, he decided to bring it with him to Oyo.

When he was nearing the city gates, several of Changó's soldiers came out. They were looking for the horse which had suddenly disappeared from the king's stables. When they saw Obatalá in his soiled clothes, holding the horse by the bridle, they immediately assumed that he had stolen the horse. They swiftly gathered around Obatalá and began to insult him and beat him mercilessly. When Obatalá tried to explain who he was they laughed at him and beat him even more.

"Imagine this thief's insolence!" they cried in outrage. "Not only does he steal Changó's horse but claims to be his adoptive father, the mighty Obatalá himself, King of the White Cloth, whose robes are always so immaculately clean."

They brought Obatalá in chains to the city of Oyo and promptly threw him in a dungeon without listening to his entreaties that they let him see Changó.

Some time passed and Obatalá languished in prison. Changó knew nothing of the affair, and naturally could not release him. Obatalá waited patiently for some time, hoping that the truth would be uncovered, and that he would be released soon. But no one came to deliver him from his humiliating situation, and he began to grow angry. Finally, his anger grew to such proportions that he caused a great drought to fall upon Oyo. Many crops were lost and a great many animals died, and Changó's subjects began to go hungry. But still no one came to release Obatalá. The orisha, who is usually the very essence of patience and kindness, threw all these tender qualities to the winds and bent his unleashed fury against the people of Oyo. This time he caused a fatal illness to fall upon the city and people began to die in great numbers.

Disturbed by the sudden tragedies that had befallen his city, Changó consulted his own diviners who told him, after scrutinizing their oracles, that all the evil that had befallen Oyo had been caused by an important personage who was imprisoned in the palace's dungeon unknown to Changó.

Upon hearing this disturbing news, Changó began a careful search of all his prisoners and he finally came face to face with Obatalá. The elder orisha was covered with grime, his white hair and beard almost unrecognizable with dirt.

Changó was horrified at the sight.

"Forgive me, *baba-mi*," he cried, throwing himself at Obatalá's feet. "I didn't know anything about this outrage. But I promise you that all those responsible will be properly punished."

Obatalá looked at Changó sternly.

"I know you knew nothing about my imprisonment, *omo-mi*," he said coldly. "But a king should always know what happens within his palace walls."

"This will never happen again in Oyo," vowed Changó, his face crimson with shame. "I swear, *baba-mi*!"

Obatalá raised Changó from the floor and embraced him. Changó immediately gave orders that a bath and new white robes should be prepared for Obatalá. Then he declared a long holiday to celebrate his adoptive father's visit, and Obatalá immediately lifted the curse he had placed over Oyo. The festivities ordered by Changó were so splendid that Obatalá soon forgot his ordeal and finished his stay in the city with a great deal of enjoyment. But he did not forget Yemmu's dream or Orunla's warning, and Eleggua's actions by the road suddenly made sense to him. It was clear that the impish orisha had simply tried to keep Obatalá from making the trip because he knew, as he always did, the ordeals that Obatalá would undergo.

Eleggua and the Two Inseparable Friends

Eleggua's actions are often difficult to understand. An incorrigible prankster, he sometimes causes havoc apparently for no good reason, like the time he destroyed the relationship between two friends who loved each other dearly.

The two friends, which the legend does not name, loved each other like brothers and vowed that nothing and no one would ever come between them. Such a statement would naturally be a challenge to Eleggua, who can disrupt any relationship no matter how close it may be. He therefore decided to put this great friendship to the test. To that effect, he dressed himself in a garment that was red on the right side and black on the left. Thus attired he walked between the two friends.

One of the men, seeing Eleggua pass by, remarked to the other on the handsome black suit the orisha had been wearing.

The second man looked at his friend in disbelief. "Are you color blind?" he asked in mocking tones. "That man was dressed in red!"

Naturally this happened because one man had seen the side of the suit that was red, while the other had seen the black side. This simple difference of opinion was enough for the two inseparable friends to start an argument which grew to such proportions that they were soon at each other's throats. The quarrel stopped there, but the two friends parted as enemies and never spoke again.

Why did Eleggua cause the rupture between two good friends? The legend does not say. It is simply that Eleggua is Eleggua and he's wont to do such things. One could say that to tempt Eleggua is to tempt fate and that in many ways is what Eleggua symbolizes.

Eleggua's actions with Obatalá are easier to understand. He was fate giving a warning, a warning that Obatalá failed to heed with near-fatal consequences. In his second appearance as the young boy, he was carrying out his fateful work and could no longer help Obatalá. He had to do what he had to do, even against his own wishes. And that is often the case with many of the actions of Eleggua throughout the many legends that feature him prominently.

Eleggua's Friendship

Although in many instances Eleggua has been identified with the devil, this identification shows a profound lack of understanding of the orisha's true essence. The devil is an intrinsically evil entity, Eleggua is not. One would have to say that Eleggua is really beyond good and evil. He does some very dastardly deeds at times, but he does some equally wonderful things when he so chooses. He simply does what he must do to keep the tides of evolution moving. But when he acts strictly as himself, his actions are invariably just and honorable. This is exemplified by another legend.

Orunla was very disappointed with his friends because he discovered that they were all more interested in his divining tray and his divination secrets than they were in his friendship. In order to test them, he decided to spread the news that he had died. He took into his confidence one of his most trusted assistants and told him what he was to say to anyone who came to inquire about his master's death.

The news of the supposed death of the diviner took the city of Ile-Ife by storm. One by one, all of Orunla's friends came to pay their last respects. Ifá's helper, who had been thoroughly instructed by the orisha, confirmed the news of his death and told everyone that his master had been buried in secret several days earlier.

"What a great loss to us all is the death of the divine Orunla!" said the first visitor. "He owed me a lot of money but I never demanded payment from him, particularly since he promised to leave me his divining tray and all of his secrets in his will. Now that I'm here, I will obey his last wishes and take the table of divination with me. Will you please give it to me."

"I would like to comply with my dear master's last wishes," said Orunla's assistant sadly. "But, unfortunately, the divining tray with all of its implements has disappeared. No one knows where it is."

The visitor stood up immediately and prepared to take his leave.

"Well, make sure that you let me know when it is found," he said coldly. "It is my property now."

This first visitor was followed by a second and a third, and by dozens more. All of them demanded Orunla's divination table and his divining secrets and claimed that he had promised these things to them as an heirloom when he died.

Finally Eleggua came to the house.

"How infinitely sad it is for me to come to this house and find it empty of my friend Orunla's presence," he said dejectedly. "There will never be a better and more noble friend! Alas! His death deprives us all of the kindest, noblest soul ever created by our father Olofi."

"Yes, the loss is great," agreed Orunla's helper. "But tell me, did my master owe you any money? Did he promise to leave you something in his will? If he did, please tell me, for my master instructed me to pay all his debts should he die before me."

"No, he owed me no money and promised me nothing," said Eleggua. "It is I who owe some money to Orunla and I will send it to you as soon as I get home. You may need it if he left any debts."

"Are you sure?" insisted Orunla's helper. "My master and you were such good friends. Surely he must have promised you something. How about his divining tray and his divination secrets? I'm sure my master would love you to have them."

"No, Orunla promised me nothing," said Eleggua firmly. "He did not promise me the Table of Ifá especially. He was far too wise to give that to anyone. The true secret behind the oracle was Orunla's great mind. Only he could interpret the mysteries of the table. I could never take his place."

Upon hearing these words, Orunla, who was hiding behind a door and had heard all that had transpired in the room, came out and embraced Eleggua with great affection.

"You are my only true friend, Eleggua," he said, his voice choking with emotion. "No one could hope for a more noble friend."

In Yoruba lore Eleggua's friendship is far more desirable than Orunla's divination powers. But Eleggua's friendship has to be earned, and it can only be earned through heroic deeds or noble effort. It may be possible to enlist his help by means of a suitable offer, but his friendship is not so easily gained.

This impish, unpredictable orisha is at the core of the Yoruba pantheon. He's the arbiter of every polemic; the final judge in every contest. He makes things possible or impossible, brings about joy and sorrow, triumph and disaster. Without his good will none of the orishas' work can be completed or their desires fulfilled. Eleggua is essential for survival, yet his essence is as tenuous as a moonbeam and just as difficult to grasp. Pure yet provocative, honest yet demanding, noble yet severe, joyous yet tragic, Eleggua is found at the beginning of every act and at its inevitable conclusion. That is why I would like to end this section with a poem in his honor.

> *Eshú, maker of destinies,*
> *The power of ashé is in your breath.*
> *You walk with the wind in high places*
> *And nurture the universe with your wisdom.*
> *The rainbow is your favored road.*
> *Grand Master of Illusion,*
> *You, to whom a dream is real*
> *And reality as fragile as a dream,*
> *Open the road of light before me.*
> *Close the gates of hell behind me.*
> *And grant me the miracle*
> *Of one perfect moment*
> *Of Truth.*

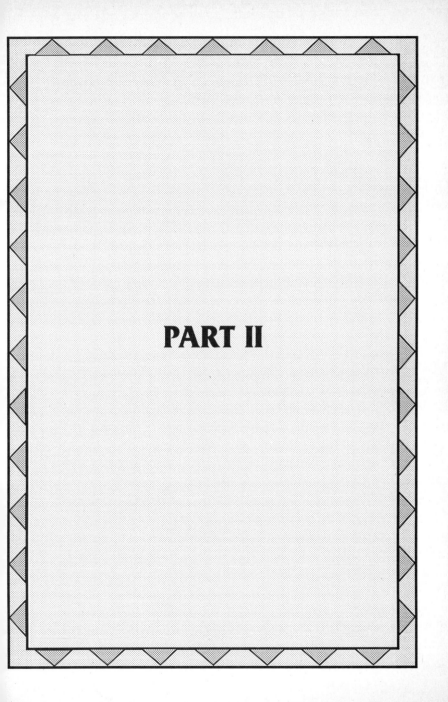

PART II

Oloddumare Creates Olosi

In Santería, as among the Yorubas, Oloddumare is the Supreme Being, the Creator, who is both omnipotent and omniscient and is the source of all that exists. The myths are vague about how Oloddumare created earth, but simply say that in the beginning everything on the planet was a marshy land that was largely covered by water. This liquid domain was the habitat of the androgynous being known as Olosi. According to this version of the patakis, Olosi was the first orisha created by Oloddumare.

After creating the earth, Oloddumare felt lonely and decided to create another being who would be his companion and with whom he would share his new realm. In order to share his possessions equally with his new creation, he gave this being powers of the same magnitude as his own. He also made him invisible and called him Olosi. But Olosi, finding himself of equal stature as Oloddumare, grew insolent and greedy. Finally, he decided to usurp Oloddumare's exalted place as Creator and become ruler of the earth. His scheme backfired because Oloddumare was, after all, the Creator and could not be ousted so easily.

Having realized Olosi's treachery and his total unworthiness, Oloddumare banished him from his presence. But having made Olosi as powerful as himself, Oloddumare was unable to destroy the creature. He had to content himself with the banishment, but had to allow Olosi to continue his invisible existence albeit on a separate plane. Because of his immense supernatural powers, Olosi was able to permeate the earth, and lie in wait until he could wreak vengeance on Oloddumare. He did not have to wait very long, for Oloddumare was already planning the creation of a new being—one who would take Olosi's place, but who would be faithful and obedient to the Creator.

Oddudúa and Oloddumare

After his disappointment with Olosi, Oloddumare decided to create another being. Although he also gave his second creation great powers and made him immortal, he instilled in this new being a great sense of peace and loyalty. In this manner he created someone who would always be true and would never rebel against the Creator's authority. The name of this new Prometheus was Oddudúa.

From the beginning Oddudúa proved to be worthy of Oloddumare's trust. He was faithful and obedient and carried out the Creator's orders without complaints. Noticing Oddudúa's loneliness, Oloddumare gave him a wife whom he called Yemmu. This first female force sprang from the waters, from the primeval orisha called Olokun.

The first task Oloddumare gave Oddudúa was the creation of solid ground. For this purpose he gave him a few grains of sand, a hen, and a pigeon. Oddudúa threw the sand upon the marshy land and put the hen and the pigeon over it. They began to scratch at the sand, spreading it in all directions. Wherever a grain of sand fell, great expanses of dry land appeared. Very soon there was solid ground everywhere and Olokun was forced to surrender much of what, up to then, had been his sole domain. Naturally he tried to recover his possessions, invading the land with huge tidal waves, but Oddudúa had been warned by Oloddumare that this might happen and he was prepared. He fashioned a huge golden chain and with it he secured Olokun and threw him to the bottom of the sea, where he still lies in wait for an opportunity to regain the earth.

Oddudúa continued to live peacefully with Yemmu in the newly created land and in time they had six children. They were Aganyú, Oggún, Dada, Eleggua, Osun, and Ochosi.

Aganyú represented the fire at the center of the earth, and is also identified in this version with the sun, known as Olorun. Aganyú's fiery anger explodes as the mighty volcano which is his main identification.

Oggún was the iron worker, patron of metals, as well as a sylvan deity, identified with the woods.

Dada was the first daughter of Oddudúa and Yemmu, and she represented intelligence and the power of the mind.

Eleggua, the fourth child, was the messenger of the orishas and represented fate and its constant changes. He was the guardian and watcher of his father's realm, making sure his wishes were carried out.

Osun was in charge of warning when danger was near and held the knowledge of the orishas' power.

Ochosi, the sixth child, represented justice and was in charge of hunting game for his father's house.

These six deities, with Oddudúa and Yemmu, were the first orishas who came into being, according to this version. Together they symbolize the primordial earth, rich in promise, still unfulfilled because humanity is yet to be created.

After the birth of his six children, Oddudúa received a second mandate from Oloddumare. He was to form many clay figures, male and female, and set them on the ground to dry. Oloddumare would come from time to time to breathe life into them. These were to be the forerunners of the human race.

Obediently, Oddudúa set to work and began to make the clay figures. But unbeknownst to him, Olosi was at work in the darkness, determined to undermine Oloddumare's plans.

One of the orishas' greatest source of pleasure was palm wine, which they drank plentifully during their festivities. Aware of the effect that palm wine had on those who drank it in excess, Olosi instilled a great thirst in Oddudúa, as he labored with the clay figures.

Driven by his thirst, Oddudúa began to drink the palm wine. Very soon his mind became clouded, and the figures that he made grew contorted and misshapened between his now clumsy fingers. Unaware of what he was doing, Oddudúa continued to make the distorted shapes. When he was finished he set them down to dry and laid next to them, sunk deeply in a drunken stupor.

Several hours later Oddudúa woke up, his mind now clear from the effects of the palm wine. When he inspected his work and saw what he had done, he was filled with great shame and sorrow. He knew that the figures were the proto-types of a new race of mortal beings who were to populate the earth. They could not be undone, for whatever he had made was to be given life by Oloddumare. Trembling with fear, he tried to straighten out some of the figures, but the clay had already hardened and he only succeeded in break-ing off some of the limbs. He had therefore made things worse. Desperate, he sat down on the ground and began to cry. He was still crying when Oloddumare came to see him.

"Oddudúa, what have you done?" thundered the Cre-ator upon seeing the twisted figures.

"Mercy, my lord!" cried Oddudúa, falling down at Oloddumare's feet. "It was not my fault!"

"If it was not your fault, whose fault was it?" asked Oloddumare, not unkindly, seeing Oddudúa's distress.

"It was the palm wine, my lord!" said Oddudúa, trem-bling with terror. "It clouded my judgment. I did not know what I was doing."

"But you are an abstemious being, Oddudúa," said Oloddumare. "How came you by the palm wine?"

"I do not know, my lord," said Oddudúa, wringing his hands in his despair. "I was unaccountably thirsty. It was a monstrous thirst, like I have never felt before. The palm wine was just there. It seemed to appear out of nowhere. I have been bewitched. Please forgive me!"

Oloddumare's eyes grew dark with anger. He knew then who was responsible for Oddudúa's downfall.

"Arise," he said softly, helping Oddudúa to his feet. "I understand what has taken place here. It is not entirely your fault. But because of your actions, the human race which I had envisioned as physically perfect will have many individuals who will be as malformed as the figures you have made. There will be cripples and hunchbacks and beings without limbs, like these forms here. What is done cannot be undone. So be it."

Sighing, he picked up the figures, and one by one he breathed life into them, creating in this manner the human race, not perfect as he had hoped, but full of many infirmities and weaknesses, as Olosi had intended.

"What about me, my lord?" cried Oddudúa miserably. "Am I forgiven?"

"Yes, Oddudúa," said the Creator sadly. "You are forgiven, but you have proven to be weak and quite susceptible to evil influences. You were the unknowing victim of Olosi, a being of great power I created in a moment of loneliness. Olosi's existence must remain unknown to the other orishas because they must resist his influence without knowing it is there. Only then can I be sure of their strength. When creation on earth is completed and the orishas have finished their missions I will tell them about Olosi, not before. In the meantime, your work on earth is done. You must return to me, and a new spirit will issue from my being to occupy your body. His name will be Oddúa, but no one will know of the exchange, not even Yemmu."

When he finished speaking, Oloddumare took a great breath and absorbed Oddudúa's spirit into his being. He then breathed out a new spirit into Oddudúa's lifeless body and Oddúa was born.

Where the Curse Was Born

Like Oddudúa, Oddúa was kind, gentle, and faithful to Oloddumare, but unlike Oddudúa, he was impervious to temptation. His soul was so pure he could do no wrong. Neither could he feel anger or a sense of outrage, which would eventually prove to be his only weakness.

Yemmu never realized the change in her spouse and their life together continued peacefully and uneventfully. Time passed, and their children grew up, and Oddúa was working hard in the fields as he had always done.

Aganyú, the handsomest or the orishas, was a source of pride to his father. He divided his time between the center of the earth, where he controlled the underground fires that nourished the planet and the smoking mountains which he used to regulate the necessary flow of lava that world otherwise endanger the earth's core.

Dada, the only female orisha which had been born so far, was also kept busy shaping the minds of the newly emerging people who were populating the earth.

Eleggua's playful nature delighted everyone around him and was a source of great joy to his parents. He was also very industrious and was a zealous overseer of his father's domain and nothing ever escaped his watchful eyes.

Osun, who was in charge of keeping things in order and watching for possible dangers, and Ochosi, who was in charge of the hunt, spent most of the time in the woods, where they had countless adventures.

But Oggún, who had been put in charge of the forge and the molding of metals, was a source of constant worry to Oddúa. He was silent and morose and it was clear that he was not happy with his work. More often than not, he would abandon the forge and escape to the woods which was the only place where he seemed comfortable.

In his sweet, gentle way, Oddúa would remonstrate with his moody son, who would answer back with increasing insolence. Oggún's bad temper was legendary, and his brothers avoided incurring his wrath. He got along best with Ochosi who was also of a retiring nature, and Eleggua, who was too clever to cross Oggún. But Olosi was still hiding, invisible in the dark, waiting for the time to strike again.

Oggún's passionate temper and his contempt of his father gave Olosi a hideous idea, one which he hastened to put into action. Up to this time, Dada was the only female orisha, and she had been promised in marriage to her brother Aganyú. Marriage between siblings was common in those times. But the other orishas, for lack of female companionship, were forced into a state of virginity. This was a natural state for them and they were happy in their ignorance of sexual dalliances. Olosi saw this as an opportunity to destroy the blissful lives of the orishas. Insidiously, he began to plant the seed of sexual desire in Oggún's mind. But he took care not to direct this desire towards Dada. Instead he planted in Oggún's mind a growing, raging desire for his own mother, the unsuspecting Yemmu.

Every day Oddúa went to the fields to tend his cherished crop of yams which were sacred to him. Yemmu remained alone at home to do her daily chores. Their children were also busy with their appointed tasks.

Oggún took advantage of Yemmu's solitude and began to drop by daily, each time with a different excuse. As she worked in the house, happy in the company of her beloved son, he watched her with burning eyes, feasting on her graceful movements and her undiminished beauty. Day by day his lust, fired by Olosi's malice, grew in intensity, until one day, no longer able to control his unnatural desires, Oggún attacked his mother.

Yemmu's horrified pleas with her son to remember she was his mother fell on deaf ears, and Oggún carried out his nefarious plans and raped his mother. This action was repeated every day as soon as Oddúa left the house, and each time Yemmu's pitiful cries were only heard by the beasts of the forest. But one day Eleggua came home unexpectedly and saw Oggún in the process of attacking Yemmu. Eleggua's footsteps are light and are only heard when he wishes, so Oggún did not hear his brother approach.

Eleggua was wiry but slight, and he knew he could not hope to best his brother in battle. Aware that he could not help Yemmu by wrestling with Oggún, he retraced his steps and went back to the front door. This time he made sure his presence was known by making enough noise to awaken the dead. When he went inside, Oggún was standing morosely by the window while Yemmu was crying softly in a corner.

Eleggua went over to her and embraced her tenderly.

"What is wrong, *Iyá-mí*?" he asked her gently. "Why are you crying?"

Yemmu shook her head and said nothing.

"Why is *Iyá-mí* crying, Oggún?" said Eleggua with feigned innocence. "Is she ill?"

"What should I know of the wiles of women?" snapped Oggún furiously. "Has my father ever seen fit to give me a wife? He's promised Dada to Aganyú, whom he favors over all. I have no experience with women. Besides, who cares. She'll get over whatever bothers her soon enough."

With a contemptuous shrug of his hefty shoulders, he turned and left the house, slamming the door as he went.

As soon as Oggún was out of earshot, Eleggua knelt down by his mother's side.

"*Iyá-mí*, please don't cry," he said, stroking her head gently. "I know why you grieve. I saw Oggún forcing himself on you before I came in."

"Oh, my son!" cried Yemmu, burying her head in Eleggua's arms. "What a terrible crime your brother has committed! I don't know if I can live with the shame and the sorrow!"

"Don't worry, *Iyá-mí*," said Eleggua. "We'll tell *Baba-mi* when he comes home. He'll know what to do."

"I don't dare tell him," cried Yemmu. "I'm afraid of what Oggún will do. He said he'll hurt his father if I ever tell him what happened. That's why I've kept silent all these weeks."

"Do you mean to tell me Oggún has done this before?" cried Eleggua, astonished.

"Yes, my son," sighed Yemmu miserably. "Every day as soon as Oddúa leaves for the fields Oggún comes into the house and abuses me in spite of my pleas. I don't know what to do, but if he continues, I may have to ask Oloddumare to end my life."

"That won't be necessary, *Iyá-mí*," said Eleggua. "I give you my solemn promise Oggún will be stopped. Leave everything to me."

"But what can you do, my son?" asked Yemmu, wringing her hands in despair. "You are not strong enough to overpower Oggún. He could hurt you. Then what would I do?"

"There are all kinds of strengths," said Eleggua with a smile. "My strength is not of the body, but it will best Oggún."

Kissing his mother gently, he turned and left the house.

The next day, as Oddúa was starting work in the fields, he saw Eleggua running toward him.

"What is wrong, my son?" he asked with a worried frown. "What is your haste? Anything the matter?"

"Yes, *Baba-mi*," said Eleggua, struggling to catch his breath. "I was passing our house and I heard *Iyá-mí* crying. I knocked on the door but no one answered. I fear she may have come to harm. I think you should go back."

"Of course," said Oddúa, hastily gathering his working tools. "What could have happened to her? She was fine this morning when I left her, but she has not been looking very good lately. Something seems to be bothering her."

"We'll find out soon enough, *Baba-mi*," said Eleggua, helping his father pick up the tools. "But we'd better hurry."

The two orishas hastened back to the house, Eleggua running in front, with his father's work implements poised on his shoulders. Knowing Oggún's habits, Eleggua had timed his own actions carefully so that he arrived at the house with Oddúa only moments after Oggún had walked in. The two orishas were, therefore, in time to save Yemmu from another of Oggún's attacks.

As they came to the door, Yemmu's cries were heard clearly through the thin wood. Frantic with worry, Oddúa burst open the door and saw Oggún trying once more to force himself on his mother.

Oddúas presence acted as an instantaneous damper on Oggún's ardors. Paling with terror, he backed away from his mother and clumsily began to dress himself, stammering with fear.

"*Baba-mi*, I ... I was just ... *Iyá-mí* was crying. I thought she needed help ... did not hear you come in ..." He finished dressing and backed away into a corner, shaking from head to foot. Yemmu in the meantime, her face ashen with terror, knelt on the floor and clung to her husband's knees.

"My lord, please, forgive ..." she faltered. Her terror was for Oggún whom she feared her husband would destroy. Her maternal instincts were still to forgive the offense and save her wayward son from her husband's wrath. But Oddúa mistook her plea for mercy and thought instead that she was pleading for herself, acknowledging in this way a guilty cohabitation with her own son.

Aghast, numb with horror and pain, Oddúa backed away from Yemmu, his terrible suspicion plainly visible in his face. Yemmu saw the look in her husband's eyes and collapsed on the floor, covering her head with her hands. There she lay, as if struck by lightning, her body shaking uncontrollably.

Not being able to feel outraged at his son's actions and incapable of punishing him for his terrible deed, Oddúa turned his eyes upward and called to Oloddumare.

"Father, my lord, take me back!" he cried in anguish. "Take me back for I cannot endure this pain!"

Eleggua, who had been the horrified witness to this family tragedy, ran over to his father and embraced him.

"Please, *Baba-mi*", he pleaded, his eyes streaming with tears. "Don't leave. Please stay, *Baba-mi*."

But Oloddumare had heard Oddúa's cries and answered him swiftly. Enraged at Oggún's actions, and knowing Oddúa was too gentle to dispense to his son the punishment he deserved, Oloddumare withdrew Oddúa's spirit as he once had done with Oddudúa, and replaced him with Ayáguna, the first of the Obatalás and the one whose rage was almost equal to his own. Thus was Obatalá/Ayáguna born, the last soul to inhabit Oddudúa's body.

Eleggua saw Oddúa's body shake suddenly and fall heavily to the floor.

"*Baba-mi, Baba-mi!*" he cried, shaking his father's body. "Please come back!"

Oggún squatted dazedly in his corner, his benumbed brain beginning to comprehend the enormity of his crime. His dastardly deed accomplished, Olosi had withdrawn again, leaving the bewitched orisha to cope with his unwitting guilt for the rest of his supernal existence.

Eleggua's anguished cries seemed to fall on deaf ears, as Oddúa continued to lay motionless on the earthen floor. But suddenly, the elder orisha's body shuddered spasmodically and his eyes opened. Eleggua, who had been staring disconsolately at his father's face, recoiled at the look in his eyes. Never had Eleggua seen Oddúa angry or otherwise disturbed, his placid gentility always a joy to those around him. But that gentle quality was now gone from Oddúa's eyes. Instead, his pupils shone with a dark fire, and an undisguised hatred seemed to permeate every inch of his body.

Shocked and bewildered, Eleggua backed away from his father. His innate intelligence told him at once this was not Oddúa. With his legendary cautiousness, he waited and said nothing, watching this new being with wary eyes.

Ayáguna, now in possession of Oddúa's body, arose slowly from his supine position and faced his wife and his son.

"Come forward, you wretch!" he hissed at Oggún, who shrank further into his corner, terrified at his father's eerie transformation. "Come forward, I say," roared Ayáguna, eyes aflame.

And Oggún, with watery knees, all his former bravado, dissolved in the face of Ayáguna's majesty, approached his father humbly, with downcast eyes.

"You worm, you foul loathsome, predatory beast. I abhor you. I curse a thousand times the day you were conceived!"

Ayáguna spat out his words, with slow, icy venom. The cold, implacable hatred in his eyes and the controlled, calculated precision in his voice were far more terrifying to Oggún than if his father had yelled and screamed at him in rage. This was a new Oddúa, one he had never seen before. Like Eleggua, he realized with sudden dismay that he was looking at a stranger, a violent aspect of his father that was alien to his erstwhile gentle ways. Trembling, he fell down on his knees.

"Please, *Baba-mi*, forgive me," he cried, tears flowing freely down his cheeks. "I don't know why I did this dreadful thing. It's as if somebody else had been acting through me. I would have never hurt *Iyá-mí* otherwise. I love and cherish her. I don't know what came over me."

His humble, contrite words found no pity in Ayáguna's raging breast.

"You dare ask for forgiveness, you contemptible, abominable creature!" spat Ayáguna, shaking with fury. "There is no forgiveness for you or for your mother! You are both repugnant and abhorrent in my eyes. Don't ask for pity for you'll not get it from me. Your detestable, unnatural passion will meet with my most severe judgment!"

"But my mother is innocent!" cried Oggún desperately. "I am the guilty one! Punish me if you must, but spare her!"

"I curse you both!" cried Ayáguna, pitiless. "Don't try to defend her. Your defense does her more damage in my eyes for I see you defend, not your mother, but your mistress!"

"Oggún speaks the truth, *Baba-mi*!" said Eleggua, falling down on his knees also. "I was witness to her forced humiliation by Oggún. That is why I went to get you in the fields. She is an innocent victim. Please believe me!"

"Silence!" cried Ayáguna, his fury increasing with each plea. "I will not believe you. I was a witness to your mother's willing surrender to her own son's guilty passion. I will not spare her!"

Yemmu, who remained lying face down on the ground, whimpered pitifully at these harsh words and tore desperately at her hair. Eleggua rushed to her side and held her close to his chest, his tears mingling with hers.

Ayáguna, unrelenting and inclement in his wrath, was unmoved by their sorrow.

"Hear my curse, you faithless and depraved woman!" he cried. "Had I the power to destroy your worthless life, I would do so in an instant. But that power belongs only to Oloddumare. So I curse your womb and your motherhood. Cursed be your name and your issue. Cursed be your soul and your life. May your laughter turn to ashes and your joy to sorrow. Cursed be every male child you bear from this moment onward, for I will kill all who come from your womb!"

"No!" cried Yemmu, rising from the floor and falling once more at Ayáguna's feet. "Mercy, lord! Mercy for my children! Don't curse my unborn sons! They are innocent! Curse only me!"

"Accursed be you all!" roared Ayáguna, the very walls of the house trembling. "Accursed forever and ever! I will kill your every son! They will be dead before they are born!"

"I am innocent!" cried Yemmu, her tears suddenly dry on her earth-stained face. She looked upward and screamed, "Oloddumare knows I'm innocent! You are merciless and blind. But I will escape your curse and bless my children. My innocence will protect them from your hatred!"

She stood facing her raging husband, regal and magnificent in her torn and stained clothes. Ayáguna, taken aback by her unexpected recovery, watched her in astonishment and for the first time, the glimmer of a doubt entered his mind. Could she be innocent after all?

But Yemmu was not pleading any longer. Her beautiful eyes, swollen by tears and veiled with sorrow, were looking inward. Her sadness was so overwhelming, Ayáguna was moved in spite of his anger. His face paled as he suddenly realized the grave mistake he had made. Yemmu's purity and innocence radiated from her like silver light. Numbed with the terrible reality of his unfair and hasty judgment, he stood facing her, rooted to the ground as if he were made of stone.

"I must leave now, my husband," said Yemmu with simple dignity. "As you did before, I must leave this body so that I may save my children from your inexorable wrath."

"No, *Iyá-mí*, no!" cried Oggún and Eleggua in unison.

"Forgive me, *Iyá-mí*, forgive me!" sobbed Oggún. "Don't leave us. I will take upon my guilty shoulders my father's curse. Don't go!"

"What will we do without you, my mother?" cried Eleggua in anguish.

"I'm not abandoning you, my son," said Yemmu. "But I must gather strength to protect you. My love for you will be my strength."

She seemed to grow in stature. And suddenly her body burst asunder and with a great cry Yemmu's spirit rushed upward toward Oloddumare's mansion in the heavens. As Ayáguna and sons watched horror-stricken, great torrents of water rushed forth from her divided body, covering everything with their tumultuous flow. At the same time, a blinding light issued from her body and ascended quickly toward the heavens. This ball of silvery light grew more solid as it sped upward until it was hanging over the earth, suspended in the sky like a cocoon of dazzling radiance.

Eleggua and Oggún held to each other as the waters covered them, while Ayáguna rose with the waters, grim and silent in his grief. And suddenly, as swiftly as they had rushed forward, the waters gathered in an awesome pillar of foam and out of its blue-green depths was formed a majestic and glorious female form. She had Yemmu's face but her body was covered with algae and strings of pearls and precious stones glistened on her long hair and her hands and feet.

"I am Yemayá Attaramawa," she said with a loud, firm voice. "I am the Mother of all. My power is supreme and my children are my own to protect and punish as I see fit. There in the sky is my other self, my sister the moon. Her name is Nana Buruku. I set her there so that with her light she will illuminate at night the deeds of humanity. Between us we will protect and rule the ways of women to shield them from the ways of men. Women will no longer be victimized by men for we will be there to guide and shield them. She as the moon and I as the sea will control the tides of this planet. Power is no longer your sole possession, my husband!"

Ayáguna listened to her words, his head sunken on his chest. He then approached her humbly and knelt at her feet.

"Forgive me, my wife. I wronged you and I shall repent through all eternity."

Ayáguna's spirit, having accomplished Oloddumare's designs, fled his body and only Obatalá remained, sad and contrite at Yemayá's feet.

"Arise, my lord," said Yemayá. "Unlike you, I have compassion in my heart and I forgive you."

The two orishas embraced as their two sons watched. Then Oggún came forward and knelt in front of them.

"*Baba-mi*, I know my sin is grievous and I must be punished," he said, his forehead on the ground. "But I ask of your mercy that I be allowed to curse myself. Your curse could never be as harsh or severe as my own. Allow this as a sign of your forgiveness."

"It was your mother you offended," said Obatalá gravely. "It is she who must make that decision."

"So be it," said Yemayá. "Yemmu is your mother, not I. But I will not allow you to go unpunished. Curse yourself and may your curse be everlasting so that you never forget your crime."

"I thank you, my lady," said Oggún humbly. "This is my curse. May I never rest throughout my life. May I toil forever at the forge while others sleep. May my work bring me no joy or satisfaction and may loneliness and tragedy be my sole companions. May love flee from me and may people fear me as the bringer of pain and sorrow to their lives. As I live in pain and solitude, so shall my curse be forever resting upon my guilty head."

Thus was the curse born in the joyful land of the orishas, while Olosi rejoiced in his malignant work.

Eleggua and Orunla

After the unhappy events leading to Ayáguna's curse and the emergence of Yemayá, life was resumed among the orishas, but a somber pall hung over them like a threatening cloud. They were all aware that Obatalá's word was law and that his oath was sacred. What he vowed to do he must carry out. Therefore they waited in dread lest they hear that Yemayá was with child. This eventually happened as Yemayá and Obatalá had resumed their marital relations. Being responsible for the population of the earth and for the birth of new orishas, who would help guide the destinies of humanity, they had no choice but to continue their fertile union.

When Yemayá was delivered of a healthy and beautiful male child, the orishas groaned in unison and waited for Obatalá to act. The elder orisha, filled with sorrow and regret, but unable to dispel the oath he had made to kill every male child born to his wife, took his newborn son in his arms and embraced him tenderly. Then he called Eleggua to his side and gave him the child.

"Eleggua, my son, I am going to ask you to help me fulfill the sinister vow I made and which I am bound by my own laws to fulfill." At this point Obatalá broke down and began to cry.

"But, *Baba-mi*," said Eleggua. "You are the law. Why can't you break your vow?"

"How can I when I'm supposed to set an example of the importance of keeping a vow?" said Obatalá, his body racked with sobs. "I must observe my own laws if I am to expect others to do the same. But I can't do this deed myself. I don't have the strength. But you, my son, are the strongest of my children in spite of your frail appearance. I need you to help me carry out my oath and destroy the child."

"But we are immortal, *Baba-mi*. How can I kill the child?"

"As the supernal father I have the power to destroy my children. This power was given to me by Oloddumare in expectation that something like this might happen. This power I convey now to you. No other life may you take. Only the child's."

"But, *Baba-mi*, how can you ask me to kill my own brother?" asked Eleggua, his gentle heart overwhelmed with horror. "He's just an innocent baby. I don't have the courage to do such a deed."

Obatalá shook his head, his eyes brimming with sorrow.

"You must find the courage, my son. It is your duty to help me fulfill my vow. Do so at once. Argue no more."

He bent down and kissed the infant softly, fighting back his tears.

"But, *Baba-mi*, he doesn't even have a name," said Eleggua, cradling his brother against his heart. "Shouldn't you at least name him? Doesn't he deserve a name?"

"I was avoiding that," said Obatalá. "I hoped in this way I could forget him sooner, but I know now I will never forget him. His name shall be Orunla."

He turned his back and walked away hastily, as if afraid to change his mind.

Eleggua sat down by the crossroad and rocked his infant brother in his arms. He tried to think in which way he could save the child without disobeying his father, as he had no intention of killing Orunla. Soon an idea formed in his fertile mind, and he jumped to his feet, laughing with delight.

"Orunla, my little brother," he said, planting a resounding kiss on the infant's face. "I have found the way to obey our father's command and still save your life. You shall be buried but you shall not die."

He opened the large knapsack that always hung across his shoulders and placed the child inside.

"Hang in there, little one, and fear not," he said gaily. "I know exactly where we must go."

Whistling merrily, now that he had found the answer to his problem, Eleggua dashed away into the woods and was soon lost among the trees.

Several hours later he was back at his father's house. Obatalá was waiting impatiently for him. He knew Eleggua's kind heart and was sure he would not carry out his father's orders. After sending him to destroy Orunla, Obatalá had repented his decision and was determined to break his own law and spare the child. He was therefore horrified to see Eleggua return without Orunla.

"Eleggua, where is your brother?" he asked, trembling with premonition. "Did you kill him?"

Eleggua, who did not suspect his father had changed his mind, bent down his head.

"Your command has been obeyed, *Baba-mi*. I have just buried my brother in the woods."

"May Oloddumare have pity on us both!" cried Obatalá, falling unconscious to the ground.

At that moment, Yemayá, who had heard the commotion, arrived on the scene.

"What is the matter, Eleggua?" she asked. Then, noticing Obatalá lying on the ground, she knelt by her husband's side.

"What has happened to your father?" she asked, cradling Obatalá's head in her arms. "Why is he unconscious?"

Eleggua decided to tell Yemayá the truth. He knew she was strong and fair-minded and could keep a secret.

"He's grieving, my lady," he said, squatting next to her in his favorite position. "He felt compelled to carry out his oath to destroy all your male children, so he sent me with the child Orunla to the woods and ordered me to kill him."

"My child!" cried Yemayá, horrified. "You have killed my child!" She let Obatalá's head slide from her arms and stood up, her body shaking spasmodically. Maddened with grief, her body began to liquefy swiftly and Eleggua saw with frightened eyes how she was turning into the ocean she personified.

"No, my lady, no!" he cried. "The child is alive. I did not kill him!"

The whirling waters stopped their rushing fury and very slowly Yemayá regained her normal form.

"My son is alive?" she asked anxiously. "Where is he? What has Obatalá done with him?"

"He's in the woods, my lady," said Eleggua, breathing a sigh of relief. "I did not know what to do at first, as I had to find a way to save him and at the same time obey my father's orders. Then I remembered Iroko, the great ceiba tree which stands in the depths of the woods. It is a kind and motherly being, created by Olofi to protect the forests. Since I had been told to kill the child, I decided to bury him to the waist and leave him in Iroko's care while I came home to tell my father I had obeyed his command. I felt I was not lying when I told him I had buried my brother since I had just finished doing so. Every day I will go to the woods and feed Orunla and keep him company and teach him what he needs to know, and one day we'll find the way to reveal the truth to my father."

Yemayá smiled, embracing Eleggua with affection.

"You have done wisely, my son," she said. "I shall always remember your kindness toward your young brother. And don't worry, Obatalá will not be told what you have done until the right time. I am sure he's grieving now over the loss of his son. I shall be magnanimous and forgive him, as he did what he felt was his duty in order to preserve Oloddumare's laws."

When Obatalá awoke from his swoon, he found a gentle and understanding Yemayá by his side and a sorrowful Eleggua to share his loss. Many years were to pass before he learned the true fate of his ill-starred son Orunla, who was destined to become the holy diviner and the wisest among the orishas.

Changó Is Born

After Orunla's birth and his "death," life was resumed among the orishas, but there was a haunted look in Obatalá's eyes which saddened Eleggua, who knew his father continued to grieve in silence over the supposed death of his infant son. The other orishas, who also believed Orunla was dead, did not mention the child and continued their labors, hoping that no other male would be born to Yemayá. Of them all, the one who toiled the hardest and grieved the most was Oggún, who, true to the curse he had placed on his own head, shunned everyone and worked without rest at his forge.

Eleggua continued to visit Orunla, who grew strong and handsome under his brother's care and Iroko's watchful and benevolent presence. The giant ceiba tree shielded the child from the eyes of all who passed by, including the other orishas and the wild beasts that roamed the forest. Soon Orunla became a young man, but whenever he asked Eleggua when he would be able to abandon his hiding place under the ceiba, his brother answered evasively and asked him to be patient a little longer.

In the meantime, several daughters had been born to Obatalá and Yemayá; among them, Obba, Oyá, and the gentle Yewá, whom Obatalá had destined for celibacy. He intended her to be a symbol of purity and modesty and for that reason he had instructed the male orishas never to look at her with lustful eyes.

Obba was sweet and beautiful and had been instructed to become the giver of mathematics and all sciences to humanity. With her, wisdom was born.

Oyá, on the other hand, was wild and tempestuous. Her beauty was savage and untamed, like the wind and the storms she symbolized. As soon as she was of age, Obatalá gave her to Oggún as his wife, in the hope that her love might sweeten Oggún's bitterness and overthrow the curse he had placed upon his own head.

He stretched out a well-formed arm and pointed upwards. All at once another lightning bolt crossed the sky and fell to the ground, narrowly missing Aganyú.

"But I've never been able to do this myself," said Aganyú, open-mouthed. "How do you do it?"

"I don't know how I do it, *Baba-mi*. I just do it."

"Well, this is a gift from Oloddumare, I'm sure," said Aganyú. "But in the meantime, don't tell your mother about it. I must prepare her first. She wasn't too happy about my giving you the secret of fire and I don't know how she'll react to this added power of yours. And don't use it until I tell you to. I don't want you to hurt yourself."

"I can't hurt myself, *Baba-mi*. I'm immortal," said Changó with innocent pride.

"How do you know you're immortal?" asked Aganyú, increasingly amazed at Changó's precocious wisdom.

"Because I have heard you and *Iyá-mí* talking when you think I cannot hear you. I know we are orishas, in charge of helping and guiding humanity, and that there are other beings like ourselves with similar powers."

"What else do you know?"

"Only that there is someone called Obatalá who is your father and who entrusted me to your care."

Aganyú sat down by the rim of the flowing volcano and pulled the boy towards him.

"My son," he said, embracing Changó, "there is something I have to tell you."

He then proceeded to disclose to Changó his true origins and the reasons why he had been entrusted into Aganyú and Dada's care.

Changó Returns

After learning the truth about his birth, Changó incessantly pleaded with Aganyú and Dada to bring him back to his ancestral home.

"Why do you wish to leave us, *omo-mi*?" asked Dada sadly. "Don't you love us anymore?"

"Yes, I do, *Iyá-mí*," cried Changó, embracing her. "But I want to see my birth parents. I long to hold them in my arms and tell them how much I love them. I know how much they have suffered and I want to bring some joy into their lives."

But Changó's insistence in returning to his parents was not only fueled by filial love, but also by the determination to avenge Oggún's offense to his mother and the supposed death of his brother Orunla. This determination he carefully kept to himself, because he knew that if Aganyú and Dada suspected his plans, they would not bring him back home.

Aganyú resisted Changó's entreaties for several years, but one day he took Dada aside and told her it was time to inform Obatalá that his youngest son knew the truth about his birth.

"But *Baba-mi* will then keep Changó with him," cried Dada, her eyes filled with tears. "I'll miss him so much. We'll be so lonely without him."

"I know," agreed Aganyú, bowing his head. "But the lad has a right to see his real parents. We'll go to see him from time to time. It won't be so bad. You'll see."

But Dada refused to be consoled and when Aganyú and Changó finally departed to return to Obatalá's kingdom, she hid herself away and refused to bid them farewell.

The trip from the earth's core to the holy city of Ile-Ife, where Obatalá and Yemayá had their kingdom, passed without incident and one day Aganyú and Changó found themselves at the frontier of their father's lands. The sentinels who guarded the frontier greeted Aganyú joyously and sent messengers ahead to inform Obatalá of the imminent arrival of his two sons. Thus it was that Changó found, not only his parents, but also his brothers and sisters waiting to greet him. Obatalá had informed all his children that Changó was not dead, as they had been led to believe, but safe and sound all those years in Dada and Aganyú's care. They all received him with great affection, especially Eleggua, who had known the truth all along and who was anxious to meet his younger brother. There was an immediate and genuine spark of mutual sympathy between the two orishas, one which would grow deeper and stronger with time.

Only Oggún, his wife Oyá, and Obatalá's youngest daughter Oshún, were not present during Changó's arrival. Oggún was at war in a far away land and Oyá was guarding their kingdom. Oshún, who was as free as the river waters she represented, was away for a few days, at a music festival given in her honor in the land of Ilesha, which was sacred to her. Oshún had been born the year after Changó's birth and was already considered to be the most beautiful of Obatalá and Yemayá's daughters.

Obatalá and Yemayá greeted their long lost son with tears of joy. They immediately declared a holiday to celebrate his return and held many festivities in his honor which lasted for several weeks.

When the celebration was over, Aganyú embraced Changó and returned to his domain at the center of the earth, reminding his adoptive son that he and Dada would expect Changó to visit them often.

After Aganyú left, Obatalá called Changó to his presence and embraced him tenderly.

"*Omo-mi*, we have been separated for many years due to a family tragedy that I don't want to sadden you with," he said. "But now that you are here, it is only proper that you should take over the lands of your inheritance, as well as the duties Oloddumare has entrusted unto you."

"I am ready to take over my duties, *Baba-mi*," said Changó, who had been instructed by Aganyú not to reveal to Obatalá that he knew the reasons for his forced separation from his parents.

"Very well, my son," said Obatalá with a satisfied smile. "I'm pleased with your development. Even though you're the youngest of my sons, you are wise beyond your years. That is why I have decided to give you the kingdom of Oyo to rule. It is large and its people unyielding, but I'm sure you will guide them well. Through your brother Aganyú, Oloddumare has conferred upon you the powers of fire, thunder and lightning, as well as the gift of prophecy. Use them wisely to rule your people."

"I will do my best to honor your trust in me, *Baba-mi*," said Changó, prostrating himself at his father's feet. "I would die gladly rather than disappoint you."

The two orishas embraced and shortly afterwards Changó left his parents to take over the rule of the kingdom of Oyo. His brother Eleggua accompanied him to his new home.

Orunla Is Freed

Eleggua and Changó had been traveling for some time when suddenly Changó reined in his horse and dismounted.

"Why are you stopping, my brother?" asked Eleggua, eyeing Changó curiously. "Are you tired?"

"I'm never tired," snapped Changó. "But I refuse to go on until you come clean with me."

"What do you mean?" asked Eleggua, assuming an innocent attitude. "I'm not hiding anything from you."

"Yes, you all are," said Changó angrily. "But I know all about the family secret you seem so intent in hiding from me. I know you killed my brother Orunla under my father's orders. I want to know how you could do such a ghastly deed with a clear conscience. There can be no friendship between us until you guide me to my brother's grave and I can pay my respects to him. Then I shall seek my brother Oggún and avenge Orunla's death and my mother's humiliation."

Eleggua sat down in his favorite place by the crossroad and pulled out a flask of palm wine and a few tobacco leaves from his knapsack. He took a long draught of the fiery liquid and offered the flask and some of the tobacco to Changó.

"I don't drink spirits and I don't smoke," said Changó, turning his back on his brother and walking to the opposite side of the road.

Eleggua sighed and began to roll the tobacco between his slim fingers.

"Well, I guess I'd better tell you the truth," he said, lighting the rolled leaves and puffing at the tobacco with an impish grin.

"Yes, I guess you'd better," said Changó shortly.

"What I am about to tell you has been my secret for many years. Only one being knows about it and she's kept silent all this time because she also cares about Orunla."

"What are you talking about?" asked Changó, looking at Eleggua with a dangerous glint in his eyes. "Is this some new intrigue you are concocting?"

"No, my brother," said Eleggua. For a fleeting moment there was a sad, introspective look in his eyes. But it was soon gone and the usual, carefree smile lit Eleggua's face once more. "It is not an intrigue, rather a happy piece of news. Our brother Orunla is not dead. He's very much alive and safe in the forest in the care of Iroko, the giant ceiba tree."

Then, while Changó listened in disbelief, Eleggua proceeded to tell his brother how he had conceived the idea of saving Orunla's life by burying him to the waist underneath the ceiba. He explained how he had brought food to his young brother and taught him many things, while keeping his secret from Obatalá and Yemayá, who believed Orunla to be dead.

"But he's growing weaker every day," he said with a worried frown. "He's too big to remain buried much longer and I fear he must be freed soon or he may indeed perish."

"But he's an orisha," said Changó. "He cannot die."

"Not ordinarily," agreed Eleggua. "But remember he has Obatalá's curse still on his head. Our father has the power of life and death. It was given to him by Oloddumare himself."

"Then we must hurry and free our brother and ask our father to lift the curse," said Changó with his usual determination. "We must go to him at once."

"But he has no reason for living like the rest of us," countered Eleggua. "The only reason for an orisha's existence is to have a gift to impart to humanity. Orunla has none. He is a living dead."

"No, he's not!" cried Changó. "I shall give him my power of prophecy. Then he'll have something to give the world."

"Capital!" said Eleggua, jumping and skipping merrily around the clearing. "That should satisfy our father."

The two brothers embraced joyfully and from that moment their friendship was sealed. Throughout their lives they would be known as Ocanini, one heart shared by two bodies.

Several days later, Obatalá and Yemayá were greatly surprised to see Changó and Eleggua return to Ile-Ife in the company of a young man dressed in robes of green and yellow.

"What has happened, my sons?" asked Obatalá, a worried frown creasing his brow. "Have you encountered trouble in your travels?"

"Not at all, *Baba-mi*," said Eleggua with a smile. "But we met this young man who had lost his way and we decided to bring him to you so you might offer him your hospitality."

"Yes, indeed," said Obatalá, who was kindness personified. "But how did he go through the sentinels unnoticed? And where does he come from? I have never seen him before."

Yemayá, who had been looking at the young man intently, felt a strange pang in her heart and felt suddenly faint. Obatalá noticed it and reached out to her with concern.

"What ails you, my lady?" he asked. "You look pale."

"It is nothing," said Yemayá, making an effort to regain her self-control. "This young man reminded me of someone, but I must be mistaken, for I have never seen him before."

Changó, taking advantage of the interruption, brought the young man forward.

"He didn't come through the frontier, *Baba-mi*," he said. "He came through the forest. He's from the kingdom of Dahomey and he has a great power. He can divine the future and knows all things hidden to others."

"But you are the only one with the power of prophecy, my son," said Obatalá. "How can such a gift be in the hands of another, unless it is through the will of Oloddumare."

"Maybe Oloddumare himself imparted it to him," said Changó. "How are we to know the will of the Creator?"

"If this is so, I must put this young man's powers to the test," said Obatalá, rising from his throne. "You may go rest now, but tomorrow you must bring him back to me so that I may determine if he has indeed the power to prophecy."

The next day, all of Obatalá's courtiers and his children were waiting expectantly for the test that Obatalá had devised.

At the appointed time, Eleggua and Changó brought the young man to Obatalá.

"Here's the test," said Obatalá gravely. "In that field across from us I have planted a row of toasted corn and a row of fertile corn. You must find both rows and tell me which has the toasted corn and which has the fertile corn. Only someone with the gift of prophecy can determine that. If you succeed, I must admit you have the gift. If you fail, then you have deceived two princes of the blood royal, as well as myself. The punishment will be severe. Are you willing to take the test?"

The young man bowed deeply.

"I am willing, my lord," he said, raising his head and looking at Obatalá with somber eyes. "And I will abide by your decision, whatever it may be."

Obatalá felt strangely disturbed and his old heart felt suddenly tired and saddened.

"So be it," he said, doing his best to hide his discomfort. "Inspect the field and tell me what you've found."

The entire court watched breathlessly as the young man walked slowly around the field, and then after a few minutes of deliberation, returned to face Obatalá.

"The row of toasted corn is planted horizontally, facing your throne, my lord," he said quietly. "The row of fertile corn is at the end of the field, and it is planted vertically, next to the young elm."

For a few moments, the court waited with bated breath while Obatalá looked at the young man in silence.

"Who are you?" Obatalá asked finally. His heart was hammering in his chest and he trembled as he waited for the answer.

"You must first tell me if I am right," said Orunla, looking at his father with steady eyes.

"You know you are right," said Obatalá, trembling with an indescribable fear. "Yet you cannot be. For if you are, then you are an orisha, and you cannot be for I don't know you."

"Yes, you know him, my father!" cried Changó, unable to keep silent any more. "You know him in your heart. And you know his name as well as you know mine!"

Obatalá rose slowly from his throne. His legs buckled under him and his son Ochosi had to hold him so that he would not collapse on the floor. At this moment, all the years of suffering seemed to overpower Obatalá and he aged visibly in front of his children. In this, his oldest aspect, he became known as Obatalá Obalufón.

"It cannot be," he wailed feebly. "I dare not hope!"

"But it is, *Baba-mi*!" cried Changó. "Dare to hope! Listen to your heart!"

But it was not Obatalá who uttered the name that was trembling on everyone's lips.

"Orunla!" cried Yemayá, rushing forward like a wild woman. "My son! Orunla!" The words poured from her mouth like a torrent of turbulent waters. Moments later she was kissing and hugging her son, crying and laughing at the same time, holding his face between her trembling fingers, as if afraid he would vanish again from her arms.

All was joy in the land of the orishas that day. Orunla soon took his rightful place in the kingdom as the holy diviner, while Changó, his first mission accomplished, went back to Oyo to plan his revenge on Oggún.

Changó's Revenge

Oggún had been gone for many months and his wife Oyá languished in her palace, bored and restless. Every afternoon she walked in the woods nearby or flew across the tops of the trees, wrapped in the whirlwind which was her mantle. But in the mornings she sat on her throne, her beautiful face hidden by the beads which hung like a veil from her crown and which were an emblem of her majesty. Sitting there, her eyes shielded by the beads, she let her mind drift to far away regions while she listened listlessly to the reports of her ministers and to the daily petitions brought to her by her husband's subjects. To all of them she had the same answer: "I shall tell Oggún when he returns."

One of these mornings, she was brought out of her ennui by one of her servants who told her that a royal cortege was approaching at the head of which was a majestic rider, dressed in magnificent red brocade. His face was also hidden by a beaded veil which indicated that he was an orisha and a member of Obatalá's family.

Oyá was stunned by the news, as her father had not attempted to contact her or Oggún since they had left Ile-Ife. She quickly made arrangements to receive her royal visitor with adequate pomp and circumstance, and when he arrived at her palace she was already waiting, dressed in her most splendid robes, aloof and regal on her throne.

"Hail, my lady," said the visitor, bowing ceremoniously. "I trust I have not inconvenienced you unduly, seeing that I failed to send my messengers ahead to inform you of my arrival."

"My father's children do not need to bow before me," said Oyá haughtily. "And they are always welcome in my kingdom, whether or not they appraise me of their visit ahead of time."

"You are most gracious, my lady," said her unknown guest. "I have come to pay my respects to you and to my brother Oggún. I have recently returned to my father's home after a prolonged sojourn with my brethren, Dada and Aganyú. As I did not have the pleasure of meeting you in Ile-Ife, I decided to visit you and place myself and my humble kingdom of Oyo at your service."

Behind the beads, Oyá's eyes lit up with interest at these words. She had heard of her brother Changó's arrival in Ile-Ife and had longed to join the festivities honoring his return. But her duties as the queen of Takúa, and her husband' absence, had made her unable to leave her kingdom unattended.

"So you are ..." she said, tilting her head encouragingly.

"Changó, my lady," said the thunder god, lifting the beads off his handsome face and looking at her with a mischievous gleam in his eyes.

Oyá had been told of Changó's unusual beauty, but she was unprepared for the devastating charm that seemed to flow from him like a river of fire. For a moment, she, who was never at a loss for words, did not know what to say. Finally, aware that her silence might be interpreted as a rude rejection of her brother, she made a supreme effort and tried to regain her composure.

"I am ... well, quite surprised, but very happy to meet you finally, my lord," she said, instinctively adjusting her robes around her body.

"You are most kind, my sister," said Changó with a smile. "But I would appreciate your words more if I could only see the charming lips that uttered them."

"Of course, forgive my discourtesy, my lord," said Oyá, lifting the beads off her face with a graceful gesture. She was aware of her own beauty and was gratified to see the look of surprised admiration in Changó's eyes.

"Your beauty far surpasses my expectations, my sister," said Changó gallantly. His eyes burned with undisguised lust and Oyá lowered hers, unable to sustain her brother's gaze.

Aware of Oyá's discomfort yet reveling in it, Changó shifted his eyes and looked around the palace room.

"And where is my brother Oggún?" he asked, well aware that Oggún was away at war.

"He's at war in a distant kingdom, my lord. I don't know yet when he will return, but I will try to provide you with every comfort while you are in our palace."

Oyá felt increasingly uncomfortable in Changó's presence, but did not want him to notice it. A subtle duel of words began between them, and Changó realized that this woman was not a fool. He had come with the preconceived plan of seducing her and in this manner avenging the wrong Oggún had done to his mother. But Oyá was not at all what Changó had expected. She was beautiful yet stately and remote. She would not be an easy conquest. And Changó, who, for all his youth, was accustomed to the unabashed adoration of women, felt suddenly uneasy. Perhaps he had made a mistake in deciding to use Oyá to punish Oggún. After all she could not be blamed for his actions.

"Maybe I should return when my brother comes back," he said, his eyes suddenly serious. "I should not like to impose on your hospitality while you are busy attending to the needs of the kingdom."

"You could never impose on me, my lord," said Oyá, her eyes betraying her interest. "I should consider it a great honor to offer you my hospitality. Besides, it is what my mother and father would want."

Changó did not answer. His heart was constricted by conflicting emotions. Oyá's beauty and exquisite charm attracted and tempted him, but his mind was tormented by his own evil intentions. How could he betray her trust and carry out his plans of revenge with a clear conscience, he wondered. Her next words decided both their destinies.

"I would feel most offended if you left now, my lord," said Oyá with a seductive smile. "Stay at least a few days."

"So be it, my lady," said Changó with a sigh. "I'll stay, but only for a few days."

But his sojourn in Oggún's kingdom was to last for more than a few days. Weeks followed months and he remained by Oyá's side. And although he had decided not to avenge himself on Oggún by seducing his wife, Oyá's growing passion for Changó rendered him vulnerable to her determination to gain his love. And one day, in spite of his decision to respect Oyá, Changó succumbed to her desire and became her lover.

Oyá's passion was like nothing Changó had known in his many experiences with women. She met his own fiery demands one by one and surmounted them with her own. Holding her in his arms was like embracing a raging tempest. She surprised him continually with the depths and ferocity of her desire and he found himself falling desperately in love with her, in spite of his determination not to do so. Time lost all sense to them and they gave themselves to their passion without regard for any consequences.

As Changó and Oyá did not trouble to hide their relationship, everyone in the kingdom was aware of it. So it was that Oggún learned about Oyá's betrayal long before he arrived in Takúa. It seemed that the entire land knew about it and everyone made sure Oggún knew about it also. Thus Changó's revenge was accomplished without his realizing it.

Oggún's rage and humiliation knew no bounds when he learned about Changó's relationship with Oyá. Not only was Changó his youngest brother, but he was already famous for his love exploits. It was therefore doubly injurious to Oggún's pride that a rake like Changó had successfully seduced Oggún's wife in Oggún's own home.

Determined to uncover the truth by himself, Oggún returned to his palace in secret, dispensing with the usual retinue of soldiers who accompanied him everywhere he went. And so it was that he walked into Oyá's chamber unannounced and found her in the midst of a passionate encounter with Changó.

Oggún's roar of fury could be heard clear through the entire land of Takúa. Changó and Oyá, stunned by Oggún's sudden and unexpected appearance, were at first unable to move. They remained locked in each other's arms staring at Oggún with shocked disbelief. This enraged Oggún even more, who lunged at Changó and grabbed him by the hair, pulling him away from Oyá.

At this moment Oyá showed the strength and pride which are her main characteristics. Undaunted by her husband's fury, she stood before him, naked and defiant, without attempting to cover her body or deny her guilt.

"Stop, my lord!" she cried, her eyes aflame with passion. "Do not chastise your brother. I was the one who seduced him. He only reacted as any real man would."

Oggún's surprise was greater than his anger. His mouth fell open and he released his grip on Changó's hair.

"You faithless, depraved woman!" he gasped, staring at her with eyes full of hatred. "What have I ever done to deserve your betrayal? Why have you humiliated me in front of the entire kingdom with this … this wretch?"

"Because you persistently abandon me and prefer to make battle than to make love!" cried Oyá, with growing defiance. "In Changó I have found the man I always dreamed of, the man you could never be!"

Oyá's contemptuous words drove Oggún mad with fury. With a snarl he jumped at her and hit her viciously with the side of his machete, sending her flying to the other side of the room with the force of the impact. She lay there, bleeding but still defiant, as Oggún turned to face Changó.

Changó had time to recover from Oggún's sudden arrival. During Oyá's tirade he had dressed swiftly and found the small gourd that Aganyú had given him and which was always with him. He dipped his fingers into the gourd and quickly put some of its fiery substance into his mouth.

Oggún swung his machete and lunged at Changó. The thunder god was unarmed, his battle ax left with the rest of his belongings in another chamber of the palace. But Changó had other weapons, as the unsuspecting Oggún would soon discover. With a loud war cry, Changó reached an arm toward the sky and brought it down swiftly. Immediately a bolt of lightning fell at Oggún's feet, igniting the skirt of palm fronds that was his sole attire. Great volleys of fire shot out of Changó's mouth with every cry. Thunder and lightning raged around him as he moved with swift grace around Oggún.

Blinded by the brilliance of the lightning and scorched by the fire that had burned his skirt, Oggún jumped around in fury, swinging his machete in the air, and missing Changó each time. In her corner, Oyá watched the uneven battle with astonished eyes. Although she knew of Changó's power over fire and lightning, she had never seen him using them. She had also seen Changó's use of the gourd a few moments earlier and wondered how he could produce fire with it.

At that moment one of Changó's lightning bolts fell directly on Oggún's head, knocking him unconscious to the ground. Changó stood over his vanquished foe while fire raged around him.

"Now my mother is avenged!" he cried exultantly.

Oyá watched him with thoughtful eyes. The first glimmers of the truth began to dawn on her slowly. Her heart constricted with an indescribable sorrow. She rose painfully to her feet. All around her, the palace and everything in it burned with Changó's fires. She had nothing left. Her husband and her palace were lost to her forever.

Changó saw the look in Oyá's eyes and knew she had guessed his true intentions. With a muted cry he ran to her and held her in his arms, the fire spent from his body.

"Whatever has happened, whatever I have done, I want you to know that I love you and forever will," he said, cradling her against his chest.

"Do you really, my lord?" said Oyá sadly. "Do you really know what love is?" She clung to him fiercely, determined to hold on to him always, but equally determined to avenge herself for all that he had taken from her.

Changó did not answer her. He knew his need of her could never equal her love for him, but he also knew that in Oyá he had met his match and that he would never find anyone like her. Thus the pataki says that Oyá, who is the wind, will always nurture fire, who is Changó, and that Changó, who is also lightning, will forever strike iron, who is Oggún.

Oyá's Revenge

After Oyá's betrayal and the devastating defeat he suffered at Changó's hands, Oggún retreated into the forest, abandoning his kingdom and his work at the forge. Oyá also left Takúa and went to live with Changó in his palace in the kingdom of Oyo.

But Oyá had not forgotten Changó's ruthless use of her in his revenge on Oggún, and had vowed that she would in turn avenge the loss of her kingdom. Her passion for the god of thunder and lightning had not abated and she tempered her fierce love for him with her thirst for revenge. But she was too clever to betray the contradictory feelings that raged within her heart and therefore she waited, keeping her growing impatience tightly reined, until the right moment to exact her revenge.

Their first months in Oyo, Changó was a model of tenderness and gallantry towards Oyá. He was aware that she had lost her husband, her lands, and her reputation because of him, and he attempted to make it up to her by putting his kingdom and all his possessions at her disposal. All his servants treated her as a queen and he gave her no reason to doubt his devotion. but this ideal state of affairs was not destined to last. Changó was, after all, Changó, and very soon he began to get restless. He missed his freedom, his wild parties and the many love affairs that were an intrinsic part of his way of life. He cared for Oyá in his own fashion, but he was not cut out to be devoted to one woman exclusively.

Oyá noticed the subtle change in her lover's attitude. He was still passionate and attentive, but there was a certain disquiet in his eyes and an increasing moodiness about him that to her experienced eyes were the first fatal indications of a lover who is beginning to lose interest. In short, Changó was bored, and Oyá knew it. This did not disturb her unduly because she understood Changó's fiery temperament well enough, and she knew that to try to restrict his freedom was tantamount to losing him. So she wisely restrained her bitter resentment and waited.

She did not have to wait very long. Finally tired of his self-imposed abstinence from his usual pleasures, Changó began to return to his old ways. At first he left Oyá alone for a few hours, and then the hours turned into days. When he came back from his escapades, he was more loving than ever and Oyá, unable to resist his charming rakishness and too wise to rail him for his inconsiderate and selfish treatment of her, did not reject his advances and appeared to believe his most blatant lies. And although this attitude only endeared her more to Changó, it did not prevent him from continuing to take advantage of her patience.

Oyá's persistence and endurance were soon rewarded, and Changó began to trust her and open himself more to her. He no longer hid himself from her when he used the fire gourd, and he did not keep it as zealously guarded as he used to. So it was that one day, after Changó had left on one of his usual merry-making sprees, Oyá entered the chamber where Changó kept the gourd. She knew Changó would not return for a while and therefore she felt safe to carry out her plans. She put some of the fire substance on her tongue and secured the gourd to her belt. She then left the palace.

When she arrived at the palace gate, one of Changó's guards approached her and asked her respectfully where she was going. She never left the palace grounds without Changó and since his fateful encounter with Oggún, the thunder god had given strict orders to his servants never to let her out of their sight.

Oyá's answer to the guard was to open her mouth and let out a huge volley of fire which enveloped him from head to foot. The sudden gust of fire and its great power knocked Oyá back and she fell to the ground, unable to control the flames that poured out of her mouth like a river. The guard's screams of agony brought other servants to the scene, all of whom watched in amazement as Oyá spouted fire with the same apparent ease as Changó. Terrified, they backed away, dragging their hapless comrade with them, scorched and covered with soot. Equally terrified, and still reeling from the power of the gourd, Oyá wrapped herself in her whirlwind and flew away, leaving a trail of fire and ashes behind her.

When Changó returned several days later, and found out what Oyá had done, his fury knew no bounds. He then realized she had been baiting him all along, waiting for the opportune moment to steal the gourd. Although he knew the secret of the gourd and knew how to prepare the substance that gave him the power of fire, he was enraged to have been so easily deceived by a woman, especially one whom he trusted so implicitly. It never occurred to him that Oyá might have good reasons for her actions because in his total selfishness he felt he had been exceedingly generous to her and even felt he had sacrificed a great deal for her sake.

While Changó paced like a caged lion around his chambers, licking his wounded pride and trying to figure out where Oyá might have fled, Oyá had had time to regain her composure and learn how to control the secret power of the gourd. Her natural intelligence told her that she had to hide from Changó until his initial anger had subsided. She knew Changó's fires never lasted very long and she counted on his innate generosity to forgive her eventually. Finding a hiding place had not been difficult. The last place Changó would look for her would be a place he frequented. That was why she chose the top of the palm tree as her refuge. The palm tree was sacred to Changó as it had been given to him by Obatalá upon his return. It was very unlikely that the thunder god would seek her there. But she did not realize that the woods had many eyes and just as many ears, and that two of those eyes and ears belonged to Eleggua.

As the messenger of the orishas and the overseer of Obatalá's kingdom, it was Eleggua's duty to know everything and be everywhere at the same time. This was a duty which the mischievous orisha enjoyed to the fullest, and there was very little that his shrewd eyes and sensitive ears missed. Everything, or nearly everything, he learned he immediately told his father, and therefore Obatalá was quite aware of the battle between Changó and Oggún, and the latter's retreat into the forest. He also knew of the prolonged affair between Changó and Oyá, a relationship which saddened and disturbed the elder orisha.

He therefore had entrusted to Eleggua the surveillance of Changó's palace, and Eleggua had been an undetected witness of Oyá's theft of the gourd and of Changó's frustration and anger at her deception.

It did not take Eleggua very long to discover Oyá's hiding place. The orisha Osain, one of Obatalá's least known children and the rightful owner of the woods, was one of Eleggua's closest friends. Osain knew every inch of the woods as well as he knew the palm of his only hand, and when Eleggua asked him if he knew where Oyá was hiding, the sylvan deity took him immediately to the palm tree and pointed upward. There, semi-hidden by the palm fronds, Oyá sat with the gourd, still probing the power of fire and learning how to use it to best advantage. By now she was fairly adept at controlling it and she already knew how to direct it at will.

Eleggua nodded with a smile, and thanking Osain left the woods. Oyá never knew her hiding place had been discovered.

In the meantime, still bristling with humiliation, Changó had sent an entire horde of his servants to enquire as to Oyá's whereabouts. He was still waiting for them, plotting with relish what he was going to do to Oyá when he finally found her, when Eleggua arrived at the palace.

Changó received his favorite brother with affection but with a sullenness that was uncharacteristic of him. Eleggua, who knew what was bothering Changó, did not comment on his brother's distracted attitude and chatted away with his usual glibness. Changó, who did not want Eleggua to know the trick that Oyá had played on him, tried to hide his frustration behind a volubility that was patently forced. After a while, Eleggua decided to drop all pretense.

"There's no need for you to go on like this, my brother," he said. "I know what's going on in your mind. Oyá has stolen the fire gourd and you are trying to find out where she's gone."

Changó jumped to feet, livid with anger.

"What is this you are saying? Does the whole world know about Oyá's treachery and the humiliation she's put me through? I curse the day I laid eyes on the lusty wench! Oggún is lucky to be rid of her!"

Eleggua raised an appeasing hand.

"Calm yourself, my brother. Nobody else knows about this. I know only because it is my obligation to know everything that goes on in our father's kingdom. Besides, I'm here to tell you I know where Oyá is hiding and to take you there."

"Where is she? Quick, tell me so that I can find her and give her the punishment she deserves."

Changó was so incensed at the news, his huge frame was quivering with excitement.

"I must warn you that she has learned to control the power of the gourd and that she can wield fire with as much ease as yourself," said Eleggua.

"We'll see about that," cried Changó, trembling with fury. "Just take me to her."

The thunder god, who has as much subtlety as a herd of buffalo, blazed his path through the woods with bolts of lightning and tongues of fire. While he had waited for news of Oyá, he had had time to mix another batch of the fire potion and he made full use of it on his way to find Oyá. Thus it was that the wind goddess knew of his approach long before he arrived at the palm tree.

But Oyá was ready for Changó and did not wait for him to arrive. Leaving her hiding place at the top of the palm tree, she slid to the ground and waited for him, arms akimbo, her entire body brazened for the inevitable encounter.

As soon as Changó saw Oyá he brought down a bolt of lightning and directed it viciously at her. Oyá jumped sideways and countered by reaching to the sky and bringing down a thunderbolt that missed Changó by inches. The thunder god was so astounded at her prowess that he barely missed the next thunderbolt. Unlike his own lightning bolt, which fell straight to the ground, Oyá's thunderbolt zigzagged across the sky and moved sideways. It never touched the ground, but it was twice as devastating as his because it could hit a moving target from any position.

Screaming with frustration and spouting fire from mouth and nostrils, Changó sought to envelop Oyá with his flames. But she was, after all, the wind and moved with blinding swiftness. Over and over he sent fire to her and missed his target, but every time she sent a ball of fire at him she never missed. Thus it was that Changó was scorched with his own fire and stung with his own lightning and was unable to retaliate.

The battle between the two orishas raged for hours until large portions of the forest were ablaze with fire. Eleggua watched them from a safe distance, munching on some of the morsels he always carried in his capacious knapsack. When he judged that the battle had lasted long enough and that the two orishas were close to exhaustion, he rose from his comfortable position and whistled.

The shrill sound served as a quick and unexpected deterrent. Changó and Oyá stopped in the middle of their struggle and looked at Eleggua. They were both covered with soot and ashes, their clothing burned off their bodies. Naked and heaving with fatigue, they glared at their brother who laughed congenially as he approached them.

"All right, so you have battled each other. Who has won? From where I'm standing, I'd say neither of you," said Eleggua ironically. "What I can see is that Changó has found out that Oyá is a worthy opponent and that maybe she had a right to be peeved. Whereas Oyá has learned that a woman, however strong, must learn to accept a man for what he is. Why don' t you kiss and make up? You're even now."

As he spoke, Eleggua took off his mantle and threw it over Oyá to cover her nakedness. She took it gratefully and looked at Changó with enquiring eyes. Her lust for revenge was now appeased and she only longed for his forgiveness.

Changó returned her look, still aggrieved but with a dawning sense of guilt. Wordlessly he opened his arms and she rushed to meet his embrace. Under Eleggua's friendly gaze the two lovers held each other and kissed passionately. From that moment onward, Oyá became Changó's staunch ally in many of his fiercest battles, wielding the thunderbolt and fire with equal power.

Changó Gets Married

Changó's defeat of Oggún and his subsequent affair with Oyá was the talk of the entire kingdom of Ile-Ife. Distressed by the scandal, Obatalá summoned Changó to his presence.

Changó had resumed his tempestuous relationship with Oyá to whom he was now closer than ever. Obatalá's summons did not worry him as he had no idea what his father wanted to tell him. He merely assumed Obatalá wished to spend some time with him, as he had not returned to see his parents since he had come to Oyo. He was therefore unprepared for the severe look in Obatalá's face and the coolness of his reception.

The throne room was empty when Changó arrived and only Obatalá was present to greet the thunder god. Changó fell at his father's feet and paid him for *forivale*.

"Hail, *Baba-mi*," he said humbly. "It is an honor and a great joy to be with you once more."

"Arise, Alafia Aina," said Obatalá, using Changó's formal title as king of fire to greet his son. This was an unusually cold greeting and Changó looked at his father with uneasiness.

"Is there something wrong, my lord?" he asked anxiously. "Have I offended you unknowingly?"

"I fear you have, *omo-mi*," said Obatalá gravely. "It has come to my attention that you did battle with your brother Oggún after he found out you had seduced his wife Oyá."

"All I did was avenge the wrong Oggún did to *Iyá-mí*," said Changó, lowering his head. "It was not my intention to offend you. I would rather die than hurt you, my lord."

"It was not your place to seek revenge on your brother," said Obatalá severely. "He had already cursed himself and I had forgiven him. Your actions were inexcusable."

"Please forgive me, *Baba-mi*," said Changó, flushed with embarrassment. "It was not my intention to offend you."

Obatalá's kind heart was moved by Changó's humility, but he was determined to curtail his son's wild ways, and did not allow his feelings to show on his face.

"Where is Oyá now?" he asked abruptly.

"She's at Oyo, my lord," Changó muttered, unable to meet his father's eyes.

"Did you know that your illicit relationship with Oyá is the favorite topic in Ile-Ife?" cried Obatalá indignantly. "You have disgraced our family and our name!"

Changó did not answer. His chest was constricted with shame and humiliation.

"Answer me!" cried Obatalá.

"No, *Baba-mi*," said Changó. "I did not know."

Obatalá leaned back on his throne and closed his eyes. He felt old and tired. Changó was his favorite son and he hated to chastise him, but he knew it was his duty to teach his wayward child a lesson.

"Oh Changó, *omo-mi*, how I wished I could change you," he sighed finally. "I have given this some thought and I have reached a decision. I want you to get married and lead a normal respectable life. You are a major orisha, destined to help humanity and guide them with their painful lives. My decision is therefore final. You must be married at once."

Changó looked at his father open-mouthed.

"But, *Baba-mi*, Oyá is already married to Oggún. How can I marry her? I thought marriages between orishas were forever."

"And so they are, *omo-mi*," said Obatalá. "You are not going to marry Oyá. You are going to marry your sister Obba."

Changó stared at Obatalá in dismay. He had met Obba who was a beautiful and gentle girl, but he could not think of her as his wife. She was too soft and quiet, not at all like the fiery Oyá who had earned his reluctant love and admiration.

"But, *Baba-mi*, I barely know Obba. I don't think I could be happy with her. And she would not be happy with me. We are much too different!"

"Precisely because you are different you should be perfect for each other," said Obatalá with finality. "Besides, I have already made the decision. You are to marry Obba at once. There is nothing more to be said."

"As you wish, *Baba-mi*," said Changó, bowing his head. I am your servant." Deep within, his heart was tormented with a thousand doubts. He knew his forbidden alliance with Oyá was over and yet he wished with all the fire in his veins that she, instead of Obba, be the woman he would marry.

Changó's marriage to Obba took place the following morning. All the orishas, except Oggún and Oyá, were present at the festivities which lasted for many days. Changó's natural lust was kindled by Obba's delicate beauty and he embarked upon matrimony, with his usual zest and vigor. Oyá's fiery passion lay dormant in his breast while he engaged in the pleasurable duties of a husband. Initiating the inexperienced Obba into the pleasures of marriage was tremendously exciting to the irrepressible thunder god, who had ceased to pine over the forsaken Oyá.

In the meantime, the wind goddess had been ordered to return to her father's home and she was an unhappy witness to Changó's devotion to his new wife. Several days after Oyá's arrival in Ile-Ife Changó and Obba left for Oyo. But Oyá was not to be disposed of so easily, and in her tempestuous heart she was already planning Obba's downfall.

Oyá and Obba

For several months Oyá lay in wait, licking her wounds and ruminating her vengeance. She knew she had to be patient and make every effort not to betray her intentions because the success of her plans lay in gaining Obba's trust and friendship. This she set out to do with consummate guile.

Obba had never left her parents' home before her marriage to Changó and was not familiar with malice or duplicity. Obatalá had carefully kept from her the scandalous life Changó had led before his marriage, and his tempestuous affair with Oyá. It was therefore very easy for the wind goddess to befriend the unsuspecting Obba. Because she knew that Changó would never allow her to come near Obba when he was at home, Oyá waited for Changó to be away from his palace before visiting her sister.

Oyá did not have to wait very long. As it had happened when he was living with Oyá, Changó began to get bored with his young wife. His interest in Obba waned even sooner because she lacked the fiery temperament of the wind goddess and her love was too tame to keep the thunder god at home. As soon as the newness had gone from his marriage, Changó began to find the inexperienced Obba an unequal match for his lustful nature and he began to frequent his old haunts. He also began to miss Oyá and her fiery love, which was something Oyá was counting on.

In the beginning Obba did not find anything amiss in Changó's prolonged absences, but very soon she began to hear her own servants gossip about his frequent adventures. At first she refused to believe what she heard, but after a while she was forced to accept her husband's infidelity. Being gentle and inobtrusive, Obba accepted Changó's philandering with characteristic forbearance, but deep within, her heart was filled with sorrow. This was the time Oyá chose to make her appearance.

Oyá's first visit filled Obba with joy. She had been away from her father's house for a long time and she welcomed her sister with open arms. Although Oyá had never paid any attention to her before, Obba did not find anything strange in her sister's suddenly friendly attitude. Her great loneliness was assuaged by Oyá's presence and she did her best to make her feel welcome. Initially, Oyá did not mention Changó and neither did Obba, but on her subsequent visits Oyá began to question her sister about her marital life. Thus she was happy to learn how Changó had already lost interest in Obba and rarely visited her boudoir.

"But my sister, how unkind of your husband," said Oyá, doing her best to hide her satisfaction. "Men are all the same. Whenever they begin to abandon their wives you can be sure they are involved with other women."

"Alas, my sister, I fear your words are true," said the unhappy Obba, bowing her head. "I am sure my husband is being unfaithful. I hear the servants talking about it when they think I am not around. I am most unhappy."

"My poor Obba!" said Oyá, putting an arm around her sister's shoulders. "Why don't you face Changó and rail him for his infidelity? Surely you cannot continue living with him under these conditions. If I were you I would leave him and return to our parents' home."

Obba shook her head sadly.

"I cannot leave my husband. A wife's place is by her husband's side. And I would never think of accusing him of infidelity. I owe him respect and obedience. All I can do is hope he will change his ways and return to me."

"My poor sister, you really know nothing about men's ways," said Oyá with a crafty smile. "Changó will never change his ways. More than likely he will get worse as time goes by, especially if you don't do anything to stop him."

This was true, as Oyá knew through bitter experience. But her words were not designed to help Obba regain Changó's love, but rather ensure that she would lose it forever.

"But what can I do?" asked Obba desperately. "I very seldom see Changó. He only sees me during our meals together, and then only when he is home, which is not often."

Obba's words gave Oyá a fiendish idea. She knew Changó was very fond of his food and that he particularly relished dishes prepared with okra and palm oil. She now knew exactly how to get Changó to abandon Obba.

"My dear sister, I know a way to ensure a husband's fidelity, but it requires a great deal of courage, and I don't think you are capable of doing it."

"Please, Oyá, tell me what it is. My love for Changó is unbounded. I'll gladly face any pain to regain his affection."

Oyá smiled inwardly. With these words Obba had sealed her fate.

"Well, you see that lately every time I come to see you I wear my headdress very low so as to cover my ears," said Oyá, adjusting her turban daintily. In reality she always wore her headdress in the same fashion, but Obba, who had no reason to doubt her sister, accepted her story at face value.

"And why is that, my sister?" she asked curiously. "Is there something wrong with your ears?"

"Before I go on you must swear that you will never reveal to anyone what I am about to tell you," said Oyá, who wanted to make sure that she would not be blamed for the nasty trick she was about to play on her sister.

"But of course," said the unwitting Obba anxiously. "I would never reveal anything you tell me. Pray go on!"

"Well, the reason I wear my headdress so low is because I have no ears," whispered Oyá. "I cut them off and used them as a condiment in my husband's dinner. A woman's ears act as an irresistible aphrodisiac, and any man who eats a dish prepared with them will be forever faithful to the woman who serves it to him. My husband Oggún used to be twice as unfaithful as Changó and now I grow weary of his attentions."

Poor Obba listened to this malicious lie and believed it. She trusted her sister so much that it never occurred to her to ask Oyá to remove her headdress to verify the story. If she had, Oyá would undoubtedly have told her that her ears had grown back after a while and Obba would have believed her.

"And how can I serve them without Changó noticing them?" she asked.

"Changó loves okra and palm oil," said Oyá. "Mince the ears and serve them to him mixed with okra and corn meal, well flavored with palm oil. He will love the dish, I assure you. But best of all, he will be yours forever after that."

Obba, desperate to regain her husband's waning affection, listened to the ill-intended advice. Changó, who is a formidable eater and swallows his food without looking at it, consumed his ghastly meal without noticing anything amiss. He did not even notice that his wife looked paler than usual and that her headdress was so low it covered her neck.

During the next few days Obba waited for the miraculous change that was supposed to take place in Changó. But instead of staying home with her as Oyá had promised, her husband took off for several weeks and did not even see her before he left.

In the meantime Oyá sent one of her servants to see Changó who was staying with a friend in a city nearby, carrying on with his parties and endless love affairs, as usual. Oyá had returned to her reconstructed palace in Takúa, and she waited there with relish for her lover's return. She was now well pleased that her malicious cunning had triumphed and her hated rival had destroyed her beauty. It also pleased her that she had avenged herself on Changó who had unknowingly eaten his wife's ears in a stew.

Changó had been missing Oyá desperately, and when he received her message he knew she had forgiven him and was willing to tale him back. Therefore he did not waste any time in hurrying to her presence.

Oyá received Changó with her usual charm and did not reproach him for his long absence. On the contrary, she made him feel as comfortable as she could and the two resumed their passionate affair as if nothing had happened.

Changó stayed with Oyá for several weeks and when he finally decided to leave, it was clear that he was loath to do so, but Oyá's insidious work was not complete.

"My lord," she said with a wicked gleam in her eyes. "How come such a handsome man as yourself, someone so choosy in his choice of women, is married to a disfigured woman?"

"What do you mean?" asked Changó angrily. "Obba may not be the perfect mate, but she is a beautiful woman."

"Is that so?" countered Oyá with a smirk. "How can a woman without ears be beautiful?"

"What do you mean without ears?" asked Changó, astonished.

"That is what I have heard," said Oyá, adding fuel to the fire. "Haven't you noticed how she never removes her headdress, not even to go to sleep? And I have heard more. Her servants are saying she cut off her ears to serve them to you in a stew."

Changó nearly fell off his stool when he heard this.

"Surely you have taken leave of your senses!" he cried, his handsome face suffused with anger. "Obba is incapable of such a horrendous deed! You will apologize to her at once! And in person!"

Oyá rose also, livid with fury.

"I'll be glad to, my lord!" she cried with a proud toss of her head. "But why don't you first go home and ask your precious Obba to take off her headdress? If her ears are in place, I'll be glad to apologize to her!"

Changó did not answer. With a baleful look at his mistress, he turned around and left the palace.

Obba was in her room, looking wistfully out of the window when her husband stormed in. As soon as she saw the thunderous look in his eyes, she knew he had learned her secret.

Changó did not waste time with words. He simply walked over to Obba and tore the headdress off her head, exposing her hideously mutilated ears.

"So it is true!" he gasped, horrified. "How could you do such a ghastly thing? How could you cut off your ears and serve them to me in my food? You must be crazy!"

Obba saw the look of rejection in his face and fell at his feet, sobbing desperately.

"Please, my lord, forgive me!" she wailed, clinging to his knees. "I only did it to gain your love. I was told that was a sure way to bring you back to me. I'm so sorry. Please don't leave me!"

Changó dislodged her arms from his body and pushed her away unceremoniously.

"Stay away from me!" he cried savagely. "You disgust me!" If you were stupid enough to believe such a blatant lie you deserve everything that has befallen you! Obatalá has decreed that you be my wife. So be it. But from this day onward you are on your own. I am leaving you!"

Obba's anguished cries did not awaken any mercy in Changó's heart. He was numb with horror, and so filled with revulsion at his wife's deed, that all he could think of was getting as far away from her as possible.

Soon afterward, Obba returned to Obatalá's palace where she remained forever. In order to assuage her sorrow and give her a sense of value, Obatalá entrusted her with the gift of science. This gift she was to bestow on humanity at the proper time.

Changó went back to his palace in Oyo and soon renewed long-time affair with the wily Oyá. True to his word, he never returned to Obba, although he continued to acknowledge her as his only wife.

Oshún

While Changó was carrying on his torrid affair with Oyá, Oggún remained in the woods, brooding over his humiliating defeat at his brother's hands. His iron forge, upon which depended the orishas' work, as well as the evolution of humanity, lay abandoned and covered with rust. Progress had come to a standstill and Obatalá was so worried he held a counsel, summoning all the orishas to his presence.

When Obatalá expressed his concern about Oggún's prolonged absence, all his children, with the notable exceptions of Changó and Oyá, volunteered to go into the forest to try to convince the mule-headed Oggún to return to civilization. Gratefully, Obatalá accepted their offer.

One after the other, the orishas went into the woods and tried to talk Oggún into forgetting the past and returning to his forge. But Oggún refused to talk to any of them, including his one-time companion Eleggua. Even his bothers Ochosi and Osain, with whom he loved to go hunting, failed to convince the irascible orisha to forgive and forget. Oggún remained entrenched in the forest.

After all the major orishas had returned empty-handed from the woods, Oshún approached Obatalá and paid *forivale* at his feet. She was Obatalá's youngest daughter and she was never consulted in any major crisis because of her youth and inexperience.

"If it pleases, my lord," she said shyly. "I think I know how to bring my brother Oggún out of the forest."

All the other orishas burst out laughing at her words. For a long while there was a great deal of guffawing and good-natured chafing at Oshún's expense. Her older brothers and sisters, who thought of her as merely a child, in spite of her extraordinary beauty and accomplishments, considered her offer ludicrous in the extreme. After all, if they, with all their considerable experience and wisdom, had failed to bring their stubborn brother out of the woods, how could Oshún, who had no experience with the ways of the world.

Obatalá had remained silent all this time, watching his young daughter with thoughtful eyes. Oshún stood in front of his father, her eyes modestly lowered, completely nonplussed by her brethren's upbraiding. But there was a tiny sardonic smile at the corners of her mouth that did not escape Obatalá's shrewd eyes.

Finally Obatalá raised his hand. All the orishas were immediately silent and waited respectfully for his command.

"My children, I think you are being unfair to your sister," he said gravely. "Up to now she has not taken an active part in our family discussions, but maybe it is time for her to take her rightful place among us. She is not so young anymore, and maybe she has an idea worth listening to. I suggest we give her the courtesy of expressing it. Go ahead, my child," he said, smiling gently at Oshún. "Tell us what you have in mind."

"I can't express very well what I intend to do," said Oshún. "I just want to ask your permission to go into the woods and try to bring Oggún out in my own way. If I fail," she added, looking at her brethren with unconcealed irony, "you can laugh at me all you want, and I'll laugh with you."

Obatalá nodded thoughtfully and a faint smile lifted the corners of his white beard. His daughter's words confirmed his suspicions. Oshún had come of age and she showed great promise.

With Obatalá's acquiescence, Oshún began her preparations to go into the forest. She dressed in her most beautiful and revealing clothes, tied a long yellow handkerchief around her narrow waist, and hid a small vial of honey, a gift of her mother Yemayá, among the folds of her long skirt. She had noticed that whenever she used honey men looked at her with unabashed lust, and with time the sweet liquid would become one of her principal symbols.

Unlike her brethren, Oshún did not set out to look for Oggún openly. On the contrary, she entered the woods as if she were just passing through. As soon as she was deep among the dark and fragrant underbrush, she took off all her clothes, keeping only the beaded belt where she carried the honey. Her golden, sinuous body moved with easy grace among the trees, and as she moved she began to sing an enchanting melody. Music was one of Oshún's many rare gifts and she sang and danced with such heart-stopping beauty that everyone who saw and heard her was enraptured.

Oggún had seen Oshún as soon as she walked into the woods and had followed her silently as she traipsed nonchalantly through the bushes. His eyes nearly popped out of his head when he saw her take off her clothes. Never had he seen such a glorious body. His heart began to do somersaults inside his chest and his body shook with unbridled lust.

Oshún, whose sharp eyes had noticed Oggún's shadowy figure following her every move, did not betray her awareness of his presence. Undaunted, she continued her dancing, as she sang her haunting melody. From the corner of her eye she saw Oggún emerge from his hiding place behind a bush. Quick as Changó's lightning, she dipped her fingers into her vial and spread some of the cloying honey on Oggún's lips.

The god of iron licked the honey and grunted with delight. He lunged at Oshún clumsily, but she slipped through his fingers like water and quickly tied one of the ends of her handkerchief around his neck. Every time he tried to grab her she laughed merrily and moved away, pulling at her handkerchief with irresistible charm. With each movement she drew him closer to the edge of the forest. Oggún begged her to let him touch her and she laughed flirtatiously, promising to do so if he came back with her to civilization. Bewitched by her beauty and charm, Oggún finally agreed.

And so it was that Oshún triumphed where her brethren had failed and brought Oggún out of the woods, as she had set out to do. From that moment onward, the goddess of love earned the respect and admiration of the other orishas, who humbly asked her forgiveness for having doubted her abilities. As for Oggún, his love for Oshún never diminished. For wise beyond her years, Oshún kept her promise and spent many happy hours in Oggún's arms. But she was careful to teach him that as the goddess of love she could not belong to only one man, and in this way ensured that his jealousy would not erupt violently, endangering the world of the orishas and the future of humanity.

Oshún and Changó

Changó's ill treatment of Obba had filled Oshún with great sadness. Obba's sweet gentility had earned her Oshún's deep affection and Oshún had bristled with indignation when Obba told her that it was Oyá who had suggested that Obba serve her ears to Changó. It was clear to Oshún, whose great intelligence rivaled her beauty, that the ill-intended advice had been prompted by Oyá's jealousy and her desire to separate Changó and Obba. The fact that Changó had renewed his scandalous affair with Oyá as soon as he had left Obba was proof enough of Oyá's guilt.

Oshún promised herself that she would avenge her sister and show Oyá that she was not as formidable as she thought herself to be.

Changó's love of partying and the *bata* drums provided Oshún the opportunity to carry out her plan. During one of the many festivities that were common among the orishas, Oshún showed up, dressed in her most daring clothes. All the male orishas looked at her with eyes filled with desire, as she danced to the *bata* rhythms with her inimitable grace.

Changó was playing the drums and paid little attention to Oshún, in spite of all her attempts to catch his eye. Finally, Oshún, who was beginning to get a bit piqued at Changó's indifference, reached inside her trusted vial of honey and spread some of it on Changó's lips. The result was instantaneous. Changó left the drums and, like Oggún before him, began to pursue the mischievous Oshún.

Oshún enjoyed Changó's attentions, but decided to whet his appetite by being elusive. For several hours she played a wicked game of hide-and-seek with him, while Oyá watched them from afar, her eyes dark with jealousy. Finally Oshún decided the game had lasted long enough and she gave in to Changó's pleas and agreed to take him to her *ile*. After Oshún's victory with Oggún, Obatalá had presented her with a handsome palace in the nearby city of Oshogbo, and that was where she brought the god of thunder.

For a while Oshún continued her elusive tactics with Changó but eventually relented and let him make love to her.

She used all her guile and her consummate expertise in love making to thoroughly ensnare Changó and by the end of the evening the god of thunder was thoroughly besotted by Oshún's charms.

Several days went by and Changó remained in Oshún's palace. The days turned into weeks and then into months and the two orishas continued their newly found passion without growing tired of each other. In the meantime, Oyá waited in Changó's palace, seething with jealous hatred. Day by day she awaited her lover's return only to go to bed at night alone and humiliated. During the daytime she roamed the palace, breaking everything in sight and screaming invectives at the terrified servants who scurried around the house in fear for their lives. At night she tossed in bed, unable to sleep, imagining Changó in Oshún's arms and ruminating her vengeance.

Several months later, Changó decided it was time to return to his own *ile* and take charge once more of his affairs of state. Oshún embraced him tearfully and made him promise to return to her soon, a promise Changó was determined to keep. But he was was not counting on Oyá's fierce possessiveness nor her determination to keep him for herself.

Oyá received Changó with a barrage of insults and recriminations and it took the god of thunder considerable time to appease her anger. But being as wily as he was wild, Changó told Oyá he had stayed at Oshún's palace because the river goddess had trouble with her subjects and needed his expert guidance in official matters. Oyá did not believe him, but pretended to accept his excuses. She had already decided what she was going to do.

Several days later, Changó put his affairs in order, and since his kingdom was at peace, put one of his chiefs of state in command so he could return to Oshún's *ile*. But he was shocked to discover that Oyá had placed several dozen Eggun at every door and window, blocking his exit from the palace.

The Eggun, the spirits of the dead symbolized by grinning skeletons, and Changó, the fire of life, are incompatible. It is not that Changó fears them, for he fears nothing, it is rather that he will not have any contact with them. Therefore he had to retreat and remain trapped in his own house. When he confronted Oyá and demanded that she ask the Eggun to leave, she merely laughed at him. Enraged, Changó dug into his gourd and put some of the fire potion in his mouth. But Oyá was ready for him and when he threw the first volley of fire she countered with one of her own. Changó, who had forgotten that Oyá had the secret of fire, was surprised to see her meet his fire with a fire of her own. For a while the two orishas battled inside the palace, turning large portions of it into cinders. Finally Changó gave up the battle, as he realized he could destroy his entire palace if the struggle continued. Furious, he retreated into one of the palace turrets to ponder the situation.

In the meantime, Oshún, who had only intended to create trouble between Oyá and Changó, had realized that she had fallen desperately in love with the god of thunder. She, who had the power to enslave any man she chose, was now enslaved by her love for Changó. Oshún was the goddess of love and riches, but now she felt destitute and miserable, her only hope and desire embodied in her passion for the thunder god. When time passed and Changó did not return to her as he had promised, Oshún despaired, fearing that her lover had already forgotten her. But a small voice in her heart said no, Changó had not forgotten her, there had to be a powerful reason for his failure to return. Finally, acting on this insight, Oshún sent several of her servants to the city of Oyo, where Changó reigned as absolute king. When they came back, the tale they had to tell confirmed her suspicions. Oyá had imprisoned Changó in his own palace, using some of the Eggun who served her to block all the exits.

As soon as she found this out, Oshún decided to rescue Changó. Being as resourceful as she was beautiful and loving Changó enough to sacrifice everything for him, she decided to sacrifice one of her proudest possessions to ensure his freedom. This possession was her beautiful hair which was rich and full and one of her attributes Changó loved most.

Once she made this resolution, Oshún did not waste any time in carrying out her plan. Handing a knife to one of her servants she instructed the girl to cut off the thick braids that crowned her lovely head. The girl tearfully resisted the order, pointing out to Oshún that she was destroying her greatest asset, but Oshún insisted severely and the girl obeyed. As soon as she had the braids in her hands, Oshún hurried to Oyo, dressed in her most beautiful robes and her head covered by a turban.

When she arrived at Changó's palace, Oshún went straight to the main entrance where she was immediately intercepted by a squadron of skeletons. Undaunted, the goddess of love put on her most charming smile and began to flirt with the Eggun. Proving that not even the dead can resist the power of love, Oshún insinuated herself among the Eggun and talked them into letting her into the palace.

As soon as she was inside, Oshún met one of Changó's servants who told her that Oyá was away at that moment and that Changó was in his tower, pacing back and forth like a tiger. This was a good piece of news and Oshún hurried to meet her lover. Changó was stunned to see Oshún walk into the tower, and after the two lovers embraced passionately, he asked her how she had managed to walk into the palace as the only people who were allowed in or out were members of the household. But Oshún shook her head impatiently. There was no time, she said, to talk. They must hurry as Oyá might return at any moment and they had much work to do.

With the help of one of Changó's servants, she affixed her braids to her lover's head. When Changó saw the braids he remonstrated with Oshún for her sacrifice, but she ignored him and proceeded with her work. Swiftly, she painted his face with chalk, and then dressed him with one of her robes which she had brought with her, hidden under her clothes. Thus disguised she led him back to the main entrance accompanied by the woman servant. As Changó and the servant slipped out the door, Oshún again engaged the attention of the Eggun. While she flirted with the skeletons, Changó made his escape. When he was safely out of sight, she said farewell to the Eggun and left the palace.

Changó was waiting for Oshún a few miles away from his house and together they went to Ile-Ife, where they told Obatalá what Oyá had done.

When Oyá returned to Changó's palace and discovered his escape, her fury knew no bounds. She was still venting her rage against the poor Eggun when news came to her that her father wanted to see her at once.

Obatalá was sitting on his throne, wearing his most stern frown when Oyá arrived at Ile-Ife. Seeing Changó and Oshún standing together next to their father's throne told Oyá she was in serious trouble.

"*Baba-mi*," she began humbly.

"Silence!" cried Obatalá angrily. "First you defied my authority and renewed your forbidden alliance with Changó and then, when he tried to end it, as he knew he should, you tried to force him to continue it by imprisoning him in his own palace. I am appalled at your audacity!"

But, *Baba-mi*, it was Oshún who instigated the whole thing. How come you do not see her guilt?" said Oyá, trembling with fear an d anger.

"How dare you question my judgment!" said Obatalá indignantly. "Oshún saved Changó from his forced imprisonment and she sacrificed her hair to do it. Am I going to punish her for the nobility of her deeds. Certainly not. The one deserving of punishment is you and you shall be punished. Since you enjoy consorting with the dead, you will be among them from now on. The kingdom of the Eggun shall be your palace and it will be your duty to decide who enters therein as it was your desire to decide who entered Changó's domain."

Oyá lowered her head. "As you will, *Baba-mi*," she said, hiding her tears. "I am your servant."

Obatalá's kind heart was moved by her humble acceptance of his severe judgment.

"So be it," he said gently. "I know you will carry out your duties well. You will be free to leave your kingdom whenever your duties allow and you will retain your power over the wind and your newly acquired gift of fire and the thunderbolt. And you will not be alone. Your sister Obba, who you also wronged, has asked to accompany you. Maybe now you can patch your differences and become friends."

From that moment on, Oyá became known as the owner of the cemetery. Her duty is to stand guard at the entrance and to oversee the dead who are brought in. Her sister Obba, with whom she reconciled, is in charge of overseeing the burial of the dead. As for Changó and Oyá, their love affair was again rekindled, as it is not possible to separate thunder from the lightning bolt. Oshún, who is love, continued to pine for Changó, who is passion, and their need for each other was finally accepted by Oyá, who understood, albeit reluctantly, that love without passion cannot endure.

Changó Meets Yewá

After his troubles with Oyá, Changó resumed his former carefree womanizing ways. He renewed his affair with Oshún, but only on his terms. This meant that he met with the love goddess whenever he felt the desire to be with her. And Oshún, who loved him to distraction, accepted this on and off relationship because she feared she would lose him otherwise. Changó had the same arrangement with Oyá, even though he preferred her to other women, and the fiery wind goddess, although raging inwardly at this state of affairs, agreed to his terms because Changó had vowed never again to live with a woman.

But Changó was bored. He had conquered the loveliest women in his kingdom and far beyond, and he was already tired of all the beauty that lay unwanted at his feet. He longed for a new woman, one who was so lofty and unreachable that he would have to use all of his considerable seduction expertise to win her. He searched everywhere for such a woman but could not find her. So he retreated to his palace in Oyo, disgruntled and ill-tempered, venting his frustration through violent thunderstorms which left the citizens of Oyo trembling with fear.

Eleggua heard of Changó's ennui and decided to pay the thunder god a visit. Changó was glad to see his brother, for Eleggua was clever and had a saucy wit that was both challenging and entertaining.

The two orishas sat in Changó's courtyard, exchanging bits of gossip and ribald jokes filled with double-entendres. Happy in each other's company, they howled with laughter, while feasting on the many delicacies that were served to them by Changó's lovely female stewards. Both orishas were fond of their food, and they ate lustily with unabashed relish. Changó, who is abstemious, sipped sparkling spring water, but Eleggua, who loves strong spirits, drank huge amounts of palm wine. Very soon the potent liquid did its work and Eleggua, ordinarily very discreet, began to loosen up.

"I hear you're bored," he said, winking at Changó. "What's the matter? Have you lost interest in women?"

Changó shrugged his shoulders and yawned.

"They are all the same. All they do is demand and complain. I'm just tired of their willingness. I'd like some resistance for a change."

"If what you want is resistance, I know of one you could not get if you stood on your head," said Eleggua, emptying his calabash and extending it to one of the servants who refilled it immediately with the heady palm wine.

Changó perked up at these words. He knew Eleggua was privy to all the secrets in Obatalá's house, but he was also aware of his brother's reticence in betraying those secrets. He decided to take advantage of Eleggua's intoxication and pry from him the name of the woman he had just mentioned.

"And who is this challenging female, my brother?" he asked, pouring more palm wine into Eleggua's calabash. "Is she attractive?"

Eleggua savored the wine and leaned back on his stool with a sigh of contentment.

"She is the loveliest woman in Ile-Ife," he said with a cagey smile "But also the most virtuous. You would waste your time with her. She is out of your reach."

"Is that so?" said Changó, barely repressing his excitement. "Who is this paragon of virtue? Do I know her?"

"I don't think so. You were away for a long time. Then, when you finally came back, you had all that ado with Oyá and Obba. Then there was Oshún … No, I don't think you know her. Besides our father keeps her secluded like a precious jewel. She is not meant for any man. *Baba-mi* wants her to keep her innocence and remain a virgin forever."

Changó's boredom had disappeared like a passing cloud. Every fiber of his body was aflame with desire. At last he had found the challenge he had been searching for.

"And what is her name, my brother?" he asked with studied indifference.

"Ah, wouldn't you like to know." Eleggua giggled and slapped his knee delightedly. "But that's a secret. I'm sworn not to tell."

"But what's the harm in revealing her name?" insisted Changó, putting an arm around his brother's slender shoulders. "What can I do anyway? If she's as virtuous as you say, she would not pay me any attention."

Eleggua laughed and stood up on steady legs.

"That's true," he chuckled. "Besides Obatalá has Yewá hidden so well that she's only allowed to go out as far as the palace gardens, and then only on Sundays and accompanied by a retinue of female servants. You could not go near her, no matter how hard you tried. But no, I could not reveal any secrets. I have been forbidden. I am very sleepy," he added with a wide yawn. "Can you direct me to the guest quarters? I'd like to rest a while."

"Of course, my friend," said Changó, jumping to his feet "One of the servants will escort you. Rest as long as you wish. My house is yours."

He watched his brother disappear into the palace, leaning on one of the stewards. Then he sat down again and roared with laughter.

"So the lovely Yewá walks in my father's gardens on Sundays attended only by her maids. We'll see how much resistance she presents to my advances."

The following Sunday, Yewá was walking as usual along one of the garden paths. Her many-hued robe clung to her slim body, revealing its sinuous curves with every movement. Her exquisite face was faintly visible through the shimmering veil of colored beads that hung from her headdress and her natural grace was evident in every step. There was an innocent voluptuousness in her full figure that was further enhanced by her modest demeanor. A large retinue of young female servants followed her at a discrete distance, allowing her ample freedom and privacy, but at the same time keeping a careful watch on her every move.

As she walked, Yewá fanned herself with a large *abegbe* made of iridescent peacock feathers. It was a present from her younger sister Oshún, who owned the sacred bird. Suddenly, as she turned around a corner, she saw a tall, handsome youth, dressed in flame-colored robes, richly embroidered with many cowrie shells. The young man, who held a small gourd in his hands, bowed deeply upon seeing Yewá.

The beautiful orisha, astonished at the stranger's presence in the garden, stopped open-mouthed. She knew the garden was forbidden to all men while she walked in it, and she could not understand how the youth had managed to enter the place. Behind her the maids in attendance stopped also and waited respectfully for their mistress to continue her walk. From their position they could not see what had attracted Yewá's attention.

The young man raised a finger to his lips, silently bidding Yewá to keep silent.

"Forgive this intrusion, my lady," he whispered. "I know I am not supposed to be here. But I had heard so much about your beauty I had to see it for myself. Please don't go," he added hastily, noticing Yewá had taken a step backwards, obviously alarmed by his words. "I am your brother Changó. You have nothing to fear. I will leave at once. I just want to give you this small present. Next Sunday I will wait for you here. Please come alone."

He bent down and placed the small gourd under a rose bush and disappeared as swiftly as he had come.

Yewá's attendants, worried by her unusual actions, called to their mistress to see what was disturbing her, but Yewá waived an impatient hand and continued walking. They went around the garden twice, and on their third turn, Yewá managed to retrieve the small gourd unseen by her maids. She hid the gourd beneath her ample robe and continued her walk.

Later that evening, when she was finally alone in her chamber, Yewá took the gourd from the place were she had hidden it and inspected its contents. Inside the gourd she found a beautiful red stone, translucent and brilliant like fire. A tiny flame seemed to dance within its crystalline heart. It had lain hidden in the gourd, covered by soft feathers, as bright and red as the stone.

Yewá held the beautiful crystal in her hands, watching its crimson light flickering with every motion of her hands. She did not know it, but she was holding a fire opal, the most beautiful and rarest gem in existence. It was Changó's very own fire that danced in its depths, and poor Yewá was unable to resist its powerful allure. She watched the opal's fire and her heart was suddenly constricted by a strange turbulent feeling that she had never experienced before. Trembling, she hastily returned the opal to its feathered nest inside the gourd, and hid it in a corner of her room.

The next Sunday, Changó waited impatiently for Yewá to appear, but the lovely orisha did not walk in the garden that day. To her anxious parents, who wondered why she stayed indoors, she said she did not feel well and did not wish to leave the palace. This reluctance to take her usual and only distraction worried Obatalá, especially when it repeated itself during the next few weeks. When he expressed his concern to Yemayá, she said that maybe Yewá was bored with the dullness of her life. It might be wise, she suggested, to create a new diversion for their lovely daughter. But that week, Yewá dressed herself in her most beautiful clothes and announced that she would go out that Sunday. Relieved, Obatalá saw her leave the palace with her maidservants and assumed his daughter's ailment had subsided and she was now ready to resume her normal life.

Yewá was sure Changó had gotten tired of waiting for her and would not be at the place of their former meeting, but her heart was hammering in her chest as she neared the fateful corner. A few steps before reaching it, she stopped and waived her servants away. She wanted to be alone for a few moments, she said. They were to wait for her until she called them. The maidservants did not see anything unusual in this request. Yewá was not like the other orishas. She tended to be distant and morose and often did and said strange things. Therefore they let her go around the corner without following her.

Yewá's face paled beneath the beaded veil as she saw Changó standing in the middle of the path. He was dressed in the same flaming robes and wore the same charming smile on his handsome face.

"Greetings, my lady," he said as soon as he saw her. "Have you been ill? I have waited all these weeks in great anguish, fearing my presence may have caused you undue worry."

Yewá lowered her eyes and reaching beneath her robes brought out the gourd.

"Here is your present, my brother," she said, extending the gourd to Changó. "It is far too precious. I cannot possibly accept it."

Changó made no movement to take the gourd.

"On the contrary, it is far beneath your worth," he said softly "I created the stone just for you. I cannot take it back. It is yours now. But if you don't like it," he added with a petulant toss of his head, "you can give it to one of your servants or throw it away."

Yewá saw the faint look of displeasure in Changó's eyes and the subtle hardening of his well-formed lips and she trembled. She suddenly realized that she did not want to incur his anger and that she wanted to stand there and talk to him, even if by doing so she would be breaking all the vows she had made to her father.

"I could never give it away, my lord," she stammered, her heart catapulting in her chest. "I will keep it if you so desire."

"I so desire," said Changó, taking her hand and kissing it passionately. He knew Yewá's innocence was his best ally and that he had to be cautious if he was to succeed in his plans of seduction.

Yewá tried to withdraw her hand but Changó held on to it with an ardor that made the inexperienced Yewá flush with self-consciousness.

"Please, my lord," she muttered, unable to meet his flaming eyes. "You're compromising me. My maids are waiting around the corner. If they saw us together …"

Changó let go of her hand at once.

"Forgive me," he said with pretended chagrin. "I am being very selfish. But it's just that I have never seen a beauty as perfect as you. You have conquered my heart forever. I will leave at once, but only if you promise to meet me here next Sunday at the same time. If you don't, I will come to my father's court and demand to see you."

"No! Please don't!" cried Yewá, horrified. "If *Baba-mi* knew I had allowed you to talk to me, I tremble at the thought of what he might do. I'll be here next Sunday, but only that one time, and then you must promise to forget all about me."

"I can only promise to try," said Changó, bowing deeply. "But I can offer you no guarantees. One cannot rule one's heart." Without waiting for her answer he disappeared among the trees with the swiftness of lightning.

The following Sunday and every Sunday after that, Yewá kept her tryst with Changó, under the unsuspecting noses of her maidservants. Each time she met the thunder god she fell deeper under his irresistible spell. But Changó was becoming impatient. Although Yewá met with him and he could see that he was gaining ground in her virginal heart, his progress far too slow for his fiery temperament. He wanted more and he wanted it fast.

In the meantime, Obatalá was growing increasingly concerned with his daughter's behavior. She was always nervous and pensive, and barely touched her food during meals. She only seemed to come alive on the Sundays when she took her appointed rounds around the palace gardens. Obatalá could not understand what was happening to Yewá, and as she seemed perfectly healthy otherwise, he decided to watch her closely. One afternoon, as Yewá sat with her mother and maidservants in the palace's recreation chamber, Obatalá went to her room and searched it. He did not know what he was looking for, but he was certain that somewhere in that room he would find a clue to Yewá's distracted attitude.

Several hours later, when Yewá went back to her room, she found her father sitting by the window, staring blankly into space. Yewá's heart leaped in her chest at the sight of her father. She stopped at the entrance of the room, frozen with fear, and her eyes flew unbidden to the place where she kept the gourd with its precious contents.

"Is this what you're concerned about?" asked Obatalá. He opened his hand and Yewá saw the fire opal gleam wickedly at her from her father's outstretched palm.

Too innocent to lie, Yewá remained by the door, unable to move or speak. Her face was pale as death and she trembled uncontrollably.

"Come in," said Obatalá, beckoning to his daughter. "Come in!" he ordered with terrifying severity, as she continued to stand like a statue by the door.

Yewá came into the room like an automaton. He feet felt leaden and her tongue clung like cotton to the roof of her mouth.

"How came you by this?" asked Obatalá with a terrible voice.

Yewá lowered her head, her cheeks ashen, and said nothing.

"This is Changó's stone. Only he knows how to make it. There is none like it in the world. How came you by it? ANSWER ME!"

Yewá fell down to her knees.

"I am innocent, *Baba-mi*! I am innocent!" she cried, her eyes wide with terror. "He gave me the stone as a gift. But nothing has happened between us. I swear it. I have only met him in the garden several times. That is all."

"You have met him in the garden several times!" cried Obatalá trembling with fury. "You have betrayed my confidence and lied to me and to your mother. You are a worthless child. You were my last hope. The only ray of light and purity in my life, and you have betrayed me!"

Unable to stand any longer, he slumped down in his seat, his chest racked with heart-rending sobs. He looked suddenly very old and frail, the very image of despair and desolation.

Yewá clung to his knees sobbing.

"But I have done nothing, *Baba-mi,*" she moaned. "Please believe me. I am innocent!"

"You have lied. You were the light of my eyes. And you betrayed my trust. I can never believe you again. I can believe no one. I am all alone!"

There was such hopelessness in Obatalá's voice, such desperate sadness, Yewá recoiled as if she had been struck. Slowly, she managed to stand up again and without a word, left the room.

The next morning, Obatalá convened a meeting where all the orishas were present. They knew their father had something momentous to say for he seldom summoned them all to his presence. But they were unprepared to see how old and tired he looked sitting in his throne, next to the always beautiful and youthful Yemayá.

"I have summoned you here to make a special announcement, "said Obatalá. His voice was sad but firm and there was a majestic glow in his countenance that made everyone shiver. "I have decided to retire. Your mother is still young and filled with Oloddumare's grace. She will continue her work as the mother of humanity. I will always be here if you should need my advice in the performance of your duties. But I will no longer be in command. You will be on your own from this moment onward."

A dismayed chorus greeted these words, as all the orishas in unison expressed their shock and sadness at Obatalá's decision. The elder orisha silenced them with an uplifted hand.

"My mind is made up," he said. "But before I give up my scepter, I want to make a last decision. My daughter Yewá, whom I had chosen to stay with me in my old age, to remain virginal and untouched by a man's hand, will no longer stay with me. I release her from her vow. I am sending her to the land of Iku to be with her sisters Obba and Oyá, to oversee the passing of life unto death. She will remain pure and untouched forever, but she will not be by my side."

A great silence followed this dismal pronouncement. Yewá, who sat by Yemayá's side, sank her desolate head on her mother's bosom sobbing bitterly. Changó lowered his eyes, filled with regret. He knew he was to blame for Yewá's banishment and his heart was overwhelmed with self-reproach. He was aware that his punishment would be the knowledge of his blame and his inability to repair the damage he had caused.

True to his word, Obatalá banished Yewá to the land of the dead and retired from mundane affairs. Yemayá, now free of her marital obligations to Obatalá, left Ile-Ife and established her kingdom in the bottom of the ocean. The orishas continued to carry on their duties as the prototypes of humanity and their intermediaries with Oloddumare.

Eleggua's Sacrifice

After Obatalá's retirement, a pall seemed to fall upon the land. There was great unhappiness everywhere and evil permeated the once happy land of the orishas.

Yemayá, bored in her watery kingdom, fell in love with a young fisherman called Inle and took him with her to her undersea palace. For a while she seemed happy with the handsome youth, then he too began to bore her. At last she decided to return him to earth, but afraid that he might betray their secret affair, she cut off his tongue. Oloddumare, feeling sorry for the poor fisherman, elevated him to the rank of the orishas and made him the divine healer.

In the meantime, Obatalá, also bored by his self-imposed retirement, decided to create eight new beings. Lesser in power than the orishas, these demigods grew envious and discontent with their condition. Finally, desirous of usurping Obatalá's throne, they plotted to destroy him. But Obatalá was immortal and his destruction posed grave difficulties. After much consideration, these ungrateful children decided to set a trap for their divine father.

Obatalá was delighted when these new children of his old age invited him on an outing several miles away. The place where the planned festivities were to take place was a lake surrounded by many mountain peaks. It was a beautiful but desolate area and to get there it was necessary to pass through a gorge flanked by two mountain walls.

Due to his old age and growing infirmity, Obatalá was traveling in a litter. When they reached the middle of the gorge, the servants who were carrying it and who had been instructed beforehand, put it down and ran away. Their actions puzzled the elder orisha, who alit from the coach and called out to the servants. Only silence met his calls. Feeling a strange premonition, Obatalá looked up and saw several of his newly created children watching him from the craggy peaks of the mountain.

"Achama! Adima! Ogan! Aruma!" he called out to them. "What are you doing up there? Come down and help me!"

The only answer he received was a barrage of sharp stone flints that came crashing on top of him, cutting him sharply. As the shards and flints came down, Obatalá increased his cries, intermingling them with pleas of mercy to his treacherous blood. But they paid no attention to his pitiful cries. After a while Obatalá's pleas grew weaker and then he was silenced by the forced avalanche that was rained on him from above.

The eight spurious semi-deities waited for several hours before daring to come down. They were aware of Obatalá's formidable powers and wanted to make sure he would not be able to punish them. But they had little to fear. The sharp stones had cut the elder orisha to pieces and, although still alive, he was unable to speak or act.

Full of joy at their nefarious action, the eight demigods left their father lying in pieces at the foot of the canyon and returned to Ile-Ife, which they claimed as their own kingdom.

The news of this tragedy soon reached the ears of the orishas who grieved their father's destruction. The warrior orishas, like Changó and Oggún, wanted to march into Ile-Ife to destroy their murderous half brothers, but Oshún, although the youngest, proved to be the wisest.

"What good will that do?" she asked with her usual common sense "Let us leave that to Oloddumare. The important thing now is to restore our father to life. Oloddumare will then make sure our father regains his kingdom."

These words were well-received by the other orishas and they all went together to the gorge where Obatalá's remains were still lying undisturbed. Among wails of sorrow they gathered their father's body and placed it in a large basket. This they brought to Oloddumare and placed it at his feet, asking the Creator to restore Obatalá to his former self.

Oloddumare looked at them with sorrowful eyes.

"This I cannot do," he said somberly. "What is done cannot be undone. But I will make a new being out of each of these pieces, and the first one will be a female deity I will call Oshanla."

The Creator then proceeded to form a new being from each of the pieces of Obatalá's body. As there were twenty-four pieces, he created twenty-four different aspects of Obatalá, the most important of them being the female form he called Oshanla. That is why it is said that Obatalá has twenty-four "paths" or aspects, each of which has a different name and different attributes and characteristics.

After the re-creation of Obatalá and the orishas natural rejoicing, Oloddumare asked them to be silent and to listen to what he had to say. Everyone listened respectfully as the Creator spoke.

"My children, I have pondered many nights what I am about to say to you. The earth is filled with an evil that is slowly destroying it. I must purge it from this seething malady and you must remain with me while I do it. Then I will reveal unto you a secret that it is time you learn."

Thus the Creator opened heaven's gate upon the earth and during many days and nights it rained without mercy, the clear waters from heaven cleansing all the evil from the planet, including the creatures created by Obatalá in his loneliness. After the deluge, the earth was clean and new and all kinds of plant and animal life began to reappear upon the surface of the planet.

Once more Oloddumare gathered the orishas. "Evil has been exorcised from the earth," he said. "It is now your duty to create human life. But before you do so, I must reveal to you the secret I have kept in my heart for many eons."

He then proceeded to tell them about the existence of Olosi and why he could not be seen or destroyed.

"He is totally evil, while you were created to be intrinsically good. You have no power over him because you would have to descend to his level in order to overcome him, and being good, you cannot do it."

The orishas listened to the Creator in stunned silence. It was clear to them now why Oggún had abused his own mother, why Changó had seduced Oyá and why Oyá had betrayed Obba. The entire catalog of their miseries passed in front of their eyes and they saw how they had all been victimized by the destroyer in their midst.

"Poor Obba!" cried Oyá.

"Poor Yewá!" cried Changó.

"Poor Yemmu!" cried Oggún.

"Poor Oggún!" cried Obatalá.

"Poor Inle!" cried Yemayá.

Eleggua had been sitting quietly all this time, whittling a piece of wood. Finally, he looked up.

"Forgive me, my lord," he said to Oloddumare. "But didn't you say that the reason we cannot overcome Olosi is that we are intrinsically good?"

"That is so, my son," answered Oloddumare. "Why do you ask?"

"It has occurred to me, my lord, that if one of us were to relinquish half of his goodness and exchange it for an evil half, he might be able to overcome Olosi. The evil half could fight Olosi on his own terms and the good half would ensure that the evil half would be kept in check and used only for good."

"And who do you think would be willing to make such a sacrifice, my child?" asked Oloddumare, looking at Eleggua with infinite compassion.

"I would, my lord," said Eleggua, bowing his head. "I would do it gladly because my sacrifice would mean that there would be hope in the world, and that my brothers and sisters, as well as my mother and father, could carry on their work in peace."

Oloddumare descended from his lofty throne and embraced Eleggua.

"You are a most noble soul, my son," he said. "And deserving of every honor. From this moment onward, you shall be known as Eshú. You will have a black side, symbolizing your power over evil, and a red side, symbolizing your power over good. You will have twenty-one aspects, each of them different, some good and some evil. With the evil aspects you will chastise Olosi and keep him in check. With the good aspects you will control the evil ones, and at the same time, help humankind overcome Olosi's influence. All the orishas, including your own parents, must pay you homage because of the greatness of your sacrifice. You will be the first one honored in every ceremony and the first one to eat. You shall have the keys to every door and without your permission, none of the other orishas will be able to function. That is my decree."

From that moment, Eleggua began his relentless pursuit of Olosi. For the first time since his creation, the spirit of evil was as hounded and persecuted as he had once hounded and persecuted others. His work of destruction no longer went undetected, and although his insidious influence was still felt on earth, many of his most nefarious plans came to naught. Frustrated and infuriated by Eshú's persecution, Olosi soon learned to fear the orisha's presence. There was no place where he could hide that his indefatigable pursuer would not find him. So it was that Olosi found his match in Eleggua, and for the first time since creation there was hope for humanity.

The Orishas Ascend to Heaven

After Eleggua's transformation into Eshú, and his subsequent control of Olosi's evil, Oloddumare decided that the cosmic design was completed. The orishas could now ascend to heaven, which was their place of origin and their true abode. But before that great cosmic event could take place, a perfect division of their duties had to be made.

Oloddumare began by establishing a new being as overlord of the planet. This deity he called Olofi, who was to be the main protector of humanity and the one to whom human beings would have recourse to in times of trouble or doubt.

As human beings were not immortal and had to die, a major orisha was also created to represent sickness and pestilence, and all the ills of humanity. His name was to be Babalú-Ayé and he was formed from the mud created by the universal deluge. This was to be a most important orisha, as he represented not only illness but also the possibility of healing.

From the union between Oyá and Changó were created the Ibeyi or divine twins, who represented joy and the pleasures of life. The duties of Obba, Oyá, and Yewá, as caretakers of the land of the dead, were also redefined. Obba would decide which of the human lives were to be ended, Yewá would deliver their bodies unto their graves, while Oyá would oversee who would enter into the gloomy abode of the dead. For that reason, she would be the guardian of the cemetery door. Oyá, in her dual roles as guardian of death and goddess of the winds, would also act as the intermediary between Olofi and humanity.

Oshún would also have a dual role as the source of both love and money. Her function as the goddess of river waters would empower her with the ability to give fertility to the womb and bring about felicitous unions. Because of her many services to the orishas, she was given the color yellow as her very own personal attribute. The only other orishas to have their own exclusive colors were Obatalá, whose color was white, and Yemayá, whose color was blue.

The color red, which represented all the other orishas, belonged originally to Changó, but with typical generosity, he decided to share it with his brethren. These four colors—white, red, yellow, and blue—in special combinations would be used to form the signatures of the orishas, through which they would be identified on earth by their initiates.

To establish a link between the orishas and humanity, Oloddumare determined that the powers of the orishas could be gathered through stones called *otanes*, which would represent the orishas on earth. These *otanes* would receive all the sacrifices given to the orishas and in turn would act as reservoirs of the orishas' energies which could then be tapped by those human beings empowered through initiations to serve the orishas on earth.

To call the orishas down to earth, humanity was provided with three drums called *batas*, which were also of divine origin and had special voices and rhythms with direct connections to the deities. The drums were to be played during special ceremonies in honor of the orishas, and since each orisha had his or her own rhythms, the drums would act as purveyors of messages to the orisha whose rhythms would be played.

To establish a further link with the orishas, humanity was also provided with twenty-one cowrie shells, sixteen of which would be used to communicate with the deities. Each orisha would have his or her own set of cowrie shells, but since Eleggua was the first orisha to be honored in every ceremony, his set of cowrie shells would be used to speak with the various orishas. Only under very special circumstances would a human being be allowed to speak directly to one of the other orishas, and then only with Eleggua's permission.

After all these rules were established, Oloddumare placed the affairs of the planet in the hands of Olofi and returned to heaven, taking the orishas with him. Only Yemayá remained on earth, and through her bounteous ocean waters the various human races came into being. Then her maternal spirit also returned to her divine abode from where she continues to watch over her human offspring.

The Orishas in Nature

The curiously bittersweet relationships between the orishas are mirrored in the forces of nature, which in spite of their disparate expressions nevertheless work in unison to populate the earth with an immense variety of living forms.

The forests are often devastated by fire and then renewed by healing rains which nurture the scorched ground and revitalize it, giving rise to new life. These same waters ravage the land in violent thunderstorms and tidal waves which are aided in their destructive work by powerful gale winds. Lightning strikes and fire decimates life everywhere, yet without fire, life could not exist on the planet.

The Yorubas, who in their millenary history had the rare opportunity to observe nature close at hand, noticed the violent interrelationship of natural forces and their alternatingly destructive and creative rhythms. In order to interact with those forces and tap their awesome energies, they chose to anthropomorphize them, investing them with quasi-human characteristics while envisioning them at the same time with supernatural powers. Thus were the orishas born and through them a remarkable bond with nature was established. This resulted is a deep understanding of natural forces and their profound connection with the human unconscious.

The sun and the stars, the mighty volcano, the voracious power of fire and lightning, the majesty of the seas and the river waters, the mountain peaks, the wind and the depths of the forest, all came alive with the cosmic energy of the orishas. In the design of the cowrie shells known as *oddi unle*, the Yorubas saw Obatalá and Yemayá dividing the earth between themselves. One-fourth was to belong to Obatalá as the solid ground and three-fourths was to belong to Yemayá as the ocean waters. This was the first pact agreed upon on the planet and it was the birth of communication between peoples.

From the interrelations between the orishas, the Yorubas wove an intricate philosophy, expounded in the stories of the lives of the deities. These legends, known as patakis, became the golden rules through which they guided their lives. In each of the *oddus* of the cowrie shells, they heard the voices of the orishas telling their own stories and teaching the world to learn through the cosmic experience.

The importance of the patakis lies in this rich philosophy of life, so closely interwoven with the works of nature. Its wisdom teaches us that in order to remain on this planet we must respect nature and attempt to preserve it. Maybe then we will realize that we are only one more species on this planet. The humility of that realization could very well be our only hope for survival.

APPENDICES

Origins of the Tales

All of the legends or patakis related here originate in the Yoruba divination systems known as the diloggún (cowrie shells) and the Table of Ifá. The legends are only a small cross section of the great wealth of patakis which are an intrinsic part of the divination systems.

The Table of Ifá, which is often mentioned in the tales as the oracle of Orunla, is the main concern of the babalawo, who is Orunla's priest. In accordance with Orunla's vow—after his problems with Yemayá and the cowrie shells—only men can read his oracle. The Table of Ifá is the most important of the divination systems and the highest court of appeals in the Yoruban religion. There are over four hundred legends connected with the table.

The diloggún is the most common form of divination among the Yorubas and the African-Cuban religion known as Santería. Both men and women can read the diloggún. They are usually priests or priestesses of one of the orishas. The priests who become very proficient in the reading of the oracle become known as *oriatés*.

The diloggún is composed of eighteen cowrie shells, of which only sixteen are read. The two that are not read are known as *addele*. The diloggún is read in a very complicated ceremony during which the shells are repeatedly thrown on a table. The shells are flat on one side and on the other side show a narrow opening, not unlike a tiny mouth. This is the side that "speaks" during the reading of the diloggún.

Each time the shells are thrown on the divining table, they fall in one of sixteen patterns, each pattern determined by the amount of shells that fall with the "speaking" side up. Each pattern is known as an *oddu*. There are sixteen *oddu* in the diloggún.

1. Okana	9. Osa
2. Ellioko	10. Ofun
3. Oggunda	11. Ojuani
4. Iroso	12. Ellila
5. Oche	13. Metanla
6. Obbara	14. Merinla
7. Oddi	15. Marunla
8. Elleunle	16. Mediloggun

Each *oddu* has a proverb and several legends or patakis which are used as aids in the interpretation of the oracle. Therefore the tales are not the result of idle storytelling, but are rather a philosophical explanation of various natural laws in parable form. To the Yorubas each orisha represented an aspect of nature while each of their actions was seen as an act of God (Olofi). The patakis explain why things are the way they are and what is likely to happen according to the immutable cosmic laws. The interpreter of the oracle uses the proverb and the legends associated with each *oddu* to decipher the diloggún.

To interpret the diloggún, the diviner throws the shells twice. He annotates the outcome of the oracle in numerical form. For example, if Okana comes first, followed by Obbara, he writes down 1-6, which are the corresponding numbers of those two *oddu*. If any *oddu* falls down twice in a row, the name of the *oddu* is followed by the word *melli*, which means twin. Therefore 1-1 is Okana Melli, 2-2 is Ellioko Melli, and so on.

When two different *oddu* come out, their combined legends have to be used in the interpretation of the oracle. Because there are sixteen *oddu* which have to be thrown twice, there are 256 combinations or patterns in the diloggún. But because there are at least two and sometimes three legends in each *oddu*, the number of legends in the diloggún are over five hundred.

Although there are sixteen *oddu* in the system, the interpreter of the oracle reads only to the twelfth *oddu*, Ellila. The reason for this is that the thirteenth *oddu*, Metanla, is ruled by the orisha Babalú-Ayé, who, according to one of the tales related to this book, was exiled by Obatalá for afflicting the other orishas with smallpox. Ever since that time, according to tradition, no one reads the diloggún past Ellila, to underline the fact the Babalú-Ayé is no longer in Ile-Ife.

When the shells come out in the configuration of Metanla or higher, the interpreter of the diloggún tells his client that he or she must go to the house of the babalawo to consult the Table of Ifá at "the feet of Orunla," because according to the legend Orunla was the one who advised Babalú in his time of trouble, and he's the only one who is empowered to speak in Babalú's name. Naturally, one of the legends of the *oddu*, known as Metanla, is the tale of Babalú's exile.

Each of the tales in this book corresponds to one of the oddu of either the diloggún or the Table of Ifá. For example, Ochosi's Curse is found in one of the legends of Obbara Melli (6-6); Obatalá Tests the Warriors is found in Okana-Osa (1-9); Obatalá's Visit to Changó is found in Osa (9); Eleggua and the Two Inseparable Friends is found in Elleunle Melli (8-8); the tale where Changó takes Oyá away from Oggún is found in Oddi-Osa (7-9); while all of Orunla's tales are found in the *oddu* of the Table of Ifá.

Changó, who is the undisputed hero of these tales, opens the diloggún with Okana-Melli (1-1). According to the legend associated with this *oddu*, the god of thunder sought a place in the diloggún, but he was denied this honor. Enraged, he went to Orunla for a consultation, and the diviner told him he had to make an *ebbo* in his *odo* (mortar) with some of his own herbs. As soon as Changó prepared the *ebbo*, he was granted a position in the *oddu* known as Ellila Chebora. It is the twelfth *oddu* in the diloggún and the third in the Table of Ifá.

Many volumes would have to be written to relate in full all the patakis connected with both the diloggún and the Table of Ifá. Such a compilation would be a formidable task because it would necessitate careful research into the mysteries of both divination systems.

In this book the tales have been interwoven to form a sweeping saga of the colorful lives of the orishas. But it must be pointed out for the sake of clarity that each legend stands by itself in its own timeless, cosmic space. Each is more than an entertaining story; it is a segment of life on a cosmic level and an attempt to breach the void between the spiritual and the physical worlds.

Invocations of the Orishas
in the Diloggún

ELEGGUA

Laroye, akiloye, agurotenteonu
Apagura, acamasese
Okoloofofo, okolonini, tonicanofo, omo orogun, ollona alayiki,
Ayuba

OGGÚN

Oggún Ñanañile, Oggún cobu, alagere owo. Oggún Yumusu,
Oggún finamalu,
engueleyein, andaloro, ekú, feyú, tana guaraguru, osibiriki,
alalá, Ayuba

OCHOSI

Ochosi odemata, onibebe, Ayuba

ORISHA OKO

Orisha Oko, ikú afefé, orógodo, gailotigüaro, Ayuba

AGANYÚ

Aganyú solá kiniba, kinibasogún, allaroro kinibaco, Egüenillo
etalá, Boyubadagúa, Ayuba

CHANGÓ

Olueco, azasain, cherere adache coconijico omo laduferini
Cherebinu, boguó, allalú coso, kabio, kabio sile, Ayuba

IBEYI

Ibeyi oro, araba aina cainde Ydeu, Ayuba

OBATALÁ

Obatalá, Obataisa, Obatallano, Obirigualano, Catike Okumi Ayé
Coffiédeno babami, Alláguna, hekua babá, dumilao duaremu, azabeyiolodu

OYÁ

Oyá allegue, ayilodda, obini yawó, agüidimule otiku
Obini Chokotovuencuen, talocueri Oyá, Oyá Yumusu, Ayuba

YEMAYÁ

Acherererere Iyá milateo, Yemayá azayabico Olokun, ibutagara dedeguato Olokun, Ocobayireo Arabaibulaomi, Cofiéddeno Iyá-mí, Ayuba

OSHÚN

Oshún mori yeye-o, obini oro agbebe oro Oshún, woni colalekeilla Iyá-mí, Koyusum, Yeye cari, guanariganari, owale kuase ana, Ayuba

OSAIN

Osain, agueniyi, tivi tivi laguodin yera, sakere kermelli melli, lesecán, melli elese omo, arubogüangüaraloco, bowo ewe, Ayuba

Proverbs of the Diloggún

1. Okana: The world was started with one.
2. Ellioko: An arrow between brothers.
3. Oggunda: An argument, a tragedy.
4. Iroso: No one knows what lies at the bottom of the sea.
5. Oche: Blood that flows through the veins.
6. Obbara: A king never lies.
7. Oddi: Where the hole was dug for the first time.
8. Elleunle: The head carries the body.
9. Osa: Your best friend is your worst enemy.
10. Ofun: Where the curse was born.
11. Ojuani: Distrust, carrying water in a basket.
12. Ellila: Failure through troublemaking.

There are no proverbs from the thirteenth *oddu* (Metanla) onward because, as mentioned earlier, these higher *oddu* are not usually interpreted in the diloggún.

GLOSSARY

Most of the words listed here are the corrupt or bastardized versions of the original Yoruba. The influence of the Spanish language can be easily discerned in some words which have been clearly adapted to the Spanish usage. But for the most part, even those words which have been most thoroughly corrupted easily betray their Yoruba origins. The reasons why the glossary is not composed of pure Yoruba words is that pure Yoruba is not commonly used in Santería. The language used by the santeros is known as *lucumi*, which is a Spanish version of the original Yoruba.

Abe: razor
Abiku: children who die young
Abo: female animal
Aburomi: brother or sister
Acara: bread
Acha: tobacco, cigar
Achaba: Oggún's chain
Ache: blessings, power, cosmic enery
Achiwere: madman
Acho: cloth, dress
Acho fun fun: white cloth
Acho tele: gown
Achulue: the police
Acuaro: pheasant
Ada: machete
Addele: two of the eighteen shells not used in the diloggún
Ade: crown
Adeye: hen
Adie: fowl
Afefe: air, wind
Afin: palace
Afofó: someone who talks too much
Afoyudi: an affected male
Aga: chair
Agbegbe: fan
Agbo: ram

Agema: chameleon
Agodo: clock, watch
Agogo: bell
Aiye: hunger
Aja: dog
Aju: tongue
Akan: crab
Akuko: rooster
Akuoti: bank
Alade: princess
Alafia: blessings; a title of Changó
Aloggura: strong
Ano: illness
Anuyú: a drunken spree
Apa: arm
Aqueté: hat
Ara: the human body
Arón: illness
Arube: old, old man
Asansa: fugitive
Ase: food
Asia: banner
Atana: candle
Atare: pepper
Ate: table
Ate ni yeun: dining table
Awado: corn
Awala: star
Awo: plate
Aya: wife
Ayaba: queen
Ayakua: turtle
Ayanaku: elephant
Aye: large sea shells
Baba: father
Babalawo: priest of Ifá, the high priest of Santería
Baba-mi: my father

Bata: drums; shoe
Bió: you
Bobo: all
Boná: hot
Busun: bed
Bobo: all
Burucu: bad
Cabo: hello
Cararu: soup
Chekete: a drink of sour oranges and honey
Chiche: work
Chilekun: open the door
Chokoto: pants
Chubu: to fall down
Corico: insect
Cuele cuele: calm down
Curu: short
Daque: silence
Daradara: good
Die: a little
Diloggún: cowrie shells used for divination
Dodo: red
Dudu: black
Duro die: wait for me
Ebbo: magical spell, ritual sacrifice
Ebon-iya: aunt
Ebure: male goat
Echin: horse
Efun: powdered eggshell
Efun aro: blue dye
Eggun: the dead
Eguon: chain
Eku: palm oil
Ekute: mouse
Eledda: guardian angel
Elede: pig
Eleguedde: pumpkin

Elekes: beaded necklaces
Elese: feet
Eletán: thief, trickster
Emi ti: what do I care
Eni: tooth
Eni-Bedeya: fish
Enu: mouth
Eran: meat
Ero/erin: head
Eru: slave
Esan: orange
Eti: ear
Etu: banana
Ewa: peanut
Ewe: herbs, plants
Ewu: cotton
Ewure: female goat
Eye: blood
Eyele: pigeon
Eyin-adeye: egg
Eyo: revolution, war
Filani: Chinese
Forivale: gesture of homage
Fumi: give me
Fun fun: white
Ibdabi: waist
Iberu: fear
Ibeyi: twins
Ibo: white
Ichaworo: tiny bell
Ide: bracelet
Ifa: love; Orunla's title
Ife: love; city in Nigeria
Ifecufe: lust
Igbako: spoon
Igua: life
Ikare: tomato

Ikoko: pain
Iku: death
Ile: house, home
Ile-Olorun: church, the house of God
Imo: belly
Ina: fire
Iqui: greetings
Irawo: star
Ire: good luck
Irora: pain, sorrow
Iruke: tail
Ise: work
Isun: sleep
Ita: legs, also prophecy or street
Iwolo: leave, get out of here
Iya: mother
Iyalocha: priestess
Iyá-mí: my mother
Iyefu: flour
Iyo-ereque: sugar
Iyuo-Yibo: Europe
Kabio: greetings
Kebofi: may it be with good health
Kobori: prayers to the head
Koide: parrot's feather
Korin: to sing
Kosika: there's none
Lalafia: happy
Lola: tomorrow
Loni: today
Maferefun: thank you
Manan manan: lightning
Mariwo: a type of thich palm leaf
Meyi: twin, double
Modupués: thanks
Mofeyadi: I want to go out
Mogbo: I listen

Molo: I'm leaving
Motimoti: drunkard
Nibolo: where are you going?
Nicoco: in secret
Nimo: smart
Oba: king
Obe: knife
Obini: woman; concubine
Obinrin: woman
Obote-mi: my wife
Ocan: heart
Ocho: witch
Ocun: sea
Odaboy: farewell
Ode: hunter
Odo: mortar; river
Ofa: arrow
Oguede: banana
Ogun: fight
Okan chocho: only one way
Oko: husband
Okonrin: man
Okuta: stone
Ole: derelict
Olobo: cat
Ologuo: rich
Olorun: God
Omi: water
Omi tutu: fresh water
Omiran: some
Omo: son
Omode: boy
Omodere: one's children, when young
Omokeke: son
Omokenkere: sons
Omo-mi: my son
Omugo: silly

Ona: necklace
Onaa ire: good path
Oni: divine king; honey
Onichegun: doctor
Onide: parrot
Onifari: barber
Onimán: a person, people
Opolopo: many
Oran: business
Oro: word; poison
Oronbo: grapefruit
Orun: heavens, sky, sun
Osogbo: bad luck
Ota: enemy
Otan: stone
Otutu: cold
Owo: hand, money
Owo pupo: a lot of money
Owuko: male goat
Oyin: skin
Oyouro: it is raining
Oyu: eye; face
Panipani: murderer
Pataki: legend
Peregun: white lily
Puecueye: duck
Pupa: yellow
Pupo: plenty
Silekun: close the door
Soro: to speak
Takata: "Stone Thrower," an epithet of Changó
Talaca: poor
Toto jun: forgive me
Wa: come
Wo mi: look at me
Yefa: powdered yam
Yi: this

BIBLIOGRAPHY

Ajisafe, A.K. *Laws and Customs of the Yoruba People*. London, 1924.

Babin, María Teresa. *Panorama de la Cultura Puertoriqueña*. New York, 1958.

Buxton, T.F. *The African Slave Trade*. New York, 1893.

Cabrera, Lydia. *El Monte*. Miami, 1971.

——————— . *Contes Negrés de Cuba*. Paris.

Dorsainvil, J.C. *Une Explication Philologique du Vodou*. Port-au-Prince, 1924.

Farrow, C.S. Faith, *Fancies of Yoruba Paganism*. London, 1924.

Garcia Cortez, Julio. *El Santo (La Ocha)*. Miami, 1971.

Garrido, Pablo. *Esoteria y Fervores Populares de Puerto Rico*. San Juan, 1984.

González-Wippler, Migene. *Santería: African Magic in Latin America*. 2nd ed. New York, 1990.

——————— . *The Santería Experience*. St. Paul, 1992.

——————— . *Santería: The Religion, St. Paul, 1994*.

Hughes, Pennethorne. *Witchcraft*. London, 1952.

Johnson, S. *History of the Yorubas*. London, 1921.

Jung, Carl G. *The Interpretation of Nature and the Psyche*. London, 1955.

Klein, H.S. *Slavery in the Americas*. New York, 1946.

Lachetenere, R. *Oh Mio Yemayá*. Manzanillo, Cuba, 1938.

——————— . *El Sistema Religioso de Lucumis y Otras Influencias Africanas en Cuba*. Havana, 1940.

Leyel, C.F. *The Magic of Herbs*. New York, 1925.

Milburn, S. *Magic and Charms of the Ijebu Province*. London, 1932.

Oritz, F. *Brujos y Santeros*. Havana, 1938.

Ramos, A. *Introduçao a Anthropologia Brasileira*. Rio de Janeiro, 1943.

_____ . *O Nego na Civilizaçao Brasileira*. Rio de Janeiro, 1956.

Rigaud, Milo. *Secrets of Voodoo*. New York, 1970.

Robbins, Russel Hope. *Encyclopedia of Witchcraft and Demonology*. London, 1959.

Rogers, Andres R. *Los Caracoles*. New York, 1973.

Verger, P. *Dieux d'Afrique*. Paris, 1928.

Williams, J.J. *Voodoos and Obeahs: Phases of West Indies Witchcraft*. New York, 1933.

Wyndham. *Myths of Ife*. London, 1921.

Stay in Touch

On the following page you will find some of the books now available on related subjects. Your book dealer stocks most of these and will stock new Llewellyn titles as they become available.

To obtain our full catalog, to keep informed about new titles as they are released and to benefit from informative articles and helpful news, you are invited to write for our bimonthly news magazine/catalog, *Llewellyn's New Worlds of Mind and Spirit*. A sample copy is free, and it will continue coming to you at no cost as long as you are an active mail customer. Or you may subscribe for just $10.00 in the U.S.A. and Canada ($20.00 overseas, first class mail). Many bookstores also have *New Worlds* available to their customers.

Llewellyn's New Worlds of Mind and Spirit
P.O. Box 64383-328, St. Paul, MN 55164-0383, U.S.A.

* * *

To Order Books and Tapes

If your book dealer does not have the books described, you may order them directly from the publisher by sending full price in U.S. funds, plus $3.00 for postage and handling for orders *under* $10.00; $4.00 for orders *over* $10.00. There are no postage and handling charges for orders over $50.00. Postage and handling rates are subject to change. We ship UPS whenever possible. Delivery guaranteed. Provide your street address as UPS does not deliver to P.O. Boxes. Allow 4-6 weeks for delivery. UPS to Canada requires a $50.00 minimum order. Orders outside the U.S.A. and Canada: airmail—add retail price of book; add $5.00 for each non-book item (tapes, etc.); add $1.00 per item for surface mail.

For Group Study and Purchase

Because there is a great deal of interest in group discussion and study of the subject matter of this book, we offer a special quantity price to group leaders or agents. Our special quantity price for a minimum order of five copies of *Legends of Santería* is $29.85 cash-with-order. This price includes postage and handling within the United States. Minnesota residents must add 6.5% sales tax. For additional quantities, please order in multiples of five. For Canadian and foreign orders, add postage and handling charges as above. Credit card (VISA, MasterCard, American Express) orders are accepted. Charge card orders only ($15.00 minimum order) may be phoned in free within the U.S.A. or Canada by dialing 1-800-THE-MOON. For customer service, call 1-612-291-1970. Mail orders to:

LLEWELLYN PUBLICATIONS
P.O. Box 64383-328, St. Paul, MN 55164-0383, U.S.A.

Prices subject to change without notice.

THE SANTERIA EXPERIENCE
A Journey into the Miraculous
by Migene González-Wippler

In this raw, emotional account, Migene González-Wippler reports her own encounters with Santería as researcher and initiate. You will meet extraordinary people and witness unbelievable occurrences. All are Migene's lifelong experiences with Santería.

Explore the truths about this magico-religious system from the inside, as Migene reveals her childhood initiation and later encounters with the real and extraordinary powers of the babalawo (high priest of Santería). Learn of the magical practices of the santeros (priests of Santería). Learn actual ebbós (offerings and rituals) that you can do to enlist the aid of the African deities for specific purposes such as aura cleansing, obtaining a raise, attracting love, and more!

0-87542-257-8, 400 pgs., mass market, illus., softcover $4.95

SANTERIA: THE RELIGION
by Migene González-Wippler

When the Yoruba of West Africa were brought to Cuba as slaves, they preserved their religious heritage by disguising their gods as Catholic saints and worshiping them in secret. The resulting religion is Santería, a blend of primitive magic and Catholicism now practiced by an estimated five million Hispanic Americans.

Blending informed study with her personal experience, González-Wippler describes Santería's pantheon of gods (orishas), the priests (santeros), the divining shells used to consult the gods (the diloggún), and the herbal potions prepared as medicinal cures and for magic (ewe) as well as controversial ceremonies—including animal sacrifice. She has obtained remarkable photographs and interviews with Santería leaders that highlight aspects of the religion rarely revealed to nonbelievers. This book satisfies the need for knowledge of this expanding religious force that links its devotees in America to a spiritual wisdom seemingly lost in modern society.

1-56718-329-8, 400 pgs., 6 x 9, photos, softcover $12.95